SEXING

THE CARIBBEAN

SEXING
THE CARIBBEAN

Gender, Race, and Sexual Labor

By

KAMALA KEMPADOO

Routledge
NEW YORK AND LONDON

Published in 2004 by
Routledge
270 Madison Ave,
New York NY 10016
www.routledge-ny.com

Published in Great Britain by
Routledge
2 Park Square,
Milton Park, Abingdon,
Oxon, OX14 4RN
www.routledge.co.uk

Routledge is an imprint of the Taylor & Francis Group.

Transferred to Digital Printing 2008

Library of Congress Cataloging-in-Publication Data

Kempadoo, Kamala.
    Sexing the Caribbean : gender, race, and sexual labor / Kamala Kempadoo.
        p. cm.
    Includes bibliographical references and index.
    ISBN 0-415-93503-2 (hardback)–ISBN 0-415-93504-0 (pbk.)
    1. Sex-oriented businesses—Social aspects—Caribbean Area. 2. Sex customs—
Caribbean Area. 3. Prostitutes—Caribbean area. 4. Postcolonialism—Caribbean
Area. I. Title.

    HQ160.K45 2004
    306.7'09729—dc22
                                        2004006467

Contents

Acknowledgments

At times while writing this book, it occurred to me that doing sex work rather than writing about it might have been a saner route. That is not to say that I consider sex work to be easy. I hope this book illustrates some of the constraints and difficulties, as well as possibilities, involved in sexual-economic transactions. Rather, I was convinced that the pressures may not have been so weighty, the isolation from public life not so acute, and the rewards more immediate and tangible, had I taken another path. Nevertheless, I persisted in writing about the subject and am grateful for the encouragement I received to stay with the project and bring this book to fruition. There are many people to whom I give thanks. In particular, Karen de Souza, Andaiye, Dusilley Cannings, and other women attached to the Red Thread Women's Development Programme in Guyana showed true patience with my outsider, ivory-tower ways, reminding me, with warmth and friendliness, about the importance of connecting my ideas to the day-to-day lives and struggles of Caribbean women. The Stichting Maxi Linder Association in Suriname played a vital part in my early development of an appreciation of Caribbean sex work, while discussions with Jacqueline Martis in Curaçao; Pauline Pennant, Anne Marie Campbell, and Leith Dunn in Jamaica; and Caroline Allen in Trinidad helped refine my understandings. Patricia

Mohammed, Rhoda Reddock, and Eudine Barriteau at the Centre for Gender and Development Studies at the University of the West Indies generously and graciously made space for me at the Mona Unit of the Centre in Jamaica in 2000–2001, and kept me grounded in Caribbean feminism. While I was in Jamaica, Julian Henriques kindly offered me the opportunity to work on my book from the desk of his father, Fernando Henriques—the Caribbean father of prostitution studies. I will never forget the synchronicity of that possibility with my stay in Jamaica, or the pride and inspiration I drew from sitting at that master's desk.

In Boulder, at the University of Colorado, where most of this book was shaped, Alison Jaggar's ongoing rigorous engagement with questions about feminism and prostitution not only created a stimulating intellectual climate for me in Women's Studies but also led to a strong collegial relationship and many wonderful discussions that kept me alert and motivated. From the Department of Ethnic Studies, Evelyn HuDeHart almost single-handedly convinced me that the completion of this book was a worthwhile endeavor, and that the academy was an exciting place to stay, even when one did not always conform to mainstream views and agendas. I could not have had better academic mentors than these two women. Several doctoral students at the University of Colorado, many of whom have now gone on to bigger and better things, were a lifeline during the writing of the first draft of this book. Priya Jha was eternally enthusiastic about my project and, despite our different academic languages, gave editorial and technical assistance that was invaluable. Shoba, Brian, Laura, Tracy, Kris, and Jeanne provided refreshing companionship and timely support. Outside the University of Colorado, Annette Dula and Rickie Solinger, whose academic lifestyles are exemplary to me, offered gems of wisdom and were deeply solicitous about my health and well-being from start to finish of this book. Their friendship, compassion, and critical intellectual stances continue to resonate with me, even though we no longer live in close proximity to each other in the Rocky Mountains.

Various ideas and arguments contained in this book have been presented at academic meetings or have appeared in earlier publications. My theoretical approach to sex work is a topic I have spoken widely on for a number of years, including at the American Anthropological

Association's 97th Annual Meeting in Philadelphia, at the inaugural conference in 1999 of the Institute for Women's Studies and Gender Studies at the University of Toronto, at a conference that same year on international prostitution at the University of Aalborg, Denmark, during a plenary session at the 2000 Annual National Women's Studies Association Meeting, and at Caribbean Studies Association meetings on different occasions. The analysis of race and exoticism I presented at conferences at the University of Colorado, the University of Havana, Cuba, and the University of Bahia, Brazil. The review of family and sexuality studies in the English-speaking Caribbean I first presented at the conference "Recentering Caribbean Feminism" in Barbados in June 2002. A visit to Indiana University in November 2002, hosted by the African American Studies Department, gave me an important opportunity to present a substantial part of chapter two. At all times I received comments, questions, and critique that have helped to sharpen my analysis. In addition, I am grateful to the two anonymous reviewers, who paid careful attention to the manuscript, and to a number of other referees who read this book in its first version and gave feedback through a more general academic review process. Ilene Kalish, my editor at Routledge until almost the end, supplied substantive comments during the most critical stages of writing and shepherded me through the sticky phases. Project editor, Andrea Demby was a dream to work with during the production period. The Latin American and Caribbean Studies Programme and the Division of Social Science at York University provided a home to complete this book.

Finally, and above all, I am indebted to the sex working women and men in the Caribbean and elsewhere who agreed to be interviewed over the years, who allowed me to hang out with them and observe their lives and work, and who frankly shared their experiences. Although many may not ultimately agree with the representations and conclusions I put forward here, and may contest or simply ignore my efforts, it is written with their struggles and futures in mind.

INTRODUCTION: THINKING ABOUT THE CARIBBEAN

The Caribbean has long been portrayed in the global imagination as an exotic, resource-filled region of the world. A hypersexual image has been construed as "fact" by social chroniclers, travelers, historians, sociologists, and anthropologists to represent its "backward" and "undeveloped" condition, and the region has been variously lusted after for its natural wealth, sun-drenched sand beaches, sparkling blue seas, and tropical sensuousness. Its perceived feral nature once evoked images of wild and savage men who ate human flesh (Cannibals) and sexually precocious women (Amazons) who were to be tamed and controlled in the name of God and the Crown in order that Europe could secure its cornucopia of riches. To many, the Caribbean continues to be an unruly and promiscuous place. Territories that once served as sex havens for the colonial elite are today frequented by sex tourists, and several of the island economies now depend upon the region's racialized, sexualized image.

While other and different representations of the region abound, those that center on its sexuality have been roundly condemned by the Church, women's movements, and many intellectuals, and, as one observer notes, "are bound to erode Caribbean integrity."[1] However, in this study I argue that we need a different lens for thinking about Caribbean sexuality—that we cannot simply view it as a fabrication of the European mind and imagination, or dismiss it as colonial discourses or metaphors, but need also to view hypersexuality as a lived reality that pulses through the Caribbean body. As Frantz Fanon reminds us, colonial discourses are deeply embedded in the psyche and behavior of the colonized; such images are a part of a broader colonial regime of oppression that is sedimented in the hearts and minds of Caribbean men and women themselves.[2] Moreover, I explore the question of whether Caribbean sexuality can be imagined as more than an externally imposed, degrading, alienating, and negating view. For example, can we read Caribbean sexuality as something greater than an expression of a repressed or distorted libido of the Caribbean native? To echo one contemporary Caribbean cultural theorist's thoughts on the matter, what if we were to consider "oversexualization" as part of our postcolonial identity? Could sex, then, become "a revealing and rebelling pillar of Caribbean society"? What if we were to accept "those alien or alienating 'traits' as postcolonial sources for a critical strategy to overcome our colonial beginnings"?[3] To what extent, I ask here, can we read the "excesses" or "vulgarity" of Caribbean sexuality not simply as European inventions that refract upon Europeanness and that negate or demean the history and agency of the Other, but also as sedimented, corporeally inculcated dispositions that are lived and practiced every day? Can we speak about embodied sexual practices, identities, knowledges, and strategies of resistance of the colonized and postcolonial subject without lapsing into notions of an essential native sexuality? Is it possible to explore the knowledge that is produced through Caribbean sexual praxis, and to ask whether sexual resistances offer a potential for a politics of decolonization or narratives of liberation?

The objectives of this book are to explore Caribbean sexuality in some of its complexity. It begins with the notion that colonial and neocolonial ideas about the region have combined with West African, East Indian, Amerindian, and other non-Western cultural traditions and legacies, and together have created a variety of sexual arrangements and practices that define Caribbean sexuality. Contrary to the Western ideal of the eternally monogamous, patriarchal, heterosexual arrangement, I propose that Caribbean sexuality is characterized by diversity, in which multiple partnering relationships by both men and women, serial monogamy, informal polygamy, and same-gender and bisexual relations are commonplace. This study also argues that prostitution as well as more fluid types of transactional sexual relations are widely practiced, and that many women and girls, and increasingly more young men, exchange sex for material goods and benefits. Nevertheless, as I also stress here, hegemonic constructs of sexuality do exist in the region and other sexual practices are informal, marginalized or criminalized, and are often publicly denounced.

An underlying theme through the following chapters is that an economy depends upon the organization and productivity of human labor, and that labor that rests upon sexual energies and parts of the body is integral to the economy, whether this is explicitly commodified in the marketplace and organized within sex industries, deployed to expand a slave-labor force, or used to fortify a national or ethnic group. I therefore trace how sexuality in the Caribbean has been and continues to be material for the reproduction of the workforce, family, and nation as well as for boosting national economies and, as such, constitutes important economic resources in the region. Sexual-economic exchanges appear as crucial for the sustenance of the region in the face of inequalities that global capitalism has created in the small Caribbean nations and territories. This sexual economy is furthermore deeply embedded in industries that are tightly integrated into the global economy, such as tourism and mining. Race and ethnicity factor intricately into this far-reaching sexual economy, and I explore how these factors shape ideals and fantasies about the exotic, engendering sexual labor migrations and sex tourism.

I propose here that Caribbean sexuality is of significance to understanding not just the past and present, but also the future of the Caribbean. Not only has the erosion of older economic bases for Caribbean peoples and the proliferation of survival strategies that involve some form of sexual labor become important to many women and men, but today Caribbean colonial and postcolonial states are increasingly incorporating sexuality into their national strategies for competing in the globalized economy. There is also a growing world population that desires and demands, and has the possibility to command, new leisure and pleasure activities that involve sex, and that makes its presence felt in the Caribbean. The following chapters therefore point to international and local relations of power that rest upon the organization of Caribbean sexuality.

On the other hand, sexualized Caribbean bodies come forward in this study as self-actualizing and transformative—as sexual agents that shape and are shaped by larger political and economic forces, social structures and institutions, and relations of gender, ethnicity, and race. These sexual subjects are neither inert nor passive. Indeed, I argue that Caribbean women and men who inhabit marginal sexual spaces resist, and sometimes rebel, against gendered and sexual regimes that privilege masculine heterosexual needs and desires, and actively work against dominant ideologies and practices that seek to deny their existence. Sex workers help to define and shape this resistance, and in this book I foreground their definitions of sexuality. And while the oppressive and exploitative nature of global-local sexual economies can be readily identified, particularly for women, I also take into account the potentially transformational dimensions of sexualities of the Caribbean.

A sociological premise that frames this book is that the complexity of Caribbean sexuality requires an interrogation of the interplay between macro- and microforces. In other words, important in this study is the intersection of, on the one side, hegemonic gendered, racialized, and economic structures of domination and exploitation, and on the other, acts of resistance and individual agency. I seek to reveal the ways in which the intersection produces new impulses, and to document resistances and movements for social change that arise from the interstitial spaces. Common, everyday understandings of sexuality and the collective strategies that arise from the complexities and contradictions embedded in sexual praxis are thus important themes in this book.

Conceptualizing the Caribbean

Over the past one hundred years, while numerous studies have been conducted on aspects of sex and sexuality in the Caribbean, little has centered exclusively on Caribbean sexuality or connects racialized sexualized practices with the economy. My examination here does not claim to be comprehensive, but rather it is an effort to trace some of the multiple dimensions and configurations of sexuality in the region that arise from the existing social studies literature on the subject, as well as from firsthand research. This attempt may lead to a homogenizing conceptualization of Caribbean sexuality and a masking of national and cultural specificities. However, while I am concerned here to examine particularities within certain national contexts within the region, I am also deeply interested in thinking about commonalities that traverse the region. This study balances specific colonial and postcolonial discourses and practices that may be located on one island inhabited by 150,000 people with cultures and politics that are shared in a geographical region with a population of around 34 million. My interest here—to address both the particular and the general and to emphasize complexities and fluidities as well as fixed categories that make up the Caribbean—connects to recent intellectual work in and about the region that crosses national boundaries and that is preoccupied with postcolonial pan-Caribbean identities and development. This work speaks to local particularities and regional generalities, as well as to relationships between the local, regional, and global. In an era where the Caribbean is almost held captive by the global economy, where older notions of national independence and sovereignty are overshadowed by global developments that erode small-nation autonomy, and in light of the withering away of viable alternatives for full participation in the global capitalist economy, this trend in Caribbean studies seeks a way to address the new configurations and to produce new meanings and ideas about Caribbean sustainability, liberation, and freedom.

The Caribbean defies static definition. It is a region constituted through a violent history of Spanish, British, Dutch, French, and Danish conquest, settlement, and colonial rule that involved the genocide of the indigenous peoples as well as a forced importation of millions of Africans as slaves and thousands of Asians and some Europeans as indentured workers. Despite the violence and disruption that characterizes its colonial history, the region is home to a vast diversity and blending of ethnicities, cultures, religions, and languages and stands today as *the* global metaphor for notions of diaspora, creolization, religious syncretism, hybridity, cultural pluralism, and transnationality.[4] Simultaneously, it has produced important black revolutionary movements, religions, philosophies, and social and political thinkers that have all critiqued and challenged white supremacy, colonial domination, and racism.[5] It is constituted by countries that are nation-states that range from Haiti, the first black republic to declare its independence in 1804, to Suriname and Belize, which gained political independence during the last quarter of the twentieth century. It encompasses territories such as Guadeloupe and Martinique, which remain overseas departments of France; British colonies such as Montserrat and the Cayman Islands; and semiautonomous areas such as the Netherlands Antilles, which, while still officially colonies and a part of the Royal Kingdom of the Netherlands, locally control their internal affairs. The name of the region derives from that given to some of the indigenous inhabitants, the Caribs, yet it has also been known as Plantation America, the West Indies, el Gran Caribe, and the Caribbean Basin. In some instances it is defined only by the islands—the Antilles (Greater and Lesser, Dutch, French, and British) or el Caribe Insular. Other times it includes territories washed by the Caribbean Sea—the Circum Caribbean coastlands of Central and South America. Toward the latter part of the twentieth century, the American mainland countries of Guyana, Suriname, French Guiana, and Belize have been commonly defined as part of the region due to a shared socioeconomic, political, and ethnocultural history with the islands in the Caribbean Sea. Throughout this flux of definitions, the Spanish-speaking territories—Cuba, the Dominican Republic, and Puerto Rico—have been included and excluded, sometimes isolated from the rest of the region as parts of Latin America. *The Caribbean* was thus created some 500 years ago and reinvents itself, according to political interests, geography, history, culture, and geoeconomics.[6]

Which peoples and cultures are indigenous to the Caribbean, and thus who and what is real or authentic Caribbean, is a matter as complex as its geopolitical definition. The almost complete decimation of the peoples who inhabited the region prior to the European invasion in the fifteenth century suggests that few are true natives or aboriginals. Others, however, have claimed indigeneity.[7] A notion of a Caribbean that has been made indigenous (is "indigenized") since 1492, visible through the emergence of nation-states and a distinct cultural, social, and political life that is greater than the sum of its discrete ethnocultural parts, is a helpful starting place. It allows us to view "Caribbeanness" as neither static nor traceable to a single cultural essence, but rather to accept it as an identity and sense of belonging that has been forged through a particular history and shaped by continual interculturation, transculturation, and negotiations between various sociocultural groupings.[8] Creole society is one way in which the region is captured to signify the blending of Western European and West African cultural and linguistic heritages lodged in unequal relations of power between the two.[9] However, particularly in the context of territories with greater ethnic diversity, some scholars have pointed to the inadequacy of such a concept, as it elides other important cultural influences and relations of power in the making and reshaping of Caribbean societies. At the start of the twenty-first century, national identity (Guyanese, Cuban, Curaçaoan, Haitian, etc.), religion (Rastafarianism, Santeria, Catholicism, Hinduism, etc.), language (Patois, Creole, Papiementu, Hindi, French, English, etc.), and ethnic origin (Chinese, Indian, African, Javanese, Lebanese, Dutch, Hispanic, etc.) are some of the main ways in which difference and belonging are articulated. The Caribbean and Caribbeanness are then not entirely fixed or closed categories. Such openness makes it possible for leading Caribbean intellectuals, such as economist Norman Girvan, to argue that diaspora communities in the metropoles, due to their extensive transnational connections to, and influence on, the region, are to be included in our contemporary definitions of the Caribbean. The Haitian 10th Department that was called into existence in the 1990s, in the United States and Canada is but one very clear expression of this definition—the overseas population is now considered an integral part of Haiti and Haitianess.[10] The Caribbean is thus at once bound, yet changing—fixed on elements of geography, history, politics, and culture, yet somewhat fuzzy and amorphous at the edges.[11] It is an inclusive, expansive definition, and it is in this open-ended way that I refer to the Caribbean throughout this book. In some instances I am clearly only referring to English-speaking countries or the Dutch-influenced geographical region, in other instances to identities, bodies, and consciousnesses that traverse the region and are common to the Greater Caribbean territories, the Circum Caribbean, and the Caribbean diaspora.

Central to this study are two concepts that are relevant to Caribbeanness: hypersexuality and heteropatriarchy. The first relates to a pervasive, long-standing ideology that holds that Caribbean people possess hyperactive libidos and overly rely upon sexuality as a marker of identity. Caribbean sexuality then is not normal, but excessive, at times pathological and at others unruly, and it is this characteristic of

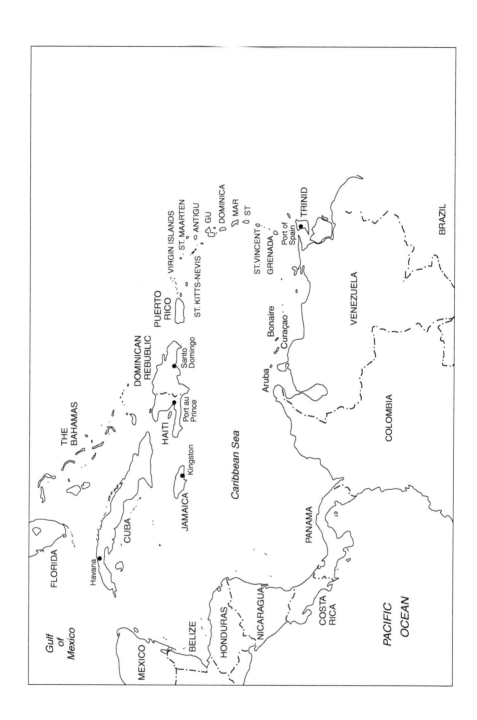

the people and its region that shapes images, policies, and economic programs from without, as well as internal ideas about self, culture, and development. The second concept captures the interplay as well as the specificity of two distinct sets of relations of power that are in operation in Caribbean societies: heterosexism and patriarchy.[12] While both heterosexism and patriarchy seem to nestle around masculine dominance, the combination, i.e., heteropatriarchy, signals a distinction and relatedness between the ways in which sexuality and gender are socially, legally, and politically organized. It is the combination that marginalizes and criminalizes gendered subjects who transgress established sexual boundaries. Heteropatriarchy is thus a concept used throughout this book to denote a structuring principle in Caribbean societies that privileges heterosexual, promiscuous masculinity and subordinates feminine sexuality, normalizing relations of power that are intolerant of and oppressive toward sexual desires and practices that are outside of or oppose the dominant sexual and gender regimes. This structuring principle privileges men's experiences, definitions, and perceptions of sexuality, whereby not only are appreciations of female (hetero)sexuality obscured, but homoeroticism and same-gender sexual relations are denied legitimacy. In this structure, coupled with a discourse of hypersexuality, lesbians, gays, transgenders, prostitutes, and other "sexual deviants" are cast not only as oversexed Caribbean subjects but as outlaws and noncitizens.

Throughout this study I also refer to the concept *race*, recognizing that it is a term that today is not widely used in the Caribbean. Nevertheless, I contend here that the region has, through its colonial history, been racialized; that is, race has been constructed as real in Caribbean life. Historically, notions of phenotypical and cultural difference were used by Western Europeans to justify the enslavement, oppression, and exploitation of Amerindians and people from Africa and Asia. People who today constitute the majority of Caribbean societies were in this history defined as different races—other times as nonhuman races— and this legacy continues. Oppressions, discriminations, and social inequalities based on phenotype and cultural origins still feature in the region, most visibly structured through labor markets and employment opportunities, educational systems, and class relations. Hierarchies marked by skin color, hair and body type, language, and facial features remain in place, with terms such as *browning*, *black*, *light-skinned*, *dark-skinned*, and *Indio* being commonly used and locally understood. Nevertheless, in contemporary academic and political discourses, race has by and large been exchanged for the notion of ethnicity, where cultural origins and physical appearance remain important signifiers, albeit with a nonpejorative overtone. Afro-Cuban or African Jamaican, Indo-Surinamese or Indian Guyanese, and Spanish Trinidadian are some of the late-twentieth-century identifiers, with each territory claiming a host of its own specific terms.[13] Throughout this study I use a variety of terms to identify difference, relying on the sociological discourse of the specific geohistorical context. By reinvoking race here, I am insisting that historical social processes and constructs that created social difference in terms of phenotype and ethnicity in the Caribbean continue to shape and inform social relations in the twenty-first century, despite the lack of single, homogeneous, region-wide discourse on the subject, and in spite of the often-heard claims that racism no longer exists in the region.

Methodology

For the past decade, I have been involved in the research and study of prostitution and the global sex trade, with a particular focus on the conditions, lives, and perspectives for and of Caribbean and other "Third World" women. My work has been and continues to be framed by a critical social studies perspective that seeks to address the continual sociological dilemma of the intersection between structure and agency—between the macro and micro, ideology and materiality—in which Pierre Bourdieu's concept of social praxeology is particularly useful.[14] This refers to a scientific activity and orientation that discloses underlying structures of social life and makes possible a thinking through of the relationship between objective structures (economic, social, political, symbolic, and cultural capital, positions, or locations, and the distribution of social resources) and the immediate, lived experience of agents and the categories of perception and appreciation that structure their action, and which reproduce and reshape objective structures.[15] It is informed by a historical materialist reading that takes social life as emerging from material conditions and the existence of real human beings, and the intercourse and relationships between and among them. My theoretical orientation is also deeply inspired by the work of such Caribbean thinkers as Walter Rodney, C. L. R. James, and Frantz Fanon, all of whom in their own different ways critically examined not only the workings of the political economy on a global scale, but also resistances and struggles for liberation and freedom from colonialism and imperialism by working Caribbean peoples. Contemporary Caribbean social theorists who continue the James, Rodney, and Fanon legacies in Caribbean studies, but also complicate these analyses due to recognition of gender and the persistence of neocolonial relations in the postcolonial, twenty-first-century Caribbean, are also important to my work. My approach is furthermore informed by Third World feminism, which draws from material-feminist traditions and centers on an examination of gender relations, yet which, as Chandra Talpade Mohanty and Himani Bannerji make clear, is lodged in the study of oppositional struggles and consciousness to hegemonic regimes shaped by colonialism, capitalism, race, class, and gender.[16]

The approach I employ here (that is at once a theory and method) seeks to make visible the perspectives, or even standpoints, and experiences and conditions of those who stand on the underside of relations of power—the subaltern, the marginalized, the dominated, the outcast, the oppressed. It involves a bottom-up approach that produces grounded theory—an inductive rather than deductive method. And while I have been trained in and have an appreciation of both quantitative and qualitative sociological and anthropological methods and techniques, the methods I have relied upon in my research are guided by the topic of inquiry. Sexual relations and prostitution, given their private and often clandestine nature, have steered me toward an almost exclusive use of qualitative methods, involving forms of participant observation, semistructured interviewing, document analysis, and participatory action-research.

This book is informed by a number of different projects and studies that I have been involved with over the past decade. My initial study of Caribbean prostitution involved the Dutch Caribbean island of Curaçao and a primary analysis of historical documents and in-depth interviews with forty-six participants in the sex industry—

prostitutes, brothel owners, police officials, medical practitioners, and clients. Fieldwork was supplemented by observations and secondary analyses of earlier studies of prostitution on the island.[17] The study in Curaçao prompted me to investigate the subject of prostitution further, for while rich as an ethnography, it also revealed the paucity of contemporary academic, including feminist, knowledge on prostitution, for both the Caribbean and other countries in the global south. It also pointed to the existence of a particular category of women (light-skinned Latinas) who were defined as the ideal prostitute in Curaçao—the "SanDom"—raising questions about the role of race in Caribbean configurations of sexuality and femininity. Moreover, the apparent voluntary and conscious migration of women from around the region to Curaçao for prostitution, and the definition by the women of their engagement as *work*, urged me to explore understandings of prostitution in the wider Caribbean and globally. These trends complicated feminist social theories and everyday conceptions of prostitution and the sex trade in that they suggested that prostitution was not only gendered in a particular way, but also racialized, and that prostitution was not simply an activity forced upon women, but also an income-generating practice women consciously engaged in. My interest to better understand these dimensions led to research about definitions of sex work around the world, through interviews with sex workers and sex worker activists, secondary analyses of documents, participant observations in various meetings on prostitution and sex work, and visits to brothels, red-light districts, and prostitution sites in predominantly "developing" or former Third World countries.[18]

A third leg of research that greatly informs this book was a collaborative, action-research project on the Caribbean sex trade that took place in eight locations spanning the English, Spanish, and Dutch Caribbean. Initially I was involved in the conceptualization, design, and fund-raising for a region-wide project but quickly took up the overall coordination and management. As project director, I worked closely with a steering committee that was attached to the University of Havana, the Caribbean Association for Feminist Research and Action in Trinidad, and the Instituto Latinoamericano de Servicios Legales Alternativos in Colombia. The steering committee trained and supervised eight teams who conducted research in sites in Suriname, Guyana, Barbados, the Netherlands Antilles, the Dominican Republic, Jamaica, Belize, and Colombia. A total of 191 sex workers were interviewed in the eight countries, and the project brought together a mix of Caribbean feminist researchers and intellectuals, national sex worker organizations, health workers, social activists, and graduate students.[19] The research project culminated in a two-day bilingual conference in Jamaica that the steering committee organized together with the Mona Unit of the Centre for Gender and Development Studies at the University of the West Indies, at which the results of the fieldwork were presented. From the two years of work we produced a research report that I later expanded with additional articles and edited into a book.[20] The collaborative nature as well as the scope of the project required continual discussion and exchange about interpretation of the data, a collective brainstorming and theorizing about the research data, and a synthesis of the outcomes. The project accumulated a vast amount of qualitative materials and data on the subject, some of which, in both raw and digested versions, was made available to me, and which greatly enhanced my own knowledge about Caribbean sexual-economic relations.

During a year spent in Jamaica in 2000–2001, while standing in as head of the Mona Unit of the Centre for Gender and Development Studies at the University of the West Indies, I conducted document research at the main university library, engaged in participant observation and unstructured interviews with sex workers at Negril and other tourism centers, and held formal and informal interviews with researchers and activists involved with sex work research and study.[21] Living and working in Jamaica exposed me on a daily basis to everyday practices and local discussions, and this was a critical period for the formulation of ideas that connected my previous insights about sex work to broader questions about the organization of Caribbean sexuality. In 2001 I was also part of a research team that conducted a study on adolescent participation and rights in Jamaica. My specific contribution was an analysis of qualitative data on adolescent sexuality that had been collected through eighteen focus group sessions among 170 young people between the ages of 10 and 19 from three, predominantly working-class, communities in Jamaica.[22] The study served to confirm many ideas and hunches I had about Caribbean sexuality and sexual-economic relations, while the age factor introduced important nuances. It was also during this period that I became involved with the Red Thread Women's Development Programme in Guyana on a project on sex worker needs and empowerment that continued into 2002 and that, due to its emphasis on sexual health, launched me into thinking further about the politics of HIV/AIDS research.

The following chapters draw from this long-term engagement with the subject of Caribbean sex work. It is a study that I hope will contribute to the production of knowledge about postcolonial Caribbean lives and subjectivities, and to thinking further about Caribbean sexualized struggles, identities, and potentialities in the twenty-first century.

2

Past Studies, New Directions: Constructions and Reconstructions of Caribbean Sexuality

A substantial body of literature exists that has produced ideas about Caribbean sexual relations, identities, and behaviors, while avoiding an explicit focus on sexuality. Studies of the "New World Negro" in the English-speaking Caribbean during the first half of the twentieth century amply illustrate this tendency. Viewed against European and Euro-American systems and cultures, the departure of black sexual and familial relations from the dominant notion of "family"—male-headed, patrilineal, heterosexual, monogamous, and co-residential—sparked intense debate and concern among social scientists. Various arguments were formulated, and varying explanations and theories sought, that would account for the particular conditions and practices of black, postemancipation New World arrangements, where marriage was not a norm among the working class and partnerships and sexual relationships followed a number of other patterns.[1] Many such studies dealt with, if not centered upon, expressions of black sexual relations, commonly defined as "mating." Concerns about "immoral" and "loose" sexual practices, "promiscuity," "unstable" or "irregular" conjugal relations, and "illegitimacy" of children often propelled early-twentieth-century studies into "the Negro" condition. Notions of black pathology, demoralization, disorganization, and deviancy pervaded the discourse. In particular, ideas of the American sociologist E. Franklin Frazier, who advanced that slavery had broken down black family life and had created unregulated, deviant behavior that included criminal activity and promiscuity, served to inform and frame research and interventions that dominated academic understandings of sexual relations in the Caribbean for several decades.[2] Ultimately, in this perspective, an accommodation to dominant European-American sexual and family norms would erase such pathologies and produce a more "civilized" New World Negro.[3]

An alternative to this perspective about black sexuality emerged through the anthropological research of a North American couple, Melville Jean and Frances Herskovits, during the 1930s and 1940s.[4] From a wide range of in-depth studies of life and customs in West Africa and the African diaspora, including Haiti, Suriname, and Trinidad, the anthropologists established a number of household, kinship, and sexual arrangements in which women were central actors, polygyny was informally accepted, and the nuclear, two-parent, co-residential union coexisted alongside extended women-only families and "keeping" relations.[5] The Herskovits' rejected the notion that racial patterns were biologically fixed or pathological, or caused exclusively by slavery and the plantation system, but instead argued that "culture is learned, rather than determined by some element in the biological endowment of a people, and that in consequence any tradition can pass from the group that has devised it to any other that have the opportunity to learn it."[6] The Herskovits' produced a body of work that affirmed the uniqueness and particularity of Afro-Caribbean culture that was seen to derive from West African customs and heritages, termed *Africanisms*. Their positive evaluation of black familial and sexual life produced a notion of informal polygyny as a culturally legitimate and acceptable relationship for African Caribbean peoples. The analysis challenged dominant ideas at the time of the unruly and deviant nature of black working-class Caribbean society, and foregrounded a specific African cultural dynamic that shaped and defined social relations in the region.

Constructing Polygamous Men and Loose Black Women

Through the early-twentieth-century studies images of the "stable" family for the elite and the emerging middle classes, polygamous behavior of men, and promiscuity of African Caribbean working people became facts. "Loose" sexuality remained associated with Africanness, and black working-class populations continued to receive most of the attention from social scientists who wished to research mating patterns. Extensive research among peasant, rural agricultural, and working-class communities proliferated from the early 1950s to the 1970s in the English-speaking Caribbean, from a variety of theoretical perspectives. One of the first Caribbean intellectuals to embark upon studies in this area in the post–World War II independence era was the Jamaican anthropologist Fernando Henriques, who published a number of studies on race, color, family, sexuality, and prostitution.[7] The groundbreaking works of anthropologist Edith Clarke and sociologists R. T. Smith and M. G. Smith are also of importance here. Their studies sought to validate the specific family forms in the Caribbean as "indigenous" or "*sui generis*"—the specific product of "the peculiar conditions of slavery," yet which included some Africanisms and which embodied its own order, principles, and structures.[8] Caribbean sexuality was defined as organized around heterosexual desire that in turn was lodged in procreative urges, dominated by masculine needs and interests. By the 1960s a movement away from rigid European definitions of "proper" family and sexual relations had occurred. Instead, the social scientists acknowledged that a variety of socially accepted mating systems, including marriage and common-law and visiting unions, were typical Caribbean constructs. Race and class were seen to differentially shape and give meaning to the various sexual arrangements. Informal polygyny such as "outside" relations or "dual marriage systems," where married men maintained a mistress or a second household, was viewed through such studies as normal. In some instances, the notion of promiscuity was redefined. Henriques, for example, took it to mean "unrestricted sexual freedom" and valorized those instances where such freedom was expressed. For him, family and sexual practices of black working-class populations were more fluid and afforded women and men greater sexual freedom than men and women of other classes and races. His studies illuminated desires and behaviors of elite men that resulted in "outside" relations, "twin" households, and prostitution with women of other classes and racial groups, while he argued that such arrangements rested on elite men's desire for sexual freedom. These relationships, he proposed, offered to the men opportunities for sexual satisfaction outside marriage, "as so many marriages are arranged on a basis of color rather than mutual attraction."[9] The tradition of upper-class men to satisfy their sexual desires with "other" women was granted normalcy through such a perspective. Men were defined as free, biologically driven social actors who had access to, and could dispose of, material or economic assets in their search for emotional and sexual satisfaction. As Henriques concluded at the end of a lavish description of prostitution practices around the world, in modern and premodern societies: "the ordinary healthy male if deprived of sexual intercourse for a long time is liable to disregard any moral conventions which impose restraint, and indulge himself where and how he can."[10] Quite simply, men needed sex and they desired unrestricted sexual freedom. Black working-class women figured in such studies of the Caribbean as the trope of the sexually free and uninhibited, and hence most sexually accessible, woman.

Male power, agency, and sexual rights remained a central preoccupation in the mid-twentieth-century Caribbean studies of family in the English-speaking Caribbean. In Raymond T. Smith's concept of matrifocality, male power was diminished and marginalized by the social prestige accorded to the mother-child bond and female-centered character of the household. A reassertion of power and authority through sexual relations with more than one woman was represented as the logical response to such marginalization. M. G. Smith identified a set of principles for Caribbean family and sexual relations, noting that there was "some modification of monogamy, while formally avoiding polygyny."[11] Men, he stated, "are permitted to have two or more extraresidential mates, women are not," with men being accorded rights of sexual access to women.[12] Women who strayed from this norm and who entered into sexual relations with two or more men simultaneously were defined as promiscuous, while men were thought to be "better able to indulge in such behavior."[13] Within these sociologists' work, sexual urges for women were located in procreative desires, and for both women and men defined exclusively as heterosexual.

Studies that followed these mid-twentieth-century masters of Caribbean social studies continued the trend of a muted celebration of a form of polygyny and an assumed natural male right of sexual access to women. Women's sexuality, if seen to be unattached to men, was defined as lasciviously deviant—"good women" were constructed as sexual for procreative purposes and as sexual servants to men. "Visiting unions," "outside" relationships, and common-law marriages, in which the man could have multiple partners and which were once viewed as aberrations or pathologies of Negro folk, were thus deemed by the 1970s to be standard Caribbean practices of sexuality and family: acceptable, legitimate, and specific to the region's own historical, cultural, economic, and social conditions. Heteropatriarchy was both normalized and made indigenous through these social scientific studies. The emergence of these ideas about sexuality coincided with the establishment of independent Creole nation-states in the West Indies during the 1950s and 1960s. New nationalist projects in the English-speaking Caribbean were profoundly masculinist, to some extent informed by black consciousness movements and struggles, yet ultimately reformist, resulting in a "considerable collusion of Caribbean men with the colonial authorities to reproduce colonial hierarchies" in which patriarchy was one axis of power.[14] The new postcolonial elite, while embracing the newly independent Caribbean as uniquely hybrid in its social and cultural structures, privileged heterosexuality and masculine dominance, upheld a modified version of the European monogamous marriage system as the dominant norm, and continued to view African Caribbean working women's sexual behavior as loose yet subordinate to men's needs.

Various policy and social-scientific initiatives from the mid-1980s have continued the focus on men in the English-speaking Caribbean. Although providing rich ethnographic detail, much of this research reiterates the image of a specific type of Caribbean sexuality that began to be constructed in the 1930s, confirming informal polygyny and heterosexuality as the accepted norm, centering sexuality in biology, and connecting sexual relations to considerations of pleasure, identity, and power for men, and to procreation, money, and status for women. Errol Miller, for example, explained male sexual "excess" and polygamous behavior in the Caribbean as arising from

the workings of patriarchy and the struggles by black men to overcome racial oppression and to obtain power, authority, and status in
society.[15] Women were defined in his theory as pawns in men's quests
for racialized power and dominance, located as passive subjects whose
gendered and sexual lives were constructed by men's desires and actions.[16] Graham Dann's study in Barbados in the 1980s attempted to
dispel the "fantasy and undocumented charges of male irresponsibility
and worthlessness" that, he argued, informed Caribbean discourses on
masculinity.[17] Women's dominance in the household and child-rear-
ing matters and her sexual "looseness" were explicitly framed here as
key to understanding the inadequacies and deficiencies of men:

> The young Barbadian male . . . is typically introduced to society by a
> woman who may have one or more boyfriends, depending upon her
> economic circumstances. In many cases there is no father figure to
> whom he can relate or on whom he can pattern his life. In such an envi-
> ronment of maternal dependence he learns that matriarchal households,
> male absenteeism and outside affairs are normal. For him they consti-
> tute an anticipatory role model for the formation of the self and for fu-
> ture expected behavior.[18]

Female promiscuity and matrifocality, to which boys were exposed, were posited as the cause for boys' future views and sexual behaviors, which included a natural sex curiosity that required
satisfaction from an early age, mutual sexual exploitation, heterosexuality as the only acceptable form of sexual expression, pregnancy as
proof of sexual competency and compatibility, and a double standard
around fidelity. The study reinforced the long-standing image of
Caribbean masculinity as embedded in a natural heterosexual drive
and pathologized women as sexually irresponsible and as producers
of maladjusted boys and men.

Socialization patterns, sexual attitudes and beliefs, and social values, customs, and behavioral norms of men represented in the study
by Dann also constitute the core themes of studies by Jamaican anthropologist Barry Chevannes over a fifteen-year period, which draw
from and confirm aspects of the earlier studies.[19] He argues that it was
generally accepted that multiple sexual relationships such as polygyny exist (in Jamaica, for example, around 50 percent of men practice

this, according to one report he cites), but notes a lack of accurate research in this area as well as the invisibility of women's multiple relationships. For adult men, he states, sexual prowess is an ideal, and sexual relations a site of contestation between women and men, with "male dominance" and "female assertiveness" competing for the upper hand. His later studies allow for some variation on these themes on the basis of ethnicity. For African Caribbean men and women, he concludes:

> Impregnation and pregnancy are the principle means by which a young male and young female respectively announce their claim to adulthood. . . . Becoming an African Caribbean man privileges one to engage in all the above forms of sexual relationships: from the promiscuous and casual to multiple partnerships (which in effect is unrecognized polygamy). A woman has no such licence. Beyond casual relationships she is stigmatized: whore, prostitute, jammette, mattress, loose. . . . A man is not a real man unless he is sexually active. But his activism must be *hetero*, not *homo*sexual.[20]

Women on the other hand need three things, "good money, good treatment, and good sex," in that order, "with sex coming last."[21]

Such studies on Caribbean masculinity in the late twentieth century provide thick descriptions of male sexual and gendered behavior, yet tend to reiterate the image of a specific type of Caribbean sexuality that has been constructed through studies of family and mating since the 1930s. Women's sexuality and sexual agency are in some instances pathologized, often simplified or obscured, while masculine heterosexual, polygynous behavior is privileged and normalized.

Procreative Women

Edith Clarke was one of the first earlier Anglophone Caribbean social scientists to produce an image of female sexual agency that went beyond notions of black working-class women as the embodiment of pure sexual freedom, or as pawns, or maladjusters of men. She documented black women's sexuality in Jamaica as exclusively heterosexual in orientation, and which, particularly for women living independently on family land and for single women who worked and lived around the sugar industry, acted autonomously from male power and masculine needs. She observed about the independent rural-based woman, "she may have a long succession of lovers by whom she bears children, without any of the men ever joining the household," and argued that despite performing many domestic duties for her male partner, a woman had the right to terminate the arrangement at her own will.[22] These women, she proposed, could determine the type of sexual relations they entered into with men, and that some even "preferred a variety of lovers to having one man and being faithful to him."[23] In "housekeeper" or "house sharing" arrangements among migrant sugar workers, she found that women provided domestic and sexual labor for the duration of the work season in exchange for keep and a place to live, making no claim to male sexual exclusivity. Male polygamy seemed acceptable. Women's sexual agency and desire, or mating, however, was defined as profoundly attached to reproduction through heterosexual intercourse: not only was sexual activity between women and men regarded as a natural occurrence, but the desire for, and logical outcome of, such activity was assumed to be children. A woman, she noted, "is only considered 'really' a woman after she has borne a child."[24] Women's sexual activity with multiple male partners, in the absence of procreation and a domesticized arrangement, remained labeled as promiscuous behavior.

The upsurge of feminist studies in the 1980s brought with it a new set of studies that both challenged and reaffirmed earlier representations of female sexuality in the Anglophone Caribbean. The Women in the Caribbean Project (WICP), for example, described in greater detail aspects of women's lives and femininity in several territories, providing the contours of a counterimage of female sexual behavior and identity.[25] Rather than defining women's sexual relationships with men as loose, promiscuous, or indiscriminate, the study argued that the patterns of visiting unions and common-law marriages were preferable for working-class, predominantly Afro-Caribbean, women because they afforded women greater economic independence than formal marriage and allowed women some freedom to organize and manage their domestic life in a manner most beneficial to themselves and their children. Marriage, the WICP study stated, was an ideal for women of all classes, with financial security and respectability important conditions for women to enter into such a union.[26] The study substantively and self-consciously foregrounded women's interests and needs. Nevertheless, certain dominant images of Caribbean womanhood remained fixed. Women's sexual interests were located squarely in childbearing and rearing, defined exclusively as heterosexual, and were seen to uphold the dominant norm of monogamous marriage. Issues of outside or sharing sexual relationships were treated ambiguously. Caribbean working women were constituted as heterosexually faithful to one male partner at a time, tolerant of outside children by their partner but not of the "baby-mother," and accepting of male polygamy as a natural condition of masculinity. "Playing around" by women was roundly condemned, although female promiscuity, particularly among working-class women of African descent, was accepted if children were the result, even if the woman had children from several different men. Multiple partnering for women was further justified on the grounds of a woman needing to sustain a relationship with the baby's father in order to ensure economic security for the family. Sexual agency and economics were through such studies firmly tied together for women, although only through their role as procreators and caretakers of the family. In the absence of children to feed, house, or care for, working-class women's sexual agency remained obscured, although the WICP data suggested that some change among middle-class women was occurring, as some women "were having outside affairs and making new liaisons" that were not tied to procreation and financial security.[27]

Women's sexual agency and their sexual needs, desires, and behaviors have for the most part been concealed in studies on family and kinship, despite some of the earlier observations made by Clarke and the WICP study. In conclusion about middle-class colored and black women in the postemancipation period, feminist sociologist Christine Barrow describes the dominant construct of female sexuality that has persisted:

> For them marriage and legitimacy became an obsession as they sought respectability for their families. They vociferously denounced what they saw as the promiscuity and immorality of the lower classes and pronounced proper family life increasingly based on western patterns of faithful marriage, legitimate children and nuclear family households.

But they were faced with their own husbands, fathers and sons, firmly embedded in Caribbean culture, for whom peer group popularity, non-domestic activity, marital segregation, concubinage and outside children had become a way of life. It remains to be seen whether the demands for marital fidelity, domestic togetherness and joint social activity on the part of young contemporary middle-class women will result in a change in these long-established structural principles of Caribbean kinship.[28]

Research in the 1990s mainly reiterated the earlier insights into family and kinship relations, yet continued to raise questions about whether the older structuring principles were undergoing change. As one team of researchers stated: "the importance of childbearing as a primary definition of femininity in the Caribbean may be simultaneously undergoing change among different groups of women in the society" as "women of all ages and socio-economic groups are gradually shifting their concepts of femininity to incorporate notions of self-fulfillment and self-actualization of their individual goals."[29] To what extent the claiming of sexual agency other than for purposes of childbearing and rearing is a part of the redefinition of Caribbean femininity is a central theme for the rest of this book.

Late-Twentieth-Century Caribbean Feminist Thought on Sexuality

Gender has, for several decades, been theorized through the counter-prism of Caribbean studies, particularly feminist studies in the Anglophone Caribbean, where it is no longer viewed as a mark of European interpretation and dominance, but complexly as a set of social relations that are produced and reconfigured through very specific histories of colonialism and patriarchies, resistances and rebellions. Gender is thus defined as not only discursively and materially produced, but also thoroughly indigenized, constructed socially, politically, and theoretically as a pillar of Caribbean identity. It is thus accepted as an organizing principle of the society, the economy, oppositional consciousness, and political struggle. Sexual desires, agency, and identity, however, have barely been broached in this body of literature, with the result that the topic of sex often remains subsumed in discussions of gender relations.

The "silence" on the subject of sexuality in Caribbean feminist studies has led to varying positions that appear in sometimes confusing and contradictory ways. The most obvious is that it becomes completely invisible, due to a disappearance of the concept of sex. Caribbean feminist political economist Eudine Barriteau, for example, notes that "at one level gender has come to stand erroneously as a trendier synonym for the biological differences and signifiers implied by the word 'sex.' Now, on almost all questionnaires there is the mandatory category 'gender' in which one is supposed to reply 'male or female.'"[30] Gender simply takes over from the older dualism of "the two sexes," and any notion of sexuality is absorbed into the gendered dichotomy. Another trend inadvertently represents sex as a passive, natural state or condition, a blank surface (male and female) upon which gender (masculinity and femininity) as social identity and role is assembled. The "two sexes" are thus socialized into gendered "values, customs and behavioural norms" where sexuality is reduced to heterosexual intercourse and becomes an expression of seemingly natural, biologically driven relations between men and women.[31] Heterosexuality is the unquestioned and naturalized norm, and gender and sex are defined in binary terms, either as oppositional or as complementary bodies. Linda Peake and Alissa Trotz, in their detailed study of Indian and African working-class women in Guyana, write of this view, "the dualist conceptual frameworks that Caribbean studies of femininity and masculinity have spawned . . . overlook the often contradictory and competing qualities of such dualisms and the individuals they purport to describe."[32] In yet other studies, gender is viewed as that which can be variously constructed from a bedrock of sexual difference, yet this difference is commonly referred to as a binary set of "the two sexes."[33] A purely social constructionist approach that refers to gender as "complex systems of personal and social relations through which women and men are socially created and maintained and through which they gain access to, or are allocated, status, power, and material resources within society" is also evident in Caribbean feminist studies.[34] Here sex is subsumed into the social construction of gender and becomes immaterial—it simply disappears. As feminist theorist Judith Butler notes about this trend more generally: "the social construction of the natural presupposes a cancellation of the natural by the social . . . if gender is the social significance that sex assumes within a given culture . . . then what, if anything, is left of 'sex' once it has assumed its social character as gender? . . . gender emerges not as a term in continued relationship of opposition to sex, but as a term which absorbs and displaces 'sex'. . . ."[35]

Despite the lack of explicit attention to sex in feminist studies, insinuated in some of the work of contemporary Caribbean feminists is an appreciation of sexuality. Social historian Patricia Mohammed acknowledges that late-twentieth-century feminism has tended to adopt Foucault's contribution to understanding sexuality as distinct from gender, as "an historical construction rather than as a natural libido arising from biological urges," and that "sex, sexuality and sexual relations must also be examined with historical specificity."[36] Her claim echoes earlier feminist arguments for the recognition of a distinct sexual system and a specific theory of sexuality in order to more precisely describe and explain erotic life.[37] She goes on to note, however, that "sexual difference is deeply embedded in subterranean aspects of culture, in mythology and rite" and is therefore "least amenable to easy change."[38] Perhaps it is this assumed difficulty of accessing, deconstructing, or transforming the subject that has convinced many Caribbean feminists to leave sex and sexuality buried in a gender analysis. Or perhaps, as occurred among black feminists in the United States, not only is it difficult to tackle a stubborn area of social relations, but efforts to address sexuality are constantly in danger of reinscribing a discourse of negativity and hypersexuality onto the bodies of women of color. It has been noted that a politics of silence has enveloped much black American feminist writings on black female sexuality, and that "to date, largely through the work of black feminist literary critics, we know more about the elision of sexuality by black women than we do about the possible varieties of expression of sexual desire."[39]

Few feminists have sought to navigate the disorderly terrain of contemporary Caribbean sexuality in any depth, although as we have seen, there is an increasing acknowledgment that it is an area warranting sustained research and study. In the few sexuality studies that do exist, we are shown complex behaviors and desires that do not always fit neatly into the dominant construct of gender. Gloria

Wekker, who extensively studied same-gender relations among working-class women in Suriname, insists that it is necessary to retain a distinction between concepts of gender and sexuality. Her study illustrates how in *mati work*—a social institution among working-class women that involves sexual relations with men and women, either simultaneously or consecutively—"it is possible to have a female gender identity, without a muted, passive, romantic, cuddly, non-genital, 'vanilla' sexuality, and also without a fixed, cross-gender sexual orientation."[40] This female sexuality does not behave in accordance with the dominant norm of femininity and therefore cannot be completely subsumed into or explained by gender. Women who express desire and passion through a sexual relationship with another woman can be seen in such studies to stray beyond the boundaries of existing gendered categories, demanding a separate space and place within Caribbean feminist discourse.

In incisive analyses of sexuality in Trinidad and Tobago and the Bahamas, M. Jacqui Alexander powerfully demonstrates that the impetus to distinguish between sexuality and gender does not simply rest in social practices between and among women and men, but is deeply embedded in state discourses and laws, pointing out that the state "also has the capacity to create new political constituencies" through the criminalization of particular types of sexual behavior.[41] Women who engage in same-gender sexual relations and those who sell sex (lesbians and prostitutes) are identified by Alexander as two categories constructed in Trinidadian and Bahamian law that are defined and treated as different on the basis of their sexuality. They are groups defined as "operating outside the boundaries of law and therefore poised to be disciplined and punished within it."[42] The state has codified difference lodged in sexual behavior and expressions of erotic desire, rather than in gender. Indeed, as studies of homosexuality in Cuba and the Dominican Republic demonstrate, while many men who have sex with men socially identify as masculine, it is their sexual activities and desires, not their gender identification, that sets them apart from other men in state policies, laws, and everyday practices.[43] In the Dominican Republic it has also been noted that sex workers and homosexuals are harassed and incarcerated for sexual behavior that breaches the law and transgresses social norms.[44]

Discrimination on the basis of gender is codified in most national laws as unjust and a violation of civil or human rights, yet discrimination on the basis of sexuality—sexual practices, desires, and identities—is still possible in many countries due to laws that criminalize anal sex, prostitution, and same-gender sexual activities. Sexual difference is thus firmly etched into Caribbean society as semiautonomous and distinct from gender, constituted through, and fully embedded in, national state discourses, laws, and everyday social practices.

The conceptual and legal distinction between sexuality and gender is, however, overshadowed by everyday understandings that lock sex and gender together into one body. Masculinity and femininity in many Caribbean societies are commonly "attributed to sex" and are located in "reproductive functions" and "immutable, biological 'facts'."[45] That is, heterosexuality is assumed to be a central component of gender identity in many peoples' lives. In their study in multiracial Guyana, Peake and Trotz conclude the following about an Afro-Guyanese community: "heterosexuality is represented as the only legitimate sexuality . . . it is sex with the opposite sex that makes a man a man and a woman a woman. . . ."[46] It is this powerful set of ideas and practices—that heterosexuality defines gender—that also serves as a reminder that any examination of Caribbean sexuality cannot be conducted completely separate from gender. Carol Vance, in her groundbreaking essay on the politics of sexuality written in the early 1980s, notes that where the contemporary feminist conceptualization of gender relates to the "cultural marking of biological sex" and sexuality to "desire and erotic pleasure," "sexuality and gender are overlapping terrains." Of particular interest, she continues, "is the articulation between specific features of each system, namely how the configurations bear on the experience of being female and conversely, how the definitions of gender resonate with and are reflected in sexuality."[47]

New Directions

Caribbean family, masculinity, and feminist studies contribute in various ways to the mapping and analysis of Caribbean sexuality, and it is from the growing tendency in Caribbean feminist social and historical studies, and the material and legal contexts in which Caribbean sexuality is shaped, that I draw on for this book. Sexual relations, as semiautonomous from gender—structured in, through, but also separately from masculinity and femininity—are foundational ideas for the rest of this study. Furthermore, I take as a starting point that gender identity and gendered relations of power are not the only axes of importance to considerations of sexuality. In agreement with early Caribbean family-studies scholars and those in sexuality studies in other non-Western contexts, I assume that social and cultural constructions of sexual meanings and identities and the ways in which specific communities structure sexual practices are conditioned by other factors: that "whom one is permitted to have sex with, in what ways, under what circumstances and with what specific outcomes are never random: such possibilities are defined through explicit and implicit rules imposed by the sexual cultures of specific communities and the underlying power relations."[48] Race and class are thus earmarked, along with gender, as primary sets of relations of power within which the sexual subject is to be explored and theorized. Important also to my project is the way in which colonialism and neocolonialism shape regimes of sexuality, and the significance of these contexts of power to the constitution of sexual categories.[49] Importantly, then, my theoretical assumptions share with many contemporary researchers and theorists the notion that studies of sexuality are conducted within and against gendered parameters and relations of power, but cannot not be collapsed into gender. In the following, I gather direction from these conceptual and theoretical developments and, while I take gendered categories, identities, and relations of power to be critical to the construction of sexualities in the Caribbean, linkages among sex, race, and colonialism loom very large and provide other contexts for analysis.

The Significance of Race

In tracing through writings, documents, and studies that address sex in the Caribbean, sexuality appears as the modality through which race is made and refashioned in specific ways. First, sex was central to colonial constructions of Otherness and for locating and defining inferiority.[50] Sexual arrangements among the conquered and colonized non-Western Others, such as polygamy, tribadery, sodomy, rape, adultery, prostitution, incest, bestiality, pederasty, and sexual profligacy as well as a perceived lack of sexual modesty were taken as prime indicators of inferiority. These sexual "qualities" placed the Other beyond the boundaries of civilization as defined in Western European Christian society, marking them as degenerate, barbaric, savage, or inhuman, and became, through the eighteenth-century scientific invention of race, embedded in theories of racial difference and primitiveness.[51] Columbus set the tone in 1492 by describing the indigenous people of the Caribbean as undeveloped, almost childlike, who "ought to be good servants" and who could be "civilized" through Christianity.[52] Such first colonial images and ideas drew from observations, or "European monologues," as well as fantasies about Amerindian culture, physical appearance, economy, politics, and gendered and sexual arrangements.[53] So while Amerindian society was divided into two camps—the Arawaks and Caribs[54]—with the former described as egalitarian and peaceful in its gender relations (and autocratic in political organization), where women and men shared many tasks and responsibilities, and the latter as highly gender segregated and oppressive to women (yet egalitarian in its political system), where women were captured, enslaved, and treated harshly,[55] there have been continual comments in historical records and documents about a lack of distinction in gendered behavior and appearance, as well as about sexual behaviors that did not conform to dominant European ideologies of what men and women should be and do.[56] Colonial, Christian-informed categories of masculinity and femininity were the yardstick for description and evaluation of Amerindian gender and sexual life, and sexual practices that deviated from this dominant norm contributed to the classification of Amerindians as inferior. As Jara and Spadaccini note in their introduction to a collection of studies that examine the legacy of the Columbian image of Amerindians: "The central feature of native inferiority was their inability to discriminate, as seen in their culinary, religious and sexual habits. Sexual deviations were explained by the generalized selection of the wrong mates, indulging in bestiality, sodomy, incest, and other unnatural practices."[57]

While the dual themes of oppression and civilization were based on ideas about race and sexuality, and were established with the first encounter between the invaders and the natives, it was the enslavement of Africans in the New World that was crucial to the consolidation of racialized sexuality as sources of power and domination in the Americas. Slave women were cast in colonial imaginations as promiscuous, "cruel and negligent as a mother, fickle as a wife," and immoral.[58] Black femininity was often represented as naturally "hot constitution'd," and sensuous in an animal-like way, lacking all the qualities that defined "decent" womanhood or women of "purity of blood."[59] The sexual imagery, leaning on associations between black womanhood and natural earthy instincts, licentiousness, immorality, and pathology, was often painted to arouse disgust and abhorrence for purposes of maintaining slavery by the plantocracy or, alternatively, to illustrate the abolitionists' cause by pointing out how slavery degraded the lives of Africans. It did not, however, deter European male pursuit of sexual intercourse with black women or fascination, delight, and pleasure with the black female body. The region often stood in European imaginations "as a land of sexual opportunity for young European males," and black women—enslaved or free—were defined as the sexual property of white men.[60] Caribbean historian Hilary Beckles states about this characteristic that slavery meant "not only the compulsory extraction of labor from Blacks but also, in theory at least, slave owners' right to total sexual access to slaves."[61] White slave owners made ample use of this "right": rape and sexual abuse were commonplace, and concubinage and prostitution were institutionalized.[62]

Anxieties and obsessions about sexualities of oppressed, conquered, and colonized populations stood at the very heart of European bourgeois debates and classifications of humanity and civilization, and conditioned strategies, policies, and laws around race.[63] These have been acknowledged by many social theorists. Chandra Talpade Mohanty, for example, observes, "the maintenance of strong sexual and racial boundaries was thus essential to the distinctions which were made between 'legitimate rulers' and 'childlike subjects.'"[64] Sander Gilman likewise points out that "laws applying to the control of slaves (such as the 1685 French *code noir* and its American analogues) placed great emphasis on the control of the slave as sexual object, both in terms of permitted and forbidden sexual contacts as well as requiring documentation as to the legal status of the offspring of slaves."[65] Sexuality was, however, not only critical in the process of the definition and control of the racial or cultural Other, but also central to the reconstitution of inferiorized and colonized groups. While varying theories of the cultural Other produced competing discourses on human difference, sexuality featured as an axis around which humankind could be reclassified. Postcolonial theorist Robert Young notes that "Nineteenth century theories of race did not just consist of essentializing differentiations between self and other: they were also about a fascination with people having sex—interminable, adulterating, aleatory, illicit, inter-racial sex."[66] "Hybridity"—manifest as "mulatto," "mestizo," "quarteroon," a person of mixed race, or a "cross-breed"—and the fecundity of the off-spring of cross-racial sexual unions were of utmost concern. If the progeny could be shown to be infertile, this could signify the presence of two distinctly different species and could prove the polygenesis of races, producing an argument for physical distance, segregation, and apartheid between races, and a legitimation for differential treatment. Alternatively, the fertility of a person of mixed race could prove the monogenesis of human races and the possibility of cross-fertilization and genetic mixing. The latter argument generated ideas that the dissemination of cultured white genes through sexual intercourse would produce a mixed group of people who stood to inherit the traits of civilization of white Europeans and who would thus be lifted out of its racially encoded place of savagery. In recognition of this dynamic, it has been noted that "according to social constructions implanted in the Americas by the Iberian colonizers, white genes mingling with Indian genes produced a 'half-breed' race of *mestizos* . . . wherein the higher status in racialist rank (white, *español*) gave superior genetic stock to the lower (*indio* and *negro*) to serve thereby as a 'civilizing' cultural factor."[67] Sexuality provided a route through which a racially inferior group could be brought into the folds of civilized society.[68]

On the other hand, such theory produced notions of the degeneration and demise of the white race. Racial pollution and contamination caused through sexual contact was a common theme in this line of thought. As Gilman writes, "Miscegenation was a fear (and a word) from the late nineteenth century vocabulary of sexuality. It was a fear of not merely interracial sexuality but of its results, the decline of the population."[69] Either way, sexual intercourse between the races has been a site for cultural mixing. The mulatto, mestizo, or metis who embodies racialized sexual transgressions, however, is commonly defined as a tragic figure, a "hybrid"—who inhabits the outer margins of respectable and civilized society, who is possibly infertile or sterile, and who is positioned as the ideal domestic, sexual servant or prostitute, and who is denied legitimacy as a social equal to whites.

In addition to the re-creation of race through sex, sexuality is a modality through which entire racialized groups were terrorized and violated in the Caribbean. Rape and the mutilation of sexual organs of conquered, enslaved, and indentured women and men were commonplace physical violations that accompanied other brutal colonial acts. Such violence was designed to oppress, control, and make submissive populations that were deemed fit for labor in the gold mines or on the plantations.[70] Sexual violence perpetrated by the European and colonial elite against racially oppressed women and men was a means through which the captive populations could be disciplined and controlled.

Historically, the reconstitution of race through sexuality has not been confined to European thought and deed, or exclusively to acts of violence. The use of sexuality by the colonized to uplift the race through whitening—both corporeally, as in producing light-skinned children, and culturally, through sexual association—is firmly embedded in the psyche and behaviors of the colonized in the Caribbean. Fanon's writings are a reminder of how deeply entwined race and sexuality were around the middle of the twentieth century. As he wrote about the colonized black Caribbean man's desires:

I wish to be acknowledged not as *black* but as *white*.
Now . . . who but a white woman can do this for me? By loving me she proves that I am worthy of white love. I am loved like a white man.
I am a white man.
I marry white culture, white beauty, white whiteness.
When my restless hands caress those white breasts, they grasp white civilization and dignity and make them mine.[71]

Of Caribbean women, he noted, "the race must be whitened: every woman in Martinique knows this, says this, repeats it. Whiten the race, save the race . . . it is always essential to avoid falling back into the pit of niggerhood, and every woman in the Antilles, whether in a casual flirtation or in a serious affair, is determined to select the least black of the men."[72]

Sexual desire of the colonized was imbued with racial meaning, and sexuality the avenue through which race could be reconfigured and "civilization" obtained. Blackness could be whitened through sexual intercourse or sexual association, and race was refashioned through embodied sexual acts. Uplifting the race meant an escape from the degraded status of black and from oppressions, discriminations, and stigmatizations of blackness. Whiteness conferred class privilege and a possibility of improved economic standing, and whiteness could be obtained through sexual liaisons. To what extent this pertains today is of course open to question and is undoubtedly more complex than fifty years ago, particularly due to the emergence of strong black consciousness and nationalist movements, and the reconfigurations of race relations within the postcolonial Caribbean. In later parts of this book, particularly in the context of tourism, I explore how the strategic use of sexuality to obtain "whiteness," and development through associating with and marrying whites, and possibly leaving the Caribbean to live as "white" in Europeanized countries, returns as a common feature of social-sexual relations today.

The Problem of Exoticism

Sexuality and race combine in inextricable yet very specific discursive and material ways in the Caribbean, and sexuality is a central prism for viewing racial oppression and violence as well as strategies for upliftment by the oppressed. Commenting about late-eighteenth- and early-nineteenth-century Puerto Rico, Eileen Findlay remarks that "racially saturated sexual norms and practices were key to the ordering of society."[73] To what extent postcolonial meanings of sexuality remain racialized in the Caribbean is explored in the following chapters. Some of what we encounter in this history refracts an exoticist discourse,

where the notion of exoticism captures the simultaneous romanticiza-
tion and domination of the racial, ethnic, or cultural Other that has
occurred through colonial and imperialist projects.[74] As an approach to
the non-Western world, it is associated with the legitimation of
European conquest, control, and domination, as well as for eighteenth-
century escapist fantasies and vicarious enjoyment of sex and violence
by European literary intellectuals and artists. Porter writes:

> The invention of the "exotic" evidently satisfied needs amongst a Euro-
> pean and, later, an Atlantic, civilization which, as it progressively ex-
> plored and dominated the entire globe with its guns and sails,
> increasingly assumed the right to define human values and conduct in
> their highest expression. Other cultures, other creeds, were not merely
> different, not even merely lower, but positively—even objectively—
> strange. It was not merely the remoteness of geographical distance in a
> world where miles counted for much, but the ineluctable sense that all
> their mental processes and logical deductions were equally as alien. La-
> beling the anthropological Other as exotic legitimated treating the peo-
> ples of the "third world" as fit to be despised—destroyed even, or at
> least doomed, like the Tasmanian aborigines, to extinction—while con-
> currently also constituting them as projections of Western fantasies.[75]

Exoticism valorized peoples and cultures that were different and re-
mote, concomitantly imposing a status of inferiority upon them. The
Orient was captured as the epitome of the exotic: a strange and unfamiliar world; both fascinating and terrifying; inviting to the curious
explorer, yet threatening to all standards of civilization upheld in
Europe; seductive in its paradise-like, unblemished "virgin" state, yet
bestial in its perceived barbaric moments. Hulme notes that the original Orientalist discourse that enveloped the Caribbean through
Columbus's initial perceptions and ideas was soon displaced by a
"discourse of savagery" that centered on the "barbarian" nature of "the
Cannibals" and had little positive or romantic to say about the native
inhabitants.[76] However, efforts to abolish slavery and to argue for just
treatment of Indians and Africans on the basis of their humanity
reintroduced an exoticist discourse, with "noble savages," "Ebony
Queens," and "Sable Beauties" appearing in the accounts of travelers,
traders, and antislavery advocates.

Nineteenth-century Europe also witnessed a flourish of art, poetry, and literature that took delight in black women. Baudelaire's "Black Venus" and poetry inspired by his mistress of color, the bust of *Venus Africaine* sculpted by Cordier in 1851, and Picasso's *Olympia* of 1901 all belong to the tradition of Europe's exoticization of African women. The eroticization of women of the different cultures or races was integral to this movement, whereby their sexuality was defined as highly attractive and fascinating, yet related to the natural primitiveness and lower order of the other cultural group.[77] According to Porter, exotic lands and peoples provided Europeans with "paradigms of the erotic." Away from the repressive sexual mores of Western Europe, strange cultures and particularly the women in them became sites where sex "was neither penalized, not pathologized nor exclusively procreative."[78] Womanhood among the colonized represented uninhibited, unbridled sensuality and sexual pleasure for the colonizer. Exoticism in its various expressions brought legitimacy to Western rule and is distinguished from other European racisms by fostering the illusion of an admiration for, delight in, and attraction to the Other, while positioning the Other as inferior and suitable for domination. Sharpley-Whiting writes about this discourse:

> White supremacy takes many forms, from extreme hatred of difference to an intensified adoration of *Other* bodies. The exoticist represents the latter supremacist. He contemplates black women as mere objects, things to be possessed, in his world of collectible exotica. In the exoticist's world, the black female provides rapturous delights, a detour from the ennui of whiteness. Black women serve as savorous spices, seasonings that come in a variety of colors and ethnic flavors to whet the exoticist's palate.[79]

Racialized dimensions of sexuality under slavery were not uniform, with the category of women of "mixed race"—the mulatto, mustee, or colored woman—being considered particularly erotic. If white womanhood represented the pinnacle of femininity, couched in assumptions of fairness, purity, frailty, and domesticity, and black womanhood the total opposite due to the presumed closeness to nature, dark skin, masculine physique, and unbridled sexuality, the combination of European and African produced notions of light-skinned women who could almost pass for white yet retained a tinge of color as well as a hint of wantonness and uninhibited sexuality of exotic cultures. The colored woman was then often described as possessing "a great physical attraction for the European,"[80] and observations such as the following echoed this sentiment:

> If I accord the palm of beauty to the ladies of color, I do not at the same time deteriorate the attractions of the fairer (white) Creoles; the stately and graceful demeanor which calls us to admire the one does not forbid us to be fascinated by the modest loveliness of the other; yet I will acknowledge that I prefer the complexion that is tinged, if not too darkly, with the richness of the olive, to the face which, however fair in its paleness, can never look as lovely as when it wore the rose-blush of beauty which has faded away. I know no prettier scene than a group of young and handsome colored girls taking their evening walk.[81]

J. A. Rogers's three-volume study of race and sex published in the 1940s also documents in rich detail various perceptions of the colonial elite and European male travelers during the eighteenth and nineteenth centuries of this particular group in the Dutch, Spanish, English, and French Caribbean, illustrating the trend of exoticization of mixed-race women in the region. Remarked a surgeon in Santo Domingo:

> When among the populations of the Antilles we first notice these remarkable metis, whose olive skins, elegant and slender figures, fine straight profiles and regular features remind us of the inhabitants of Madras or Pondicherry (India) we ask ourselves in wonder while looking at their long eyes, full of strange and gentle melancholy and at the black rich silky gleaming hair, curling in abundance over the temples and falling in profusion over the neck—to what human race can belong this singular variety.[82]

Interestingly, a commonality in the perceptions, desires, and passions of European men toward women in the East and West was lodged in this particular image. The construct of "strange beauty" consisted of a light brown complexion, silky and loosely curling hair, facial features that approximated the European ideal (straight profile), and a slim physical build. The description by the surgeon suggests not simply a racialization of non-Western peoples, but again a fascination and delight in European male minds with foreign, exotic races. This social category, which itself arose from the exercise of power over black slave women, was, however, legally and ideologically placed outside of white society, representing to Europeans racial impurity and moral, racial, and social degradation, constituting an "unnatural transgression of the rules of social propriety."[83] The mulatto woman (*la mulata*) represented the erotic and sexually desirable yet was outcast and pathologized and emerged during slavery as the symbol of the prostitute—the sexually available, yet socially despised body; the eroticized Other, the trope of the exotic.[84]

The introduction of indentured workers from India, after the abolition of slavery, into countries such as Trinidad, Guyana, Suriname, and Jamaica signals another social group that was subject to an eroticizing, sexualized colonial discourse. While stereotypes of a "docile, insipid, tractable shadow of a being with no mind, personality or significance of her own" dominated Caribbean understandings of Indian womanhood, an Orientalist representation of her—as a highly sexual being and a temptress—followed close behind.[85] Historians and sociologists have observed that in discussions about the recruitment of female labor from India in the indentureship program, British colonial government officials held that many of the female immigrants were prostitutes, social outcasts, and women who had abandoned marriage and domesticity, all of whom were considered to "have gone astray," to be "prone to immoral conduct," to exercise a "corrupting influence" on "respectable" women, or were tempted into "abnormal sexual behavior by single men with money."[86] In the eyes of officialdom then, the women were highly sexual, of dubious character, and stood outside the boundaries of decent colonial womanhood. The skewed perception of Indian womanhood held by the British reinforced patriarchal tendencies within the Indian community in both India and the Caribbean, which found the women not only "immoral" but corrupted sexual servants to non-Indian men.[87] Often labeled and categorized as lewd and lascivious, or as prostitutes, working-class Indian women were cast as "loose" elements who disrupted dominant notions of decency and proper family values. Thus while conditions of indentureship in the colonies provided Indian women with "a great degree of sexual independence and freedom" and little incentive to enter into legal marriage, their sexual behavior and relationships were viewed with great suspicion by British colonial authorities as well as by Indian men who favored and attempted to inculcate domesticated, docile femininity.

Sexuality and the Economy

Apart from viewing sexuality as semiautonomous from gender and profoundly connected to constructions of race, Caribbean sexuality is also deeply linked to the economy. With the advent of Columbus's "discovery," the region was raped both metaphorically and figuratively, for the benefit of colonial powers and capitalist interests. Exploitation and oppression that produced racial hierarchies that were in part constituted through sexuality were not simply due to notions of superiority of one group, but most evidently lodged in the pursuit of riches—for the accumulation of wealth and profit by Western European elites. To cite Young in some detail on this issue:

> [I]t is clear that the forms of sexual exchange brought about by colonialism were themselves both mirrors and consequences of the modes of economic exchange that constituted the basis of colonial relations: the extended exchange which began with small trading posts and the visiting slave ships originated indeed as much as an exchange of bodies as of goods, or rather of bodies as goods; as in that paradigm of respectability, marriage, economic and sexual exchange were intimately bound up, coupled with each other from the very first. The history of the meanings of the word "commerce" includes the exchange both of merchandise and of bodies in sexual intercourse. It was therefore wholly appropriate that sexual exchange, and its miscegenated product, which captures the violent, antagonistic, power relations of sexual and cultural diffusion, should become the dominant paradigm through which the passionate economic and political trafficking of colonialism was conceived.[88]

Forced labor in the Caribbean took precedence over genocide—it was not the destruction of the Other that lay at the heart of colonialism in the region, but rather the need by capitalists for docile, productive bodies as a source of low-cost labor power—and it was through the classification of inferior races, in part through naming their sexual practices and norms as uncivilized, abnormal, and deviant, that enslavement and indentureship could be realized. Sexual difference lay at the heart of racial difference, and it was upon this difference that the Caribbean was inserted in the globalizing capitalist economy. Under slavery, black and brown women in particular were commanded to sexually service slave owners, plantation managers, travelers, sailors, clerks, and businessmen, and the region served as a site for sexual adventures and a taste of the "forbidden." Enslaved African women were often pimped by their owners—men and women—to bring money in to the plantation household at times when the plantation economy slumped. "Slave breeding" was a strategy employed by plantation owners to increase the number of slave hands at particular times, requiring black male and female sexual intercourse for procreative purposes. The creation of the categories "black male stud," who could impregnate women irrespective of an emotional or marital attachment, and "black female breeder," who could effortlessly bring multiple children into the world to serve as slaves on the plantation, were some of the consequences of this history.[89] Profits accruing from the exploitation of sexual energies and labor of the working class in the region, attached to the pursuit of pleasure by dominant groups, echo in the twenty-first century in the tourism industry, as we shall see in chapter 5, where young brown women and black men sexually service richer (predominantly white) tourists and the region marketed on the basis of its racialized sexuality.

Sexual Agency

The crucible of race, sexuality, and the economy has forged a specific consciousness of sexual subjectivity and agency, and it is in this domain that I speak of sexuality as embodied practice and as a "rebelling pillar" in Caribbean society. This analysis then moves beyond locating Caribbean sexuality as an exclusively ideological or cultural construct to one that is materially constituted or embodied. By this, I am not referring to sexuality as anatomical differences of the sexes or to a biological sexual drive located in a naturally sexed body, but rather to the ways in which sexual desires and passions are lived through, experienced, and refashioned by bodies of flesh and blood. The "lived body" and "embodied subjectivity" then are of relevance, for it is with these ideas that the physical body becomes more than an entity that is inscribed or marked by discourse, or is seen to exist as a fixed or presocial natural condition, but is conceptualized as an organism that actively responds to change and contingency, that is self-organizing and a self-actualizing agent, constantly in process of transformation and development. The definition I use here to speak about the body reflects several decades of feminist thought on the subject through which the female body in particular has been reclaimed from its abjected, despised, and naturalized location in Western intellectual traditions. The struggle to bridge the gulf of man (read the mind, reason, and objectivity) versus nature (read woman, the body, and emotionality) that has been deeply structured in Western European thought has prodded various feminists to explore alternatives to traditional, mind-centered approaches to knowledge and to revise the body's role in systems of knowledge.[90] In some instances this revisioning has fled away from biology, producing a somataphobia—a fear of the body—and led to an erasure of sex. In other ways feminist inquiry has reiterated biological essentialism through a celebration and valorization of female bodily potentialities and feminine sexualities and ethics. In yet other feminist work, an emphasis on the discursive construction of the body has produced a theory of embodiment that takes into account sexual as well as other differences—race, class, ability, etc., in short, "the specific contextual materiality of the body."[91] Finally, resting on ideas that the body is not simply constituted through perception and ideas, but also by blood, tissue, and cells, feminist biologists have reintroduced the need to include thinking about the constitution of the body and about internal biological operations that produce, form, and transform corporeal reality. In conceptualizing the body from this approach, this most recent feminist work encapsulates the body as structure and agency and as a continual process of regeneration and activity within a set of constraints and systems through which the sexed body is viewed not as prior to gender or as an exterior surface upon which gender in mapped, but as shaped by and contingent to gender. Put another way, this recent trend in feminist thought locates processes involved in creating and continually re-creating bodies as "partly material and partly social/experiential" where nature and culture are co-constituted as "simultaneously semiotic as well as material."[92] As feminist biologist Linda Birke remarks, "We need to insist on thinking about the biological body as changing and changeable, as *transformable*."[93] Moving away from biological fixity and natural states, the body becomes an indeterminate and uncertain construct—a site of potential, transformation, and fluidity, yet is seen to materialize within physically, socially, and culturally produced limits. The body is thus "sexed" within a specific context, from both internal and external processes.

And What about Love?

In exploring Caribbean sexuality in the following chapters, my attention focuses on the significance of sexual-economic relationships, particularly prostitution and transactional sex—a term used to denote sexual-economic relationships and exchanges where gifts are given in exchange for sex, multiple partnerships may be maintained, and an up-front monetary transaction does not necessarily take place. In some feminist probings a conclusion has been reached that there is something intrinsically intimate in expressions of sexual desire that makes turning sex acts into an economic relationship oppressive or degrading, particularly for the female body and psyche. Such an argument rests upon assumptions that the use of vaginas, wombs, breasts, nipples, buttocks, and sexual and erotic energies to create and reproduce our world makes sexual acts more precious, vulnerable, and sacred than those that make use of hands, arms, brains, feet, and intellectual or physical energies to make our daily bread or to satisfy needs. Intimacy and desire, as fundamentally located in the sexual body, are viewed as universal qualities and experiences. Yet I argue that sexed bodies, constructions of sexuality, and sexual desire do not stand outside of specific social, cultural, and political contexts. In speaking to this problem, Sharpley-Whiting inverts Fanon's question of whether the black woman can authentically love across racial boundaries given the historical configuration of racialized sexuality, to the question of whether the reverse is possible:

If the feeling of inferiority often pervades the black female psyche, whisking her into the arms of a white knight who alone can endow her existence with value, and thus, inadvertently inhibiting authentic love, can the white male psyche escape the feeling of superiority, his birthright as purveyor of value, and transcend the temptation of self praise for his openness to difference, and really love a black women?[94]

Both Fanon's initial question and Sharpley-Whiting's inversion of it raise the matter of whether desire can be stripped naked of its history of unequal relations of power that are infused with notions of inferiority and superiority. Is it truly possible to seize that universal, essential quality called love that transcends socially constructed meanings? More than a century ago Frederick Engels argued that romantic love and desire were created as bourgeois fabrications in the drive to consolidate patriarchal capitalism.[95] More recently it has been advanced that meanings of love and romance are enmeshed with consumption patterns and discourses, and have been transformed over the past century through social and economic change to become a part of the mass market and mass media culture.[96] Can, then, histories of gendered, racialized, sexual relations be simply erased through the invocation of the supposedly universal quality called love? The work of a number of anthropologists has greatly contributed to this discussion. Among rural women in Haiti, for example, it is found that "having sex with a man without requiring or being offered tangible (economically valuable) benefits in return, is considered inconsequential/frivolous/disreputable, stupid, or deviantly sensual/lascivious."[97] "Giving sweetness for sweetness"—to invoke a Guyanese phrase—is neither the norm nor a highly valued interaction in this experience. Elsewhere, sexual energies are deliberately inserted into a relationship in exchange for some form of security, a future out of poverty and neocolonial conditions, to travel or "go a foreign," to obtain consumer items and goods, as a survival strategy for street kids, or as a way to appease evil spirits.[98] Heterosexual relationships are also secured as protection against homophobic, antigay and antilesbian sentiments and hostilities, or as a way to maintain a spouse who is not a lover.[99] Sexuality has multiple meanings in such contexts, not all of which have to do with a reciprocity of sexual desire or feelings of love. What may be desired by one party may not be experienced or perceived in the same way by another, yet both or all parties may be satisfied through the act, for quite different reasons, and may love each other for the satisfaction they are able to realize through the relationship. Sex, love, and desire thus emerge in Caribbean accounts as variable in meanings and value, some of which coincide with and reproduce hegemonic heterosexual regimes, and others offering a counterhegemonic interpretation.

Other Directions in Caribbean Sexuality Studies

The focus in historical and social studies on the black pathological family, deviant, or lascivious female heterosexuality and masculine sexual prowess and promiscuity, as well as the feminist silence on the subject, leaves little of substance about other sexualities. In the rest of this book, my attention centers on only one area of sexuality that has been obscured: sexual-economic relations, the majority of which are heterosexual. Same-gender sexual relations, identities, and desires do not feature centrally here, although they do enter into the discussion throughout. They remain, however, an arena of Caribbean sexual life that requires a far more thorough and fuller exploration than I am able to give, and have been clearly underrepresented in historical and contemporary Caribbean historical and social studies. As sexuality scholars Antonio De Moya and Rafael Garcia note:

> Historical records from the sixteenth century onwards suggest that bisexual and homosexual behavior involving adolescent/adult partners was probably relatively common in the Spanish colony of Santo Domingo. Because of homophobia, most of these transgressive relations had to be clandestine, relatively impersonal and publicly denied . . . . It is not clear when adult men in the colony started paying poorer adolescent males for sex, but it is likely that up until 1844, when slavery was abolished, some masters used to have sexual relations with enslaved adolescent males.[100]

Same-gender sexual relations have been depicted elsewhere in various ways. Although indigenous societies have been represented primarily as male dominated, heterosexual, and gendered into two opposing or supportive roles for over five hundred years, there is a continual undertheme of sexual and gender "otherness" of Amerindian peoples that slips through the pages, speaking mutedly about possible living arrangements and practices among Amerindians. For example, the construction of the Caribbean Amazon concerned women-only communities, which were said to annually organize heterosexual raids on neighboring islands or villages for procreative purposes.[101] What this construction suggests about Amerindian women's sexual practices during the rest of the year is left to the imagination and could conjure up images of same-gendered sexual and sensual relations between the women. Sexual intercourse between men has received a little more attention, with early invaders to the Caribbean writing that both Caribs and Arawaks were "largely sodomites."[102] One interpretation of such recordings, other than signaling an attempt to demasculinize and discredit Amerindian men as "real" men, is that among native Caribbean peoples rape of men by men over time became normalized in social and domestic settings, producing transsexuals, transvestites, eunuchs, "berdaches," and other third-gendered groupings.[103] Other interpretations are yet to be written.

In studies of the Caribbean family in the twentieth century other observations are made. In the 1940s the Herskovits' documented knowledge of homosexuality among working-class Afro-Trinidadians in the village of Toco, writing that "the homosexual is an object of ridicule and abuse . . . among women, it is termed 'making zammi (friends)' and there is much talk and 'plenty song' about such persons."[104] Dann's study in Barbados in the 1980s recorded attitudes toward homosexuality, indicating that such practices were not unfamiliar to the population under study. He noted that homosexuality was never considered "right" by Barbadian men, but rather was commonly perceived as an "abomination," evil, or sin, and "transgressions of natural law"; it was sometimes viewed as "a form of madness" and in other cases a natural malfunction or a bad habit.[105] Same-gender sexual relations were confirmed for Barbadian and Trinidadian societies in the pre- or early postindependence period of the twentieth century through these studies, and Chevannes' work extends these insights into Jamaica. "Female homosexuality," he notes, was first described in social studies in 1952. In the mid-1970s a study of bisexuality among men concluded that homosexual practices were considered a "pleasurable diversion" among this group of men, but that a disapproval existed of feminine-like behaviors in these male-to-male sexual relationships.[106] Chevannes also cites a health study that was conducted among 125 "homosexual and bisexual" men in Kingston in 1988, with the note that although the data suggest that the men were drawn from more affluent sectors of society, "this, of course, cannot be taken to imply that homosexuality is mainly a middle class phenomenon".[107, 108] More recently, in-depth studies of same-gender and bisexual relations for men in Cuba, the Dominican Republic, and Martinique have contributed to these insights.[109]

The issue of homophobia, as a critical element of the Caribbean heteropatriarchal discourse, has gained some attention. One researcher writes, "one of the most frustrating things I have found in trying to explore sexualities, is the silence that surrounds homosexuality," although she is not referring here to a silence in the dominant discourse.[110] Jamaican dance hall and reggae music, for example, is known to be replete with violently antigay sentiments, which advocate hostilities toward "Chi-Chi Men" or even the murder of the "battybwoy." It is a violence that is boomed loudly across the world. Male homosexuality is explicitly and violently renunciated and defined as a corruption of masculinity, where anything considered feminine is seen to damage the "Real Man" identity of Caribbean men. Such extreme vocal hostility toward gay men is echoed by various religious leaders and journalists, heard in other popular culture arenas, and is reiterated within government and state institutions.[111] For some, the intense paranoia of male homosexuality is a reflection of the hyperheterosexualization of Caribbean masculinity, most apparent among the black lower and working classes.[112] In such accounts of Jamaican homophobia the lack of access to resources around which poor young black men can legitimately develop their masculine identity is seen to force men to use their sexuality to exploit and dominate women. Heterosexual conquests and a hatred of homosexuality are then a way the men "access their entire cache of masculinity and manhood."[113] An aggressive masculine heterosexuality that includes "nailing" or "stabbing" a woman, as well as "battery" (gang rape) and incest, as acceptable modes of sexual behavior[114] is regurgitated through dance hall music and signals the counterpoint of the intense dislike and condemnation of male homosexuality—a dismissal and disrespect that is refracted in laws, religious beliefs, and academic discourse.

Recently it has been noted that there is an acute absence of material dealing with lesbianism in the English-speaking Caribbean, that "the little that is written about Caribbean homosexuality tends to focus on men," and that in the dominant discourse "female homosexuality is seen as a deviation from the natural, superior heterosexual option" where a lesbian stands to be corrected and punished by "real women" for being a "gender traitor." A majority of Caribbean studies locate lesbianism as a corruption of femininity, powerless and nonthreatening to men, and as less of a challenge to heteropatriarchy than male homosexuality. However, despite the despair voiced about the lack of studies and research on gays and lesbians and the disrespect of lesbianism in popular cultural expressions, an important breakthrough of the silence surrounding lesbian relationships in the English-speaking Caribbean came about in the 1990s, with the publication of Rosamund Elwin's collection of stories of Caribbean lesbian lives.[115] These coincide with writings about same-gender relationships for women in other parts of the Caribbean, such as in the Dutch-speaking Caribbean. In the collection foregrounding Caribbean women living both in the region and abroad, Elwin claims a uniqueness to Caribbean lesbianism and writes:

> Twenty years ago ... I did not know the word lesbian. Women made zami or zami was your closest friend. Whether the word was used as a noun or a verb, it was understood that a zami was intimate with other women or another woman.[117]

She points out that dominant global definitions of *lesbian*, particularly those found in the North, in which particular codes of behavior are lodged, would not necessarily be inclusive of Caribbean lesbian practices, particularly those among older women, since "intimate sexual liaisons with women were hidden and not spoken about".[118] However, she notes of the Caribbean in the 1990s, "the word lesbian is gaining political strength," signaling an increasing public appearance of women who love women.[119] Whether the traditional word *zami*— a name reclaimed and also made popular by Audre Lorde—*homosexual* or *man royal* is used for lesbians in the Anglophone Caribbean, these writings locate same-gender sexual relationships among women across race, class, and ethnicity as an integral part of these societies for many decades. They break the academic silence on the subject, foregrounding women's sexual desires and claiming a sexual agency for women that exists autonomously from men's needs and male power.

A study on identity formation of lesbians in Jamaica constitutes part of a new set of explorations in Caribbean social studies that explicitly address dominated sexualities in the region. The research in the "gay, lesbian, transgendered community resident in urban Jamaica" stresses that lesbianism is often seen as "play" between women or as "erotic kindling" for heterosexual men's sexual fantasies, but that this image, although a hindrance and an annoyance to lesbians, does not deter the formation of a positive self-image or of an active gay community in Jamaica.[120] In my own study, several Jamaican teenage girls expressed an awareness of lesbianism and discussed sex with another girl or woman as something girls their age might try out of lack of access to boys (in an all-girls school) or out of curiosity.[121] Other girls in the same study couched lesbian relations in terms of transactional sex, as a way to gain material benefits and access to symbols of a higher social status. The young women were far more accepting of same-gender relationships than were adolescent boys, a tolerance that is reflected in what has been regarded as a greater continuum among Caribbean women between homosocial and homosexual bonds than among Caribbean men.[122]

Adolescence is an arena that has also produced new insights into sexual agency and subjectivity in the Caribbean. A 1995–1997 survey of sexual attitudes and behaviors among 945 adolescents in Jamaica signals important departures from the dominant constructions, pointing out that for some girls, sexual activity in and for itself is symbolic of adulthood: that as boys regard sex as integral to their definition of masculinity and manhood, so too do girls identify sexual activity as important to becoming a woman.[123] Girls' femininity rests, in part, upon their sexual expression and behavior, despite the social stigma of "sketel" (loose woman) and the social disapproval that attaches to such activity. In addition, unlike adult women's ideas, this notion of sexuality is not tied to childbearing: adolescent girls are quite adamant about not wanting to become pregnant during their teenage years. Sexuality is for the girls far less attached to procreation than it is to curiosity and notions of love. These findings echo in a survey in Jamaica in 2000, where less than 30 percent of the young women between the ages of fifteen and twenty-four expressed the view that pregnancy and childbearing make a girl a woman, and for around 20 percent of the young women, being sexually active in itself defines womanhood.[124] In my study of adolescents, the second most common reason for girls' sexual activity, after money, was enjoyment. "It nice" captured the girls' notions of sexual pleasure and fun: a sentiment that is usually reserved for men's appreciation of sex. Moreover, among many of the girls, sexual activity with a man, and preferably a "big man" (an older boy or man who has some social standing, disposable income, or outward trappings of wealth), was claimed as a way to be accepted as "one of the girls" and to gain popularity among their peers. Sexual activity in this instance was not strongly tied to bearing children in order to prove or claim womanhood. Pregnancy and children, in such studies, are not viewed as desirable by teenage girls and do not figure prominently in their constructions of self, gender, or sexual identity. For the Dutch Antilles, Jacqueline Martis writes:

> A pervasive attitude exists on the islands, particularly among young people, that sex is not a big deal and that it can and should be used to get what one needs, such as nice clothes and shoes for a party, or drugs. There are numerous pickup sites for these types of liaisons, such as parties and discos.[125]

These expressions of sexuality by young Caribbean women underscore the tentative conclusions drawn in other Caribbean feminist studies about changing constructions of femininity in the region. Questions about what girls/young women find attractive, erotic, or pleasurable in heterosexual activity, however, require far more exploration in studies of adolescence. Nevertheless, the range of studies that indicate that sexual agency and sexual desire among younger Caribbean women from various communities and backgrounds are conceived differently than by older generations of women and men illustrate new ways of thinking about sexuality in the region.

Underexplored Areas of Caribbean Sexuality

Above I have touched upon areas of Caribbean sexuality that have to some extent been documented and theorized, especially in the English-speaking Caribbean, even though there are many gaps and much room for reanalysis, reinterpretation, and further theorization. There are also some areas that are still quite invisible. Amerindian sexuality in preconquest eras is one that is perhaps the most difficult to un-cover, given the genocide of indigenous Caribbean peoples. Same-gender sexual relations and desires under slavery and indentureship also remain a question and could use careful documentation and ex-amination.[126] Sexuality of white women in the colonies is described more often in fiction than in social studies, and while much has been made of the sexual violence, as well as attractions, between white Eu-ropean men and black or brown women in the colonies, sexual rela-tions between white women and black men are greatly obscured. Apart from conventional understandings that white women were the symbols of moral purity and ideal domesticity in Caribbean colonial society and required protection by white men, it has been proposed that during slavery, because children followed the condition of the mother and that the male planter's interest was to reproduce the slave population and not the group of free people of color, black male sexual access to white women had to be blocked so that "the progeny of black males were not lost to the slave gangs."[127] Whether this expla-nation holds true across the Caribbean is still to be researched. How-ever, black men are known to have received punishments such as castration, dismemberment, and execution for having sexual relations with white women, and the women in turn "were socially disgraced and ostracized."[128] Sexual relations between white women and black men are also claimed to be more common than we are generally led to believe.[129] Such insights, while perhaps hinting at some dimensions of the sexual relations between white women and black men, and

emphasizing the ways in which white male patriarchy and the plantation economy shaped white women's sexual behavior, fall short of
describing the full complexities of white female sexuality. The char-
acterization of European women as morally corrupt and degraded
through interactions with black men and black women has left little
space for the interrogation of white women's sexual agency and desire
in the context of colonial relations of ruling, although some recent
attention has been given to the more general construction of white
womanhood in Caribbean colonial societies.[130] Thus, while some
emphasis has been given to black and Indian female sexuality, and to
the ways in which colonial policies aided in the creation of notions of
Afro- and Indo-Caribbean women's "hypersexuality," little has been
done to examine the other ethnic categories of female sexuality.
Likewise, the lack of critical attention to black male sexuality obfus-
cates the history of the construction of the "black male stud"—as
important impregnators of women in order to breed slaves, independent
of an emotional or marital attachment.

Despite many gaps, the records, documents, and data I have collected over the years and draw on for this study illuminate a complex
interplay of various factors—racial discourses, indigenized traditions,
colonial policies and laws, heterosexist-patriarchal paradigms and
practices, and capitalist economic interests. Sexuality stands as a central prism for viewing racialized colonial oppression and domination
and the refashioning of race, as well as for reading Caribbean struggles
for emancipation, both historically and contemporarily. Racialized sexuality in the Caribbean is at once a colonial discourse inscribed upon
the bodies of the colonized and the ground for empowerment and
freedom for many Caribbean women and men. In its complexities, I
argue here, Caribbean sexuality also offers a potential for producing
new challenges to contemporary sexual regimes of power and knowledge, visible through everyday and organized activities of women in
sexual-economic transactions.

3

SEX, WORK, GIFTS, AND MONEY: PROSTITUTION AND OTHER SEXUAL-ECONOMIC TRANSACTIONS

An exchange of sex for material benefits or money has been evident in the Caribbean region for several centuries. Under slavery such transactions were lodged at the nexus of at least two areas of women's existence: as an extension of sexual relations (forced or otherwise) with white men and as an income-generating activity for both slave and "free colored" women. In Barbadian society in the early 1800s, for example, slave women were frequently hired out by white and free colored families as "nannies, nurses, cooks, washerwomen, hucksters, seamstresses," yet "the general expectation of individuals who hired female labor under whatever pretense was that sexual benefits were included."[1] Concubines served as both mistresses and housekeepers and were sometimes hired out by their owners to sexually service other men in order to obtain cash. Furthermore, in times of economic slumps on plantations (particularly in British colonies), when enslaved men and women were commanded by plantation owners to provide for themselves or to bring in money to sustain the plantation through work outside the plantation, slave women were placed on the urban market as prostitutes by sugar planters. In one of the most thorough studies to date of women's labor in the English-speaking Caribbean, Rhoda Reddock notes for Trinidad: "For the most part women were hired out as domestic slaves, field laborers, as concubines, to temporary male European settlers, or were made to work as petty traders or prostitutes handing over most of their earning to their masters."[2] Black women's manual and sexual labor was, in effect, "pimped" by the slaveholders. European women were not exempt from the position of "pimp," as they may have owned and managed as much as 25 percent of Caribbean slaves, and many "made a thriving business from the rental of black and colored women for sexual services in the port towns."[3] Cases mentioned in historical records of slave women in the French Caribbean who, besides their marketing activities, were able to profit financially from selling their own or their daughters' sexual labor have also been remarked upon by some historians, indicating that besides being pimped by slave owners, slave women also took up sexual-economic activities in order to make a living independent from slavery.[4] In some instances, sex was provided by slave women in exchange for weapons that could be used to attack the plantation system, and prostitution was a means through which women, inside and outside of slavery, could establish a semblance of autonomy from the harsh conditions of agricultural or domestic labor and work independently. Lodging-house proprietresses—who were predominantly "mulatto"— "turned their weaknesses into strength by capitalizing upon white men's sexual desire for women of color."[5] Lodging houses run by the free women of color became places "flocked to" by white men who sought their sexual services. In some accounts it has been noted that the brown women diversified their services "so that they not only increased their incomes but eventually became women of importance."[6] Lucille Mathurin Mair, whose study in the early 1970s on the "rebel slave woman" was pathbreaking with regards to claiming subjectivity and agency for women under slavery, wrote about this phenomenon:

> The mulatto female was relatively well placed in creole society to name a high price for her favours. For the dominant male group, applying its racist aesthetic, made it clear that browns, being closer in physical appearance to whites than black, were the more desirable mates. In the absence of white women, the law of supply and demand thus gave mulatto women some bargaining power.[7]

Racialized configurations of sexuality, in such instances, were resources for women to secure emancipation and economic security or to obtain freedom from violent and oppressive racial systems of labor.

Arrangements under slavery that involved sexual labor were exacerbated by other practices initiated by slave owners, planters, and traders. Slaveholders throughout the region freely, and often forcibly, engaged in sexual relations with their slaves, as did their staff, retainers, and guests. Large urban centers had many nonslaveholding males who sought sexual intercourse outside of marriage, and nonagrarian trading centers such as Bermuda and Curaçao were places that single merchants, sailors, and traders visited or resided, and who often desired to have sex with local women. Some women whose services were sought as either prostitutes or sexual servants were rewarded with economic benefits, freedom, food, clothing, and petty luxuries. Women slaves, historian Marietta Morrissey concludes, "were petty cultivators, and marketeers in the early days of Caribbean slavery. They were domestics, healers and prostitutes—all positions that brought cash, favours and other items of exchange."[8] Service work and trading, including sexual transactions, were activities through which women could autonomously improve their economic positions and survival chances.

Although studies of prostitution in Caribbean colonies are scarce, specific policies and regulations for sexual relationships were laid down by colonial governments in conjunction with trading companies, colonial armed forces, and plantation owners between the early seventeenth and mid-twentieth centuries, fostering informal sexual relations. Historical research on slave women's lives in the region points out that absentee ownership of plantations often meant that young, enterprising men were sought to manage and administer affairs in the colonies. Employment for European men was promoted as a way to get rich quick and involved only a temporary stay, and the Caribbean represented in recruitment efforts in Europe as a place for sexual opportunities for young males. Marriage in the colonies was not common practice, or as one historian remarks, "most Europeans believed they were only in the West Indies for a few years to make their fortune, and thus saw matrimony as a 'bar to their expectations.'"[9] European women were not initially encouraged to settle in the colonies, and relationships between European men and enslaved and free women of color were commonplace, with systems of concubinage and informal polygynous relations becoming established and tolerated by the colonial elite. In colonial territories where marriage between Europeans and slaves was officially prohibited—such as in

the Dutch Caribbean until 1817—plantation managers and over-
seers commonly kept slave housekeepers as concubines. After this
date, sexual relations between white men and slave women were unregulated by the state, although proximity to Europeanness continued to play a part in defining which women were considered eligible
for marriage by white men and which for concubinage.[10] Unions then
were often entered into by single white men and women of color, but
rather than being based on a formal marriage contract, they were established in common law, sometimes continuing to exist alongside
formal marriages. As already described, an outside relationship with a
woman became an institutionalized, permanent, and recognized relationship, a complementing marriage of convenience among the elite.
Writing about Jewish men in nineteenth-century Curaçao, Eva
Abraham-van der Mark points out that "concubinage gave them the
benefits of a category of children which, if necessary, provided labor but
could not make any legal demands and were excluded from inheri-
tance."[11] A woman in this scenario could aspire to a nonmarital relationship with a "shon" (master) of the Sephardic merchant elites in
exchange for material and financial security for both herself and their
children, and the shon could expand his cheap labor force. Colonial
policies and practices served to separate women into racialized categories of respectable wives, on the one hand, who were members of the
ethnically dominant group, and mistresses, servants, and slaves, on the
other, who were colored or black. Simultaneously, patterns of informal
polygyny for the colonial male elite were consolidated.

The period immediately following slavery in the Caribbean has
been characterized as a time when women established autonomy of
work from the plantations and where gendered relations were transformed under changing relations of production.[12] Waged labor for
women took on greater importance with European middle-class patriarchal family ideologies and laws gaining acceptance among freed
slaves, yet many dimensions of women's lives that had been established under slavery survived. Domestic service, marketing, and prostitution, for example, continued to be constituted as black and colored
women's activities, since these women sought to escape destitution
and poverty. Henriques also notes that "emancipation did not fundamentally alter the patterns of sexuality which had been established

under slavery. Women might no longer be bound to masters but the 'white bias' in the society still facilitated illicit sexual relations between white and colored."[13] Black and other women of color under slavery and in the postemancipation period were ideologically located as persons with whom the colonial elite could enter into extramarital and "loose" sexual relations, some of which involved direct cash transactions. In other instances, the nature of the relationships rested upon other material considerations, freedoms, and livelihood security matters. Prostitution was institutionalized in Caribbean societies for some slave and free colored women as an income-generating activity, and was a means to obtain freedom for themselves or their children from slavery, or to economically survive once slavery was abolished.

Late-Twentieth-Century Studies of Prostitution

Despite the beginning work undertaken by Henriques on prostitution in the Americas in the early 1970s, Caribbean prostitution was not taken up as a full subject for study until the 1990s. Nevertheless, a number of studies in the twentieth century have made some dimensions visible. Sex tourism in countries such as Barbados, Jamaica, the Dominican Republic, and Cuba, with the involvement not only of adult women, but also men and youth as sex providers, has drawn attention. The trafficking of women for the sex trade, both internationally and regionally, is another important arena through which prostitution has been addressed. It was, for example, the topic of several conferences and meetings in the region, among them the Caribbean Conference on Prostitution held in Bonaire in 1978, and a report to the UN Special Rapporteur on Violence Against Women in 1996.[14] Public sexual health is another subject area that has made prostitution visible. While sexually transmitted diseases and infections, particularly syphilis, were of earlier concern, HIV/AIDS during the latter part of the twentieth century produced another round of interrogation into prostitution practices throughout the region. Several doctoral studies in the 1990s—on Curaçao, Barbados, and the Dominican Republic—focused on the general living and working conditions, rights, and perspectives of prostitutes themselves.[15]

In these studies, issues of migration within the region and between the Caribbean and Europe and North America are highlighted, as well as the role of the global economy in structuring local arrangements. In addition to these academic studies, a publication from the first sex workers' conference in the Dominican Republic presented extensive analyses and testimonies by Caribbean sex workers themselves, and the sex workers' organization in Suriname produced several studies and reports that reflect experiences and views of sex workers.[16] The challenges by sex workers to some of the myths and stigmas that surround prostitution in the region have contributed to the creation of a new social space in which sexuality is publicly addressed. Finally, flowing from international governmental attention to the situations of children and youth, a few studies have appeared that deal with prostitution among minors in the Caribbean.[17] In this area the topics of adolescent sexuality and child labor have been raised for the first time from perspectives that seek not to condemn young peoples' sexual behaviors, but rather to gain better insights into the meanings of sexuality within specific social, economic, and cultural contexts.

The focus in the majority of the studies on prostitution—on sexually transmitted diseases, forced prostitution, child prostitution, and sex tourism—while important for revealing and representing hitherto unnamed or taboo social practices, also emphasizes the social problems associated with the sex trade, reinforcing an image of prostitution as a social problem. Simultaneously, these studies reinscribe the notion of the Caribbean as a profoundly heterosexual space, and of women's sexuality as intimately tied to economic considerations and interests. However, they also tend to obscure other dimensions of the everyday lives of female and male prostitutes in the region, such as their own sexual agency and subjectivity, their roles as mothers or providers for the family, and their hopes and aspirations, with the consequence that whole arenas of social life are overlooked. This obfuscation in social studies of the actors' own experiences and involvement in prostitution is strange, given that within the Caribbean arts—literature, theater, and music—and in everyday story-telling and anecdotes prostitutes are invariably portrayed as integral to and active in village and town life.[18] There can be little doubt to anyone familiar with the region that widespread common knowledge of and experience with prostitution is a part of Caribbean society, yet this is barely reflected in academic social studies or public debate. Moreover, many other gaps in our knowledge about prostitution in the region remain. Prostitution around military bases in the Caribbean—both historically and contemporarily—has been paid scant attention despite the international connection that exists between prostitution and militarization.[19] Influences of male migration on constructions of prostitution can also only be gleaned from scattered sources. Both militarization and male migration and their relationship to prostitution are, however, important, particularly in light of the remilitarization of the region in the beginning of the twenty-first century by the United States, and the continuing migrations in the face of changing local economies under new forms of globalization.

From Prostitution to Sex Work:
Shifting Definitions

Prostitution has typically been the concept used to describe the relationship that involves "sexual acts, including those which do not actually involve copulation, habitually performed by individuals with other individuals of their own or opposite sex, for a consideration which is non-sexual . . . ."[20] And as pointed out in studies of mating and the family, a Caribbean woman who engages in sexual relations that are not tied to childbearing or marriage is commonly stigmatized and condemned. Nevertheless, in more recent studies and through prostitutes' own definitions of their activities, the concept of "sex work" has been adopted by various prostitutes, researchers, social workers, health practitioners, and policy makers to depict prostitution and other related activities in a less judgmental and more self-determining fashion. The notion of prostitution as work is reflected in the terms that emerged in the region in the 1990s, such as *trabajadoras sexuales* in the Dominican Republic and *sekswerkers* in Suriname, which explicitly locate prostitution as an income-generating activity and as labor. For Belize, Kane argues that prostitution "is a gender-specific form of migrant labor that serves the same economic function for women as agricultural work offers to men, and often at better pay."[21]

"Sexing for money" that emphasizes women's conscious participation is sometimes defined as a job. In Jamaica, one woman described her activities in the following way:

> I mostly do the cruise ship and every morning I leave out at 10 o'clock. . . .
> and every evening I come in back at 5 because the ship leave at 5 o'clock
> . . . . It's just a normal routine thing . . . like a person working at a bank,
> she know she has to reach the bank at 9 o'clock and she knows she has
> to leave when the bank is closed. It's just a normal routine job.[22]

Prostitution is commonly viewed as an alternative to other jobs such as domestic work, assembly work in manufacturing plants in Free Trade Zones, or security guard work—all jobs that have a set of parameters that allow a woman to go to a workplace, conduct her necessary income-generating activity, and leave. In some instances, men and women describe sex work as more lucrative than these other jobs, and in others, less demanding or less hazardous to their well-being. In Cartagena, on the Caribbean coast of Colombia, and in Sosúa in the Dominican Republic, for example, it has been noted that the humiliations, abuse, and hunger experienced in domestic work were reasons enough for a woman to state that she preferred prostitution as a way to make a living. One young Colombian woman described her experience as a domestic worker in the following way: "it was a starvation diet, and then I could not live with that . . . . I am not used to living on just lunch without dinner or breakfast."[23] Sex work enabled her to escape the drudgery and hunger that domestic work forced upon her. Another sex worker framed it as such:

> I like my job because of di money; you get money more faster, if it wasn't
> that fass money, of my job, I wouldn't have done this . . . . For instance,
> yuh have a work like yuh working at a Free Zone, yuh can't pick up
> certain amount of money fuh di week, and I pick up $4,900 already for
> one week.[24]

In most instances, there is little confusion between commercial transactions and an intimate relationship in the minds or lived experiences of women who engage in prostitution, As one Guyanese woman stated: "I will say is a job I doing . . . . I don't go fuh feelings, I does go fuh me money."[25] The distinction between sexual acts for money and sex as intimacy is also defined in terms of the different negotiations that take place with the client and a steady friend or lover. For example, whereas many sex working Caribbean women declare that condoms are regularly used with clients, once a client achieves the status of a steady partner, boyfriend, husband, or "man" in a woman's life, condoms are more than likely to be dispensed with. Sex work, thus, is associated with condom use and the likelihood of sexually transmitted diseases, while familiarity is considered safe or healthy.[26] Also, in an intimate relationship sex workers stress the possibility of finding tenderness and sexual pleasure for herself or himself. With a client, providing sex is seen as a job—to satisfy the client according to rules that the sex worker implicitly or explicitly applies. Sexual service to a customer occurs most often in a clearly defined time period and is limited to specific sexual acts. For sex that is considered uncommon, which varies from country to country, the client may be refused or asked to pay an additional amount. In Guyana, the Dominican Republic, Belize, and Cartagena, various parts of the body are defined as off-limits to the client, commonly a woman's breasts and lips. As one woman described, "some a dem [men] does want suck yuh bubby, some does want you kiss dem, I does tell dem no, no I ent deh suh, you not me husband, yuh come fuh an affair and we finish wid dat."[27] The long-term sexual partner is allowed access to different parts of the woman's body than is a client. That intimacy is not necessarily connected to the vagina but to other parts of the body points most clearly to the difficulty of conflating sexual intercourse with intimacy (or love), as sometimes occurs in feminist studies of prostitution, and to the necessity of an ongoing exploration into how conceptualizations of sexuality, sexual desire, and love are deeply informed by specific cultural and social histories.

Situations in Guyana, the Dominican Republic, and Belize also illustrate the emotional distance that sex workers maintain while on the job—of clearly distinguishing between providing sex and becoming personally involved, of performing a certain job without having to involve the emotional self. The distancing described by Caribbean sex workers is not unusual or specific to sex work. It has been argued elsewhere that boundary maintenance is a typical strategy that people develop in a variety of jobs that rest upon emotional and sexual labor, and that rather than being a destructive element, it allows the professional to control the extent to which public life intrudes into the private.[28]

The overriding definition of Caribbean prostitution as work by those who explicitly provide sexual services for material benefits, usually cash, echoes experiences and perspectives in various parts of the world. In recognition of this phenomenon, various scholars have argued for a conceptualization of prostitution as a form of labor that begins with the premise of the employment of sexual and erotic energies for production and reproduction of human social life in both material and nonmaterial ways.[29] Thus, as a human resource, sexuality nourishes and sustains life and is organized, among other things, for pleasure, to meet material, economic, and spiritual needs, and for procreative purposes. Given the particularities of specific political, economic, and cultural contexts, there is little claim to a universality in the social organization of sexuality in this conception of prostitution. Nevertheless, studies of women's lives under capitalism and patriarchy point out that sexual labor power in this gendered economic system is commodified, hyperexploited, traded on the market, bonded, and sold and exchanged as a service. It is the product from which the sex sector, including brothels, Eros centers, sex theaters and nightclubs, the adult film industry, telephone sex industries, and massage parlors, profits, and which is subordinated to masculine needs and interests. Female sexual labor power has also been relied upon for the revitalization and renewal of male labor and military forces in such places as the Philippines, Korea, Indonesia, and Belize, where in some cases sex workers have been subjected to slavery-like conditions. On the other hand, sexual energies are independently organized: the female sex worker is "self-employed"—a characteristic of women's work in the region that is commonplace.[30] Sex work is experienced and viewed as a human activity that contributes to the production and reproduction of labor and the economy.

In discussing contemporary North American and Western European feminist conceptualizations of prostitution, Marjolein van de Veen points out that this often hinges on Marxist theory and concepts, some of which stress the commodification, alienation, and objectification of the female body. Prostitution is thus regarded by some feminists as "the selling of the body and as an inherently self-estranging activity" where the self is seen to be a unified essence, and where "sexuality serves as a defining feature of the self."[31] This conceptualization of the prostitute as a commodified body rests, she notes, in Marx's earlier work on commodification as a defining feature of capitalism, which itself was lodged in a humanist discourse that claimed ideas about the universal nature of humankind and relied upon a subject/object binarism.[32] The idea of prostitution as sexual labor, according to van de Veen is instead better derived from an analysis of the appropriation and distribution of surplus value produced by labor under particular conditions, as addressed in Marx's later work. She writes, "It is in these later writings that we see Marx conceptualizing prostitution in a different way: no longer as selling a *body*, but as selling the service of *labor power* in the production of a *service* sold to the client."[33] The focus on labor power, production, and processes of capital accumulation is important here, for it is these that allow for a shift of focus from a fixed or static essentialized entity or object—the prostitute, body, or self—to a process through which these entities are produced or made. Class relations under capitalism are of particular importance to van de Veen, although she acknowledges the significance of other factors in configuring sex work. Important to her is the organization of sexuality into a service that is both embodied and produced and that, under capitalism, is exploited for profit or gain by the self and others.

However, whether prostitution can be exclusively analyzed and explained within the framework of capitalist class relations is debatable. Sexuality is organized in different modes of production, but also underpins various other social relations that are not necessarily rigidly tied to the economy, and is often categorized as a human need. Feminists who have focused on patriarchy as the central organizing principle in social life posit masculinity as critical to any understanding of prostitution. Prostitution, it is argued, is an expression of the control of women by men, where female sexuality is organized in public and private spheres to satisfy male needs, interests, and desires.

My argument here is that while existing theoretical constructs and frameworks are extremely helpful for making sense of and explaining the social world, the experiences and situated knowledge of those who live the daily realities may not always fit neatly into existing bodies of work or theories, and may suggest new ways of thinking and new knowledge about the subject. As pointed out in the foregoing chapters, the historical racialization of social relations in the Caribbean was central to the construction of sexual-economic relations, and prostitution in the region cannot be viewed outside of this matrix. Moreover, especially in the Anglophone and Dutch areas, prostitution is commonly defined as "wuk," the meaning of which is important here. Extensive research on women's work through the Women in the Caribbean Project in the early 1980s concluded that "wuk" stands for all activities, except for leisure, "which contribute to human welfare, and not merely those which are linked to a particular form of economic accounting."[34] Child care, household chores and duties, and other activities that are necessary for the maintenance of women and their households are considered work. In addition, "Caribbean women employ many different strategies to harness the resources they need to sustain themselves and their families and that all of these together constitute what might be classed their 'sources of livelihood.'"[35] Thus, the conception of work includes not just waged labor but also survival strategies and ways in which women make do, which may include a strategic use of their sexuality. Wekker writes about Suriname, "in a situation where women, carrying the main and often exclusive economic responsibility for their children, have to struggle to keep their heads above water, sex becomes one of the strategic assets women can command and control in a market situation."[36] Heterosexual relationships in Suriname, she points out, are sometimes couched in terms of financial security and "chamber obligations" by women, and that "when he gives you money, you give him sex" a common experience.[37] Sexual activity with a man who may even be a husband is then sometimes described also as work.

Caribbean sex *work*, as used here, then, is not exclusively tied to gendered service work or waged labor under patriarchal capitalist relations of production, although in some instances it is performed in this way. Sexuality may be inserted into an economic strategy, but it may also be deployed in an individual or collective struggle to counter racial oppression. These definitions of sex work do not rigidly conform to dominant ideas about prostitution, but rather rest in very specific cultural and social practices involving sexuality that are at once economic, gendered, and ethnically contextual and are specific to Caribbean history and circumstances. Nevertheless, the Caribbean concept of sex work overlaps and connects with other contemporary constructs current in various parts of the world that usually foreground gendered economic capitalist relationships. It is the overlap in definitions and understandings that forms a common ground for political alliances between organizations and groups around the world in their struggle for legitimation and the decriminalization of certain practices, laws, and ideologies that surround female sexuality.[38]

Women's Participation in Sex Work

One of the most striking findings in my research in the Dutch Caribbean island of Curaçao was the fluidity and porousness of forced and voluntary participation in sex work. Broader structuring factors nestled together with women's personal and conscious decisions and acts, producing situations where women were simultaneously bound and free, coerced and constrained, victims and agents. The stories of migrant women who worked in the main brothel in Curaçao revealed this complexity. Ana, for example, recounted that she "began to train as a prostitute in Colombia" and knew she had applied for work in a brothel prior to her arrival in Curaçao. She felt that she could no longer afford to study, could find no other employment, and had cast around to find a way to support herself and to help provide financially for her mother and aunt. She had heard about work in the brothel from a girlfriend and at the time of the interview was there for the first time. She was enthusiastic about the work because she found she earned good money and had not encountered any insurmountable problems in the job. Her idea was to save enough through sex work to secure a house for her family. Similarly, for Alicia, it was her first time in a brothel at the time of the interview. She was an experienced sex worker in her mid-twenties and the mother of one child. Although holding a high school diploma, she could find no other lucrative employment at home—even prostitution in her home locale was difficult due to the discretion needed. She too had heard about the Curaçao brothel from another woman, had applied to work there through the government authorities in Curaçao, and had mortgaged her parent's house in order to finance the trip to the island. Although the conditions and earnings were different than she had originally expected, she nevertheless stated that she planned to return to the brothel at another time of the year and to continue with prostitution until she had earned enough to buy a home and settle. As with Ana, responsibilities for income generation and security for the family, yet economic distress in the local economy and the gendered employment structures, made prostitution in Curaçao an option for her, into which she consciously entered.

Although not all the women's accounts revealed this level of consciousness about engagement in sex work, police records reveal that approximately half of the women who were issued visas to enter Curaçao and work at the state-legalized brothel between the late 1940s and mid-1990s were returnees: women who had once served a legal term for work at the brothel and who returned at a later date for another three months of sex work.[39] Other research in the region confirms this apparent voluntary participation of Caribbean women in the sex trade. Personal autonomy that sex workers—both female and male, young and old—claim and their control over a large part of their activities and earnings are central dimensions to the organization of the sex trade in the region.[40] Pimps and traffickers are usually absent in their stories and accounts. For example, thirty-five women interviewed in Sosúa in the Dominican Republic who worked in the tourist resorts and several women who worked in Orange Walk bars and clubs in Belize were freelancers, that is, women who managed their own affairs.[41] For twenty male beach hustlers interviewed in Barbados, and the thirteen young women and teenagers in Cartagena, a similar situation existed: their services were not mediated by a manager or brothel keeper.[42] In Guyana, women described themselves as self-employed, with none stating they gave money to a pimp, although many of the women paid men for protection from potential violence from clients.[43] In the main brothel in Curaçao, the women I interviewed were not directly managed by a single, ever-present, all-controlling pimp, but rather they described different levels of pimpage, where a number of individuals—men, boys, and women—private enterprises, and state departments managed and profited from their sexual labor in a variety of ways.

Other scenarios, however, also exist. In the Curaçaoan brothel, some women stated that they were uninformed about the nature of work prior to their arrival on the island—some believed they had applied for a job as entertainer. In a very few instances, women claimed to be under the impression that they would be involved in work completely outside the entertainment industry, such as in the food business. Also, despite the women's eagerness to find work that pays well and their willingness to move temporarily to another country for employment, some were recruited under false pretenses and were forced to engage in sex work in order to pay back the debts they had incurred to obtain a work permit and visas or to travel. The women are in such instances debt-bonded within the sex trade. Situations for Amerindian women in Guyana indicate that this particular population is extremely vulnerable to recruitment for sex work under false pretenses and that their work and clients are closely regulated and managed by the proprietors of entertainment establishments.[44] In a 2002 study, the following was found:

> While no sex worker claimed to have been tricked or coerced into sex work, this was clearly a risk, especially for Amerindian girls and women. None of the Amerindian women in the study had been "hijacked," but several said they knew that it happened. One story was told of "Christine," a woman who was known to kidnap girls and beat them with her heavily ringed hands . . . . In Skeldon, Corentyne, one woman reported that the proprietor of one brothel kept the women's earnings, and that if they wanted to go out they would have to leave G$2000 with him. These women were also subjected to a curfew and had to be in the brothel at night. Three women interviewed at the Borderline Bar on the Corentyne Creek, reported not being allowed to go out without the "boss-man's" permission and when the business closed at night, of being padlocked into one room to sleep. They had been there for six months. The Red Thread team also visited Santa Rosa in Albion, Corentyne, following a report that two Amerindian girls were being held against their will. This was supported by a report by another woman who said that she had escaped from Santa Rosa, with the female proprietor owing her G$15,000.[45]

Sex work in the Surinamese interior reveals a mixture of both self-employment and coercion.[46] Some women working in clubs and camps and as occasional sex workers independently control their work and earnings. Among camp-cooks, some are mislead into sex work. Brazilian women are commonly recruited and paid by mining operators and foremen to service miners, although up to 80 percent of the women in this category report to know beforehand that their travel to Suriname is for the explicit purpose of earning money through sex work. In Maroon communities, women and teenage girls work independently, although initially some mothers send their daughters into the business.[47] Where the line between autonomy and coercion lies is neither rigid nor always easily discernible.

In general, Caribbean sex work reflects a high degree of autonomy on the part of the woman with some instances of direct male control and coercion—a situation that appears similar in many respects to that in sub-Saharan African countries where "freelancing" is a common occurrence and where female sex workers often independently manage and control their own resources and capital.[48] However, as in the rest of the global sex trade, it is, for the most part, men who accumulate the largest financial profits from the sexual labor that is expended, controlling the sites where sex work occurs—as bar and hotel proprietors, tourism industry operators and managers, recruiters and traffickers of women, or direct intermediaries between client and prostitute. Female sexuality is thus an integral part of many small- and large-scale moneymaking enterprises in the region that are run by, and are profitable for, men. It is also heavily attached to the specific type of Caribbean heteropatriarchy described earlier, where women are expected to cater to male sexual desires and needs, and where men legitimately may engage in multiple sexual relationships.

The Organization of Sex Work

Sex work in the region is loosely organized around hotels and guest houses in downtown districts, where clients meet sex workers, rooms are used on or off the premises, and the proprietor is not involved directly in money transactions between clients and sex workers. In the capitals of Guyana and Suriname, for example, sex workers rent a room on the premises, independently seeking customers either outside the hotel or guest house or in the hotel bar. In the Dominican Republic in some instances women live on the premises attached to a bar and are paid weekly by the proprietor rather than by the client. In such a scenario, if clients wish to take the sex worker to another location, an exit fee is paid to the bar owner. In Belize, arrangements at a hotel combine with the "ficha" system (in which the sex worker is paid a commission on the number of drinks that the client buys), and the sex worker lives in rooms on the premises. Here the hotel or bar owner charges a set amount from the sex workers' earnings instead of rent. Hotels or guest houses where sex work takes place are often closely connected to a bar nightclub or go-go dance club, which is where the majority of sex workers meet their clients (tourists and nontourists). The ficha system ensures that the woman would not necessarily have to have sex with the client, since she is guaranteed an income from entertaining guests at the bar. The cabaret system in the Dominican Republic operates in a similar fashion. Women are recruited by a bar owner to attract men to the premises to drink, although in some instances the bar owner directly employs women on a weekly basis.[49]

In Ocho Rios in Jamaica a variation exists where, in some instances, sex workers pay an entry fee to nightclubs in order to meet clients inside, yet in Belize City and Sosúa in the Dominican Republic freelance sex workers visit bars and nightclubs to meet clients without having to pay the bar owner.[50] In Curaçao at the open-air "snacks" that sell drinks and fast food the counter serves as a site where sex workers meet clients.[51] Not wholly unrelated to the bar and nightclubs are entertainment establishments where the primary job of the sex worker is exotic dancing, lap dancing, or stripping (noted in Guyana, St. Maarten, and Jamaica). Commercial sexual intercourse is in these cases a sideline.

A location that is important to the organization of sex work is the gold mining industry in the interiors of Guyana and Suriname. In Suriname the sex trade encompasses several arrangements. One, referred to as the sex-on-credit system, takes place within the miner's living quarters. Brazilian women are recruited and hired by the foreman

of a mining operation to live for a three-month period with one
miner who pays 10 percent of his total earnings to the foreman, who
in turn pays for the woman's travel into the camp, all her lodging expenses, and a fixed salary in gold.[52] In effect, the woman becomes a domestic partner or a temporary wife, providing the miner with not
only sex but also domestic labor for the three-month period. Another
arrangement is where women are not allowed to live in the mining
camps. In such cases they travel to the interior and reside in so-called
women's camps—a designated area of huts nearby the mining camps,
where miners visit them. Hotel and bar complexes (called clubs in
Suriname) also exist around the mining camps, where women are
more likely to be recruited and employed directly by the bar or club
owners. In Guyana around various mining camps women work in a
"kaimoo"—a wooden, zinc, or tarpaulin structure consisting of a series of small rooms, with just enough space for a bed, in which the
women live and receive clients. Women who travel from the coastal
areas to work in the interior often do so for around two to three
months at a time. While there are small concentrations of sex workers in the interior, the number of women working around gold, bauxite, and diamond mining areas is generally low, except when there
has been a recent "shout" or find. In one particular bauxite mining
site, the decline in the bauxite industry more generally and a conse-
quent drop in employment and spending power among men in that
industry specifically were the main factors that contributed to a decline in sex work activities in the early twenty-first century.[53] Gold
mining sites have also fostered sex work by women and adolescents
who reside in nearby Maroon and Amerindian villages.[54] Dominant
features in sex work in and around mining operations are, however,
the migration or trafficking of women into the mining areas for a set
period of time (usually three months) and payment in gold.

Tourist resorts—hotels and beaches designed primarily for North
American and Western European tourists that are located at a distance from the center of town—constitute another site where sex
work takes place. Sex tours arranged by a travel agency or tour opera-
tor that deliberately promote sex as part of the vacation package or organized visits for the tourists to specific hotels, brothels, or nightclubs
are not visible in the region. Instead, the beaches, bars, casinos, and

nightclubs within tourist hotels and resorts function as sites where tourists individually meet sex workers. Characteristic of much of the sex work in and around the resorts are the longer-term relationships that are forged between client and sex worker that in many instances last for the period of stay of the tourist, but sometimes extend into a situation where the tourist sustains the relationship through gifts, a ticket, and money after returning home. Such relationships approximate transactional sexual relations. However, as described in Jamaica, in some instances, highly professional sex workers rent a room in an all-inclusive resort hotel in order to have "short-time" clients.[55] The tourist resort is also the only site where heterosexual male sex work has been frequently observed or noted.

Docks for both cargo and cruise ships represent another site where sex work is common. In Curaçao, the brothel *Campo Alegre/Mirage* continues to operate for the service of sailors who disembark in the deepwater harbor. In Georgetown, Guyana, women gain permission to board freighters to service their clients on board.[56] In Ocho Rios, Jamaica, crew members of cruise ships visit specially designated lounges near the pier where sex workers rent a room to conduct their business.[57] Throughout the region, sex work is also street based, occurs out of women's homes, and occurs through escort services. Special red-light districts are not apparent, nor are places that are designated exclusively for prostitution. Only one site exists where non-sex working women are banned from entering on specific days—Campo Alegre in Curaçao. In all other places, clients and nonclients, sex workers and non-sex workers can mingle, dance, drink, and socialize freely together.

Sex work in the Caribbean region, across language and cultural distinctions, indicates an interrelationship between different domains of sex work. Workers do not necessarily stay in one site or in one type of arrangement, but often operate in various systems simultaneously or at different times in their lives. Also, categories of sex work easily overlap; for example, hotel- or club-based sex work occurs in both tourist resorts and mining areas. However, not all sites are open or accessible to all sex workers. Some places are highly controlled by men, for example, foremen at the gold mines or bar owners; thus, access to these workplaces is conditioned by factors well beyond the sex worker's control. Other arrangements rely on multi-lingual skills or expensive attire, which often goes hand in hand with a higher level of education and a middle-class or elite status. Since many sex workers in the Caribbean, while not illiterate, are not highly educated and are poor, such avenues are closed to them. For the most part, those who work in tourist resorts do not work else-where (the money and conditions being better than in other places), indicating a hierarchy based on location and type of arrangement. Even so, advantages that go together with tourism-oriented prostitu-tion do not guarantee a desire for upward mobility. Young street-walkers in Cartagena, Colombia, for example, have claimed that they did not seek to move up the hierarchy, for while tourism-related sex work was more profitable to them, the streetwalking areas around the tourist resorts were far more restricted by the police than downtown neighborhoods, and foreign clients more demanding than local men.[58] The young women and teenagers thus preferred the downtown areas even though it required more clients on their part. Treatment by the state and clients in this case conditioned the young women's choices in sex work.

A characteristic of the organization of female sex work in the re-gion is the high level of mobility of the women. This can be national, regional, or international, involving movement between sex work sites within a specific country, or from country to country, and has been specifically commented upon in studies in the Dominican Re-public, Curaçao, Barbados, Guyana, and Suriname. This characteristic positions the sex worker as continually outside the immediate local context within which she works, as the "Other" who can be more eas-ily taken advantage of due to her lack of a social network, or knowledge of language or local politics and practices. It also serves to confound attempts to quantify the population, and to complicate health and social policies designed especially for sex workers. In Guyana, move-ment within the national boundaries is primarily determined by where sex workers can earn money: that the women's choice to work at a particular site or geographical location is conditioned by shifts and changes in the local economy and the amount of disposable income men have at a specific time.[59] The temporary nature of gold mining "shouts," for example, in Guyana and Suriname, draws sex

working women into the interior to gold mining camps for short periods of time, after which they may return home to work from a hotel
in the city or to another more lucrative site in the interior. In the Dominican Republic, the internal movement is primarily from rural
areas to tourist sites or to the capital.

Transactional Sex and Sponsoring

There are a number of activities in which women and men engage in
sexual-economic transactions without ever acknowledging or referring to themselves as sex workers. The mistress is one such category,
represented by terms such as *outside woman, buitenvrouw, deputy, bi-
jzijd,* or *sweetheart,* yet sometimes described by self-defined sex
workers and other members of society as sex work. Transactional sex,
sometimes referred to as red-eye sex or sexual activity for gain, is another.[60] One schoolgirl in Jamaica described it in the following way:

> Sometimes the girls looking material things . . . lets take a boy for ex-
> ample if they pass on the road and dem a walk or push bicycle and him
> call out to a girl, she will say, go weh, a who you a talk to boy. Don't chat
> to me. But mek the same boy start roll up in a Honda tomorrow. You will
> hear what happen . . . . You understand. So it is like, material things.[61]

Some stress the importance of acquiring "hot" (trendy) clothes and
hairstyles through transactional sex; others need food or lunch
money. Other than with young men, Jamaican schoolgirls and
schoolboys from working-class neighborhoods and backgrounds may
be sexually involved with older men and women—"Big Men" and "Big
Women" or "Sugar Daddies" and "Sugar Mummies"—for considerations other than sex.[62] Drug dealers, community and gang leaders in
inner-city neighborhoods, or men who drive expensive, flashy cars
are also considered particularly attractive by the girls. Often schoolboys are perceived as not having the financial wherewithal to attract
girls, and the theme of the inadequacy of the schoolboys' lunch
money is one that in Jamaica schools plays an important role. As one
young girl put it, "Especially the girl dem who just turn thirteen, dem
say schoolboy carry lunch money and big man work. Schoolboy caan
mind them because them lunch money dun from 12 o'clock."[63] Men

in the domestic setting—stepfathers or a mother's boyfriend—may also extract sex in exchange for money from a teenage girl: "Some a dem say a di stepfather a give dem di money, so, dem have sex wid 'im."[64] Dunn concludes about this in Jamaica:

> In general girls were either required or encouraged to have relationships with older men in exchange for material goods to ensure their "better-ment." As such, school fees, lunch money and busfare, school books and supplies as well as graduation-related expenses (hairdo, ring, gown, dress shoes etc) emerged as material goods and educational support that were exchanged for sex.[65]

For teenage boys, similar patterns occur. Dunn's study found that "boys are involved in similar relationships, but on a much smaller scale. There were reports of older, affluent women who daily pick up their 'chapses' from high school in expensive vehicles, take them home, take them on holidays, and provide gifts in exchange for sex. In some cases, their family receive financial support."[66] However, while transactional sex for adolescent girls is explicitly talked about by both girls and boys as attached to material goods and social and economic benefits, boys couch their activities in terms of sexual pleasure. A common perception among boys in Jamaica is that while girls "just want to have money," "man do it for free."[67] The construction of sexuality as sexual pleasure for boys/men and as economically motivated for girls/women remains a dominant theme. For few young people involved in transactional sexual relations does the notion of sex work play a role. A counselor with the Jamaican Family Planning Association recalled a discussion with a client about the similarity between transactional sex and sex work:

> She was at one of the local high schools ... she found this man who was quite willing to give her whatever it was to take her to school, and when he comes at the weekend she has sex with him and she gets her money. He buys her a gift—probably a pair of shoes or whatever—and she said if she needed something extra, she asks for it and she always gets it. I said to her, "what do you call that?" And she said "he's just my boyfriend" . . . so I said, "wouldn't you call that prostitution?" And she was all quiet . . . I said, "you are trading sex for whatever . . . if this man stops giving you

the money and the gifts and whatever, would you still have sex with him?"
She said "Miss, you must be mad! Why would I be having sex if I don't
get nuttin' from him?"[68]

In a similar fashion, in Curaçao, sponsoring describes a transaction in
which richer, older men provide financial support to younger women,
outside of marriage. Several men during interviews I held in the
mid-1990s described sponsoring as applicable to professional women
who may have a regular job and income and are middle class by all
standards, providing them with those consumer goods and trappings
deemed necessary for the modern woman and that visibly enhance
her status and class in the society (such as a cell phone, car, expensive
jewelry, etc). However, whether termed *transactional sex* or *sponsoring*
that involves "boyfriends" and "girlfriends," such relationships are
clearly defined by the men and women involved in them as entirely
dependent upon sexual-economic exchanges and as such approximate sex work, although they occur in different sites and without an
up-front negotiation of money for sex. The extent of such relationships has not been systematically researched in the region, although
they overlap with arrangements within the tourism industry as well
as with other types of sexual relations that are historically specific to
the region.

Sex and Drugs

The use and trafficking of illegal substances are also closely inter-
twined with sex work in various ways. In the 1960s in Curaçao, for
example, men would visit the brothel and pay the women not for
any sexual service but instead to imbibe alcohol or smoke marijuana, at a time that both were banned in the brothel.[69] A former
client recalled the situation when he frequented Campo in that
time:

> [A]t the end of the month the rich people would come in, buy a bottle
> of whiskey, and could say to a woman, "here, we'll pay you two hundred
> guilders and you won't have to work tonight. You just need to keep us
> company, bring a few girlfriends and we'll pay." . . . They [the men]
> would become blind drunk, kept pouring drinks . . . .

While alcohol has since been legalized in this particular site in Curaçao, undercover drug use has increased on the island. "Base" (a
form of crack) and pure cocaine were the preferred drugs in the mid-
1990s.[70] During my interviews with sex workers, most of them declared to use some kind of drugs, particularly the younger women.

In other cases, in order to support a drug habit, women and men
will trade sex. An eighteen-year-old woman in Curaçao described
the situation:

> I had a friend and he was good friends with a dealer, and he got [co-
> caine] free. And I am his girlfriend, yes, so I get too. Gratis.
> But there are other things . . . . It's like this. The people who buy drugs
> come with cars. They see you, you are a girl. They want you to go with
> them, so you go with them, and you get the drugs.

In Curaçao, "chollers"—base users—often form a family, a tight
group, a closed network of men and women where sex is exchanged for
drugs and protection. A choller explained that if he had a few packets
of base, he could exchange one for a woman's sexual companionship.
Although she would then be considered "his woman," their relationship was primarily based on his supply of drugs. Another scenario was
where, in a steady relationship, the woman solicited clients from the
street. She provided the money for both herself and partner to buy
more drugs.[71] In one particular drug-using "family" consisting of fourteen men and two women, the women provided domestic and sexual
services for the men and in addition were expected to bring in some income to the group. The women were out from 7 P.M. to 2 A.M. every
evening working the streets, selling sex for as little as two guilders.

In the mid-1990s, women who used base and provided sexual services in order to support their habit were a well-known phenomenon
on the island. The majority were Dutch Antillian girls in their late
teens. However, several older women were obviously still active as
base prostitutes. One woman I encountered was gray-haired, emaci-
ated, with bones protruding through wrinkled skin, and barely able
to rise from her cot, yet still accepting customers. While the general
impression in Curaçao at the time was that the majority of the
women's clients were other chollers or drug users, male participants
in the sex trade (clients, managers, etc.) stressed that it was just after

payday that men would visit the main brothel or the more organized
sex houses downtown. At other times, streetwalkers, who invariably
were chollers, would be sought out by the men. As one client put it,
"Your own pocket determines it. You have money, you go to Campo,
have a drink with friends and so on. And later, when you have no
money . . . you go to the street."[72] The link between sex work activities
and a desire for, or dependency on, illegal substances did not always involve a strict sexual-economic transaction, although female sexuality
was clearly employed to sustain the use and traffic of the substances.

Male Hustling

An area where the distinction between sex work and transactional sex
is equally as blurred is male "hustling." While women sex workers
usually have little problem in identifying themselves as such, men involved in similar practices do not necessarily self-define in the same
way. Rather, the terms *beachboy*, *gigolo*, *sanky panky*, *rent-a-dread*,
rental, or *hustler* are most common, with few men explicitly acknowledging the economic nature of their activities. Nevertheless, some
men recognize the proximity of their activities to prostitution:

> I would call myself gigolo, you know, . . . [but] normally people don't
> know the meaning of gigolo. Gigolo is a person . . . what go to the woman
> and say "Listen babes, I need a car, I need a home" . . . a male prostitute.[73]

In Curaçao, where gay and heterosexual men also contribute to the
general picture, they are also less recognized in their capacity as sex
workers than women. In the nightlife, some are quite visible, working
from popularly known places in town, invariably soliciting from the
street. Others associate behind closed doors, attending parties and
working more discreetly. However, during the 1980s around sixty
male prostitutes were regularly checked at a state venereal disease
clinic, many of whom became licensed sex workers and thus were officially designated as prostitutes.[74] The registration of men as prostitutes by the police was incidental and only implemented from
August to December 1982. The registered men were solely of Dutch
Antillian origin, ranging between the ages of sixteen and thirty-five,
with the majority under the age of twenty. These young men were

often grouped around a "chief" who not only organized house parties, ran the snack bar, and ensured a clientele, but also took care that
the men attended their weekly medical checkup. The men either
worked at the house, went with their clients to cars or a hotel, or occasionally spent the time at the client's home. Others worked from
different sites. According to respondents at police and health departments in 1993, the majority of the formerly registered male sex
workers had left Curaçao by then and lived in the Netherlands. The
gay bar/meeting place that was also in operation then on the
Pennstraat had also been closed.

Despite the registration practices in the 1980s in Curaçao, the category of male prostitute is not officially recognized in government
documents and pronouncements, and prostitution on the island remains identified with women. The distinction between sex work and
friendship thus remains extremely blurred. As reported by one man:

> We don't have a Campo Alegre [state-legalized brothel] as you do . . . .
> We don't have the opportunity of meeting other homosexuals in bars
> and open places, because it's not done here, although lately there are
> some bars in Otrabanda that are becoming social centers for homosexu-
> als. But many will say that he has a "steady friend."[75]

The tourist industry is the premier site that supports male sex work,
homosexual, bisexual, and heterosexual. In Curaçao, a response by a
police officer who knew almost every sex worker in his patrol area confirmed a general impression: "You mean a gigolo? Ah, we have many
here, in the hotels or here [outside Park Hotel]. You know where the
tourists are, you find a lot . . . it's primarily for the money." Studies on
tourism in the region reconfirm the impression from Curaçao and have
created a distinction between romance tourism (involving men as providers of sex to female tourist clients) and sex tourism (involving female sex workers and male tourists).[76] These distinctions invoke the
differences in general understandings and definitions of male and female sexuality in the Caribbean. Women, for example, are marginalized, scorned, and disrespected as loose women within local cultural
logic if they appear explicitly sexual and engaged in multiple sexual relationships, without this being attached to procreation and economic
needs of the family. They are generally viewed as whores if they engage

in explicit sexual-economic transactions in the tourist industry. For men, hegemonic constructions of Caribbean masculinity are not questioned or denied to a man who does the same, particularly in a heterosexual relationship. An exchange of sex with a female tourist instead reaffirms understandings of "real" Caribbean manhood. As described in the foregoing chapters, the notion of Caribbean masculinity, as legitimately attached to multiple partnering and sexual prowess, is powerful, and this idea dominates popular as well as academic understandings. Distinctions between constructions of male and female sexualities within the sex trade and the divergent ways women and men self-define in heterosexual sex tourism work also reflect different gendered sites of power and oppression for Caribbean men and women. Women are marginalized on the basis of their sexuality, but racially are seen to be performing their "expected" role, as hypersexualized subjects, and may be tolerated because they are seen to be "making do" within the tradition of working-class women to support their family. Men, however, do what is sexually normal for men—they are promiscuous or informally polygynous, heterosexually active, and engaged with multiple female partners. Stigmatization and marginalization of the men occur around different axes, such as their unemployed, semicriminalized hustler status, as well as on the basis of race, in societies where work in the formal sector is considered superior and blackness remains marked by notions of inferiority.[77] Stigmatization and marginalization on the grounds of sexuality begin to occur for men when they depart from the dominant construction of masculinity, when, for example, they engage in same-gender or bisexual relations. The heteropatriarchalization of many Caribbean societies that is inscribed in law, religion, and various social institutions, and the intense homophobia that is articulated in popular culture, remarked upon earlier, place men who have sex with men in a marginalized or criminalized position vis-à-vis the "real" Caribbean man and may lead to an explicit denial of an engagement in sex work.

Race and Sex Work

The shift from a discourse that was primarily articulated through the white European masculine colonial consciousness about Caribbean

female sexuality to one that is embedded in the imaginations and desires of the colonized man has been a subject of interrogation and
discussion by anticolonial and Third World intellectuals such as
Albert Memmi and Frantz Fanon, explored through black American
perspectives, and slightly touched upon in Caribbean gender analyses.[78] Besides the profound influence that colonialism has had on notions of the superiority of whiteness (including white femininity)
among the colonized, it has also imparted a legacy of the exoticization and eroticization of the brown woman. This was infused into
new relations of power and privilege structured through anticolonial
and nationalist struggles for political independence that appeared on
the Caribbean landscape in the twentieth century. One encounters
attitudes and ideas that reflect both a racialization of sexual desire
and an exoticization of cultural difference within the Caribbean
itself, much of which revolves around the brown female body and
identity. In Cuba, for example, the *mulata* was not only considered
exotic by foreign men, but male Cuban writers, artists, and poets "en-
shrined the erotic image of Cuba's *mulatas*" during the nineteenth
and early twentieth centuries.[79] The image of the "SanDom" was
constructed in Curaçao to represent foreign, brown, culturally
"Other" women as prostitutes.

Similar notions of the exotic, erotic brown woman have been recorded in research on prostitution around the region where light-
skinned Latin American, Brazilian, and Spanish-speaking Caribbean
women are positioned as migrant workers in the sex trade, thus
highly exploitable and highly vulnerable in relationship to the resident population, yet are defined as hypersexual within local dominant gender ideologies. In the interior in Guyana, Brazilian miners
have stated that they prefer Indian, Amerindian, or "mixed" girls—
that they did not like black women.[80] In Haiti, the male sexual preference for the lighter-skinned, silky-haired Dominicans is seen to be
a part of a culture of exoticism that includes beliefs that Spanish is
"the language of love" and that women from the Dominican Republic
are more professional and more attractive in sex work than Haitian
women.[81] However, complexities of race/color and sexual desirability
in the postcolonial Caribbean societies remain a contested subject.
Noting the shift around beauty ideals in the Caribbean during the

1960s, Miller, for example, points out that attractiveness was no longer seen as constituted by white femininity, but rather "the beautiful girl has Caucasian features and is Fair or Clear in color," yet "the paradox of the situation is that even the most vehement of Black Power leaders in both the Caribbean and the United States tend to have white wives."[82] This is not unlike earlier trends in Curaçao. As a Black Power advocate noted in the late 1960s:

> At Campo Alegre [the central brothel] I have noticed that there are only white women, and the Black woman who might be among them has to work double the hours to make the same money as her white colleagues . . . . I have seen how our revolutionaries and young men who are full of Black Power are the first in the line to go to bed with a white woman, or to marry a white women . . . . I have noticed that when they screw a Black woman she becomes their whore, but if they screw a white woman, it's as if she has done them a favor . . . . [W]hy is our Black woman used by the white man and rejected by the Black man?[83]

While *creolization, mestizaje, blanquemiento, browning,* or *whitening-up* have received extensive attention in studies of Caribbean colonial history, intersections of sexual desirability with ethnicity and race in postcolonial nationalist discourses remain underexplored.[84] Nevertheless, Brackette Williams's analysis of a Guyanese village concludes that while ethnic identities of various cultural groups are historical residua and national identity rests upon ideas of equal rights of all members of society, another, contradictory process is at work. Hierarchies, she notes, are constructed on the basis of notions of an ethnic group's contribution to society, where a definition of ethnicity rests upon notions of "differences in innate intellectual and physical capabilities" and where members of inferioriorized groups are viewed as "innately lazy, incompetent and promiscuous."[85] Thus, while the former colonial ideology of Anglo-European superiority no longer dominates, new hierarchies of race are in place, which include ideas about sexuality. In an extensive examination of racialized sexualities in Spanish Caribbean literature, Claudette M. Williams points out: "Vestiges of the original white racial bias persist today in the representation of light skin and 'white' (Caucasian) features as the ideal of female beauty," which she argues follows from the "well-known saying" in Latin America and the Caribbean that the white woman was for marriage, "the mulatto woman for a good time, and the black woman for work."[86]

> The white woman descendent of the European colonizer is idolized and prized as the sexless model or purity and beauty. The light-skinned mulatto or brown woman, hybrid product of the sexual liaisons between European men and African women, represents the Creole middle groups, but is tainted racially and, by extension, morally. Therefore she can only be the provider of those taboo sexual pleasures that would tarnish the "fair lady."[87]

On the other hand, it is noted in the Dominican Republic that "popular male and female opinion reveres the beauty of the *blancola*, yet popular sexual myth inbues the *negrola* with vigor and skillful prowess."[88] It is Afro-Dominican women who are defined as lower-class street sellers, prostitutes, and single mothers, and darkness is heavily associated with unbridled sexuality.

Hierarchies around racialized sexualities resurface in postcolonial Caribbean contexts, albeit in much more varied forms than under colonialism, and in far more complex arrangements, where skin color, ethnicity, and nationality are critical in the construction of race. Ongoing explorations into contemporary social constructions of racialized Caribbean masculinities and femininities may unpack other dimensions of this dynamic. It may also lead to a more fuller apprehension of the hierarchy that exists in prostitution around the region in which "brown-skin girls" or the category "mixed," "mulatto," or "Latina" holds the better paid, more lucrative work, with African Caribbean women most commonly located in the most poorly paid sectors.[89]

Diversity

Despite the commonalities in various types of sexual-economic transactions, the sex worker in the Caribbean is not a homogenous category. Hierarchies exist according to sites of activity, level of education, and, as discussed above, race/ethnicity and nationality. Many of the women and men who participate in sexual-economic relations are not full-time sex workers: for some the sale of sexual labor is a way to support a drug-use habit; for others it is classified as "opportunity" work—that which is done on an irregular basis—and for yet others, it is a means to secure the latest in consumer goods. Saleswomen and cooks in the interior of Suriname, hotel employees and "muchachas de su casa" in the Dominican Republic, entertainment coordinators in all-inclusive hotels in Montego Bay, waitresses in Ocho Rios, nurses and teachers in other parts of Jamaica, bank tellers and secretaries in Belize, and odd jobbers or beach vendors in Barbados who are engaged in sexual-economic transactions do not necessarily identify themselves as sex workers, yet will acknowledge the incorporation of sex work into their range of income-generating activities. Age also mediates the category. Young people, girls and boys, as pointed out above, do not always self-define or are not defined by others as sex workers. Moreover, in some Spanish-speaking Caribbean territories definitions of a sex worker or prostitute are closely interwoven with Catholic standards of womanhood.[90] Chastity until marriage and monogamy constitutes critical elements of decent femininity in this religious context. Once a girl or woman has sexual intercourse outside formal marriage, she is considered ruined and no longer fit for marriage. To what extent this is paralleled in Hindu or Muslim communities throughout the region where sexual relations, particularly for women, are tightly bound to marriage, and virginity until marriage highly prized, remains to be fully explored.

The number of different locations where sex work takes place, the various patterns around the organization of sex work, and the diversity of ways that the work site and arrangements are connected also contribute to the idea that Caribbean sex work cannot be discussed or represented in a monolithic way. Trends in the region indicate distinctive patterns that embody a high degree of heterogeneity, fluidity, and movement. Women often participate in formal prostitution willingly and knowingly—taking their own steps to work in a brothel, migrate around the region to locations known for lucrative prostitution activities, and deliberately combine sex work with other forms of income generation. Others are attracted into the sex sector through false promises of work and are forced to stay in prostitution due to debts owed to those who recruited or trafficked them. For many more women and some men, however, formal prostitution does not take place. Some engage in sex work on the side as a supplement to other income-generating activities, others to obtain material goods that are otherwise out of their reach. The deliberate exchange of sexual services for material benefits occurs in a variety of ways for adult and adolescent women and men, some of which is defined as prostitution, the majority as sexual relations with "boyfriends" and "girlfriends." A distinction between sexual relations that are attached to marriage and love and those attached to economic relations is extremely blurred. Chevannes concludes about this fluidity that a continuum exists around sexual relations, ranging from those that are explicitly attached to the very deliberate and conscious exchange of sexual services for money (prostitution) to arrangements that are based on economic security (marriage), with forms of transactional sex in between, maintaining that transactional sex refers to a "negotiated sexuality" that is "not quite as cold as prostitution."[91] Such a lineal description and analysis of sexual-economic relations can, however, be misleading and obscures the great complexities that are practiced throughout the region. The "mati work" arrangement described for Suriname where a woman "fulfills her obligations" to society by taking a husband, bearing children, setting up a heterosexual household, etc., yet simultaneously engages in same-gender sexual relations, or the distinction made by prostitutes of work with clients and safe sexual relationships with a boyfriend or husband, present other dimensions to the equation. A woman's sexuality, in the body and life of one person, is in both instances drawn upon self-consciously as a resource that enables her to find social and economic security, while on the other hand it is the source for pleasure for herself and others. Whether the two arenas are always kept separate is difficult to determine. Many a sex worker in a tourist setting "falls in love" or marries her client, suggesting some form of pleasure and satisfaction for the woman in the encounter. Not all prostitutes classify their clients as nasty, and in transactional sexual relations for adolescents, sexual pleasure could be a part of the equation.

Sex work, as we have seen throughout this chapter, has multiple dimensions and meanings, as well as several contradictions, yet it remains a central way in which sexuality is organized in the region. It may occur as prostitution or as transactional sex, inside or outside the context of intimacy and friendship, and is widely practiced by poor and not-so-poor women. Moreover, despite national and international efforts to curtail, limit, and control working women's sexual-economic activities, sex work has a long history and is deeply embedded in social relations. It is thus also likely to continue to be an integral part of the Caribbean landscape into the future.

4

THE HAPPY CAMP IN CURAÇAO: LEGAL SEX WORK AND THE MAKING OF THE "SANDOM"

While sex work takes place in a number of places and locations throughout the Caribbean, the Netherlands Antilles is one of few territories where sex work can legally occur, and the island of Curaçao is host to the largest brothel in the region. *Campo Alegre*—the Happy Camp—as the brothel was christened in 1949, is still in operation today, and, although it changed name in the mid-1990s to *Mirage*, is still well known on the island as "Campo."[1] Ask any adult Curaçaoan about the brothel and he or she will effortlessly direct you to an isolated place, not far from the international airport on the Hato plain on the north coast of the island. The brothel is hidden from the main road at the end of a dirt road, appearing from the outside as a fortressed army barrack or even a "concentration camp"—a bare compound surrounded by a solid, high wall with several rows of low zinc-roofed barrack-like buildings with rooms to accommodate over a hundred working women.[2] The starkness of the compound is emphasized by a lack of any vegetation, even of cacti—the most commonly found form of undergrowth on the island. An iron gate with a number of guards continually on duty is the only entrance point. The compound is a small, self-sufficient entity, containing not just rooms with beds, but also a bar and stage, casino, store, restaurant, health clinic, and administration buildings, all located in a dusty, shadeless environment far removed from the daily island activities and a distance from the capital, Willemstad. The air of a detention or army camp is further accentuated by the rule that the women may not leave the site between 6 P.M. and 6 A.M., and after sundown guards patrol the compound to check that the women are all inside and are available to serve clients. Only migrant women are allowed to work in the brothel. They apply for work at Campo through state channels, are registered with the immigration, health, and police departments, and are given work permits for a maximum of three months at a time. The brothel, while originally designed to sexually service and entertain Dutch and American militaries, crew from freighters and oil tankers that docked at the deepwater harbor, and migrant male oil refinery workers, caters today mostly to Antillian clients.

As not just the largest brothel in the Caribbean region, but also as one of the few state-regulated legal places for sex work, Campo is unique. Through the years, thousands of migrant women have been granted permission by the government authorities to work in the brothel, yet it remains a contested site for it violates laws that govern the island. The construction of a legal state-regulated brothel has also created a category of women on the island known as the "SanDom"—a synonym for prostitute—and has not only fostered a divide between local and migrant women, but also given rise to religious and feminist movements to abolish sex work altogether. The creation of the state-regulated brothel illustrates some of the main tensions and contradictions that exist in the region around the issue of sex work.

The Colonial Backdrop

The legalization and regulation of sex work in Curaçao has a long history and can best be understood in the wider discursive context of a coupling, in the mid-nineteenth century in Western Europe, of rationalized medical science with middle-class Christian-inflected morality about sexuality.[3] More specifically, however, policies and legislation in Dutch Caribbean territories toward prostitution are embedded in laws and ideologies in the Netherlands. Under the Napoleonic code, during French occupation, prostitution had been permitted and regulated in the "low countries."[4] This entailed the registration of and a regular medical check for prostitutes and was deemed necessary by Napoleon for the sexual servicing of his (male) military troops. The regulations remained formally and informally in force in various districts in the Netherlands until 1911, when articles 250bis and 250ter of a new penal code were introduced. These were intended to control the trafficking of women for the sex trade, while criminalizing the facilitation of prostitution by a third party and banning brothels. The code, however, did not outlaw prostitution once it was self-organized, or criminalize the prostitute.[5]

The penal code, when combined with Victorian Christian morality and early-twentieth-century Western European scientific discourses, produced a curious situation. On the one hand, brothels, pimps, and others who economically profited from activities of prostitutes were made illegal. On the other hand, the self-organization and self-actualization of prostitution were not criminalized under the law and the prostitute could exist as a legal subject. Prostitution was accepted as a social inevitability, yet it was deemed a threat to public decency and health, and prostitutes were subject to heavy policing and control if they worked in public areas. Patriarchal norms that secured male dominance in public and private affairs meant that women were not given free reign to organize and economically profit from their own activities or business. Instead, a sex industry managed by men was clandestinely allowed. A national policy of tolerance emerged, whereby the state turned a blind eye to prostitution activities that were facilitated or managed by a third party, took place inside dedicated sex houses, and were perceived by the authorities to cause little nuisance or obvious disruption to public life or health.[6]

The Dutch laws contravened the League of Nations conventions on prostitution of 1910 and 1933. The Dutch government also did not ratify the 1949 United Nations Convention for the Suppression of Traffic in Persons and the Exploitation of Prostitution of Others that developed from the earlier conventions, on the argument that the 1949 convention took as a premise the complete abolition of prostitution and was thus inconsistent with Dutch legislation.[7] It was also seen to contradict the regulations that were already in place in Dutch colonies in the East and West Indies, which by then allowed prostitution to legally take place.[8] In the early nineteenth century, the two articles in the Dutch penal code had, for example, been introduced to Dutch colonies in the Caribbean: Suriname, Aruba, Curaçao, Bonaire, St. Maarten, St. Eustacius, and Saba.

Regulationism in Curaçao

Curaçao, the largest of the six Dutch Antillian islands, was established in the seventeenth century as a commercial colony and a depot for European food products, arms, and slaves, and has since developed primarily on activities centering on its large natural deep-water harbor and its geopolitical position in the Caribbean region.[9] Due to its close proximity to Venezuela, it was identified as an ideal offshore refining site by the Royal Dutch Shell company, and during WWI it served as a fuel depot for Allied forces in the region. With a harbor that could allow large ships to dock, by the 1920s, approximately twenty thousand sailors from tankers and cargo ships disembarked on the island every month. At the same time, Shell recruited five thousand single male migrants to work in the oil-refining industry, and in the 1940s during WWII, the Dutch colonial marine force stationed on the island was joined by two thousand to three thousand U.S. military troops in order to protect the oil industry. The demand by the large number of single able-bodied men for sexual activity while on the island was seen by the colonial government as a need that had to be met, while local women were to be protected from what were defined as immoral and depraved acts.[10]

The main legislation concerning prostitution in Curaçao, introduced by the colonial government, was the 1917 penal code with articles 259 and 260, which replicated articles in the 1911 penal code in the Netherlands. These articles were liberally interpreted within the Curaçaoan context. Correspondence between the minister of the colonies in the Netherlands and the governor of Curaçao between 1928 and 1936, for example, reveals that despite the apparent increase in the single male population and their demand for sexual activity, prostitution in Curaçao was considered by the local authorities to take place within legal limits. In 1928 and 1929 in response to a League of Nations investigation about the existence of brothels and "the means employed in their respective countries with a view to protecting public order and health against the dangers arising from prostitution,"[11] the island government described a situation where prostitution activities were acknowledged but were not defined as a transgression of any laws or diplomatic agreements:

> The police in Curaçao do not know of any brothels. The renting of rooms occurs often, yet in only a few instances can it be established that the landlord has knowledge that the rooms are used for sexual offenses. In the past year only one conviction was made on the basis of article 259 of the Curaçao Penal Code, in which the person involved was sentenced to four months imprisonment.[12]

In 1935 the League of Nations solicited further information regarding the regulation of prostitution in its effort to collect information to support the abolition of brothels worldwide. Again the answer from Curaçao sketched a situation that was considered by the local governing authorities to fall within its legal boundaries:

> There is no system of regulation of prostitution here . . . the brothel system is not in vogue . . . no measures are necessary . . . the law orders anyone who suffers from venereal disease to seek treatment from a medical doctor . . . [and] appointed government-specialists are charged with treating these patients.[13]

The information delivered from Curaçao indicates that during this period, while the colonial government acknowledged that prostitution was taking place on the island, it did not define the situation in a way that warranted any further state intervention, control, or prohibitionist measures. Thus, despite the evidence of prostitution on the islands, the colonial governor seemed quite content to leave things as they were. As the attorney general at the time succinctly stated, "In this tropical harbor town, vice flourishes, but is not a crime."[14]

Colonial state tolerance of prostitution activities and the sex trade continued. In a response to a 1936 inquiry from the League of Nations about the rehabilitation of prostitutes, the governor of Curaçao responded to the minister of colonies in The Hague that the information up to that point about Curaçao was accurate and as complete as possible, was comparable to that submitted by the United Kingdom, and that the inquiry from the League of Nations was not, in the first place, intended for the colony.[15] As far as the colonial government in Curaçao was concerned, the matter had been adequately defined and dealt with. The system in operation in the Dutch colony was considered not to breach any national or international laws or treaties, to provide adequate treatment for contagious and venereal disease for whomever might become infected, and not to require any specific policies or laws or the abolition of prostitution. A variety of sex work activities were thus tolerated.

It was during the 1940s, with a perceived increase of prostitution activities and the rise in the number of cases of sexually transmitted diseases, that the colonial government took steps to control explicit forms of sex work.[16] On May 8, 1942, a five-man commission, two members of whom were Roman Catholic priests, was formed to investigate the problem.[17] That same year, after a series of four meetings, the commission submitted a short report and recommendations to the governor of Curaçao in which they stressed the need for government control of prostitution activities.[18] The recommendations included changes to the health regulation to specifically address "persons of the female sex who make a habit or profession of engaging in fornication with persons of the other sex."[19] Prostitutes were explicitly identified by the state as vectors of sexual disease, and the government was advised to place prostitutes under supervision of the police and health departments in both Curaçao and Aruba through a registration system. Simultaneously, recommendations were made to designate particular hotels for prostitution and to license foreign women to work at the hotels. The advice and recommendations were made for a variety of reasons, but protection of the nation "against the physical and psychological consequences of an evil" was paramount. The corruption of morals on the island was defined as detrimental to the general public, especially to women and children, and prostitutes perceived as a threat to public health.

The report and recommendations were studied by the governor, attorney general, and director of the Department of Public Health and presented to the government council as a proposal for amendments to an earlier regulation on contagious diseases.[20] The governor of Curaçao argued that the "evil" was a phenomenon that no government had the power to eliminate, and thus even though the government council agreed not to change the articles of the penal code, the deliberations resulted in various procedures to limit the spread of contagious diseases through the control of prostitutes.[21] Health officers for the U.S. and Dutch troops stationed on the island supported the introduction of any measures that would work toward the control of sexually transmitted diseases "both for the military and civilian population," and a prophylactic distribution center was set up at the U.S. military base.[22]

In light of all these considerations, on September 23, 1944, and "In the Name of the Queen," Governor Kasteel approved amendments of the regulation of contagious diseases.[23] The amendments included the stipulation that the local chief of police in Curaçao and Aruba create a register of prostitutes in which name, age, home address, and other particulars would be recorded and supplied to the Department of Public Health. All women engaged in prostitution were mandated to report to the police and register themselves as prostitutes. Registration was to occur within a week of the introduction of the regulation or, for those taking up sex work at a later date, within a week of their engagement, and for foreign women, within twenty-four hours of their arrival on the island. Registered sex workers were required to report weekly to appointed medical doctors at the Department of Public Health, and all foreign women on the first working day after their arrival on the island. Failure to visit the health authorities meant that a woman was to be reported to the police, who in turn were to intervene and ensure that the woman was examined by one of the appointed doctors. The amendments furthermore forbade men to drink with a prostitute or for a prostitute to allow the use of alcohol in her place of work, and required a person who had contracted a venereal disease to seek medical treatment. If the disease was diagnosed as incurable within forty-eight hours, the doctor was to report this to the director of the Department of Public Health. Lack of adherence in reporting cases of disease would subject the offender to a prison sentence of a maximum of one month or a fine (at the time stipulated as Naf250).

Creation of the "Happy Camp"

With the passing of the amended contagious disease act in 1944, the government began to regulate prostitution in a number of ways. A

specific department, the Child and Morals Police (Kinder-en Zeden
Politie, KZP), was established, whose tasks included the registration
of prostitutes. The registration process was set up in conjunction
with services of the Department of Public Health (Geestelijk en
Gezondheids Dienst, GGD) and the immigration department, and
an intricate system of control was created, residing directly under the
authority of the governor, the "gezaghebber," of Curaçao. Nonetheless, even with the creation of a regulatory system in 1944, the stated
objective of the colonial government—to protect the morality and
health of the nation—was not easily achieved. The situation barely
changed in downtown Willemstad. Registered prostitutes were assigned to specific hotels for work, yet many women and men continued to engage in "open air" prostitution. Marie Pompoen was in
particular an area where it was publicly evident that paid heterosexual
transactions were taking place. The belief that local women and children were still being exposed to overt sexual interactions outside the
confines of marriage and the home, and the poor hygienic conditions
under which many sexual activities took place, resulted in a police report in 1945 that proposed several further interventions. Among
them were the concentration of prostitutes in a specific zone. The
proposal was taken up by the governing council of Curaçao and a
plan devised to create an enterprise where women could rent a room
and operate in seclusion and away from public view.[24] A plot of land
to house a "hotel" and a director for the new business were conse-
quently sought. A site in Seroe Fortuna, that at the time was well
away from the main residential and commercial areas of the island,
was secured in 1947 with a mortgage provided by the Post Spaarbank
(the Dutch National Savings Bank), and a hotel license granted to a
local businessman, Mr. Bakhuis, to operate the business. The one-
hundred-room "hotel" Campo Alegre became a reality.[25] To organize
and streamline male visitors, special permits were issued to around
thirty bus drivers to deliver clients from the town and harbor, with
the marine and army forces providing their own transportation. Permits were issued to foreign women to work at the hotel for a limited
period and according to the space available. Women with Dutch Antillian nationality were barred from entering or working on the premises,
other than as medical professionals, cooks, or other service workers

for the prostitute population. A small government health clinic opened within the brothel compound.

Campo Alegre was established in 1949 as the largest brothel in the Caribbean region, designed to exclusively house foreign, migrant women as prostitutes. Women holding Dutch Antillian nationality were not allowed to work in the brothel and instead were left to their own devices to find work elsewhere. A clear hierarchy was drawn between foreign, migrant sex workers, who could work in a regulated, secluded environment, and those who were "of the nation" but had to fend for themselves on the streets and in clandestine brothels and who were more readily exposed to the public as "fallen" women.

In 1949, the attorney general alerted all the airline companies servicing Curaçao to allow women passengers who were known to have previously stayed at certain hotels to enter the territory only if in possession of a work permit for Campo Alegre. Once having arrived at the airport, the Immigration Service collected the women's papers and forwarded them to the police registration bureau. The women retrieved papers and passports from the authorities in town and registered with the police department. Immediately upon arrival or, at the latest, the next morning, the women were to report to the GGD medical doctor at the Campo clinic. The women's movements were tightly monitored and controlled by the state authorities.

Incongruencies

During the early 1950s government debates about prostitution on the island reopened due to questions raised by the public about the legality of the government practice of regulation. The debates produced a new investigation by the local government authorities into the matter, and an order from the attorney general on November 27, 1953, which defined several new and very specific measures.[26] The results were announced as follows:

> The commission advises the continuation of the confinement of prostitution in its present form, with a number of specific conditions . . . in keeping with this policy, the Ministry of Public Affairs will not prosecute the owner of *Campo* under article 259 given that such action would cause

the closing down of *Campo Alegre* . . . abolition of article 259 is not a consequence of this position . . . it is just not applied when tolerance of the
confinement of prostitution is necessary in order to enforce the measures which are intended to prevent open-air prostitution . . . the suspension of article 259 is then possible only when there is another
objective.[27]

In effect, the government recognized that the operation of the
brothel was in violation of its own penal code. However, it argued,
this would not lead to a change of law but rather to the suspension of
article 259 for the purpose of accommodating the brothel. In practice, the criminalization of the facilitation of prostitution by a third
party was set aside by the colonial government in favor of state regulation of prostitution activities.

The colonial government also maintained that it was not breaking any
UN treaties or international conventions:

The activities of the proprietor of *Campo Alegre* do not contradict the
international agreements on the trafficking of women . . . Women are
not recruited, abducted or procured from foreign lands . . . the proprietor
of *Campo Alegre* only rents rooms to prostitutes on arrangement with
them . . . [and] there is no organization that brings the women here
from other countries.[28]

In addition, the government held that prostitution "is recognized in
different degrees, as a necessary and established fact in most societies"; thus,

given the fact that on our island the reality of prostitution is accepted,
the question could be reduced to: open-air prostitution or confined
prostitution? Experience shows that the present encampment system
has stamped out open-air prostitution.[29]

Every effort was made by the colonial state to legitimize the brothel
to the public, stressing the inevitability of prostitution and the need
to protect the local (female) population from the "social evil" through
strict control and confinement of prostitutes.

The state's approach to prostitution was supported by some members of the Roman Catholic Church. For example, Monsignor A. van

der Veen Zeppenfeldt's response to the question of whether the government should officially sanction prostitution was that "the Government can tolerate prostitution and even take measures that serve to lead it into the least detrimental forms for the community, once it has been established that it is an evil in the community which the government cannot eliminate."[30] Father M. Hulsman, the chairman of the original commission on prostitution in 1942, also declared that "*Campo Alegre* is an inevitable evil that must be tolerated by the government to prevent immoral excesses elsewhere in the community."[31] The Church was entirely complicit with the colonial state in regulating prostitution on the island.

Regulated Sex Work, 1944–1999

The regulations that were established in the 1940s, premised on the state control of sexualized women's labor and bodies, were still in place at the end of the twentieth century. They required foreign women to enroll in a police register as a prostitute, giving name, address, date and place of birth, nationality, and occupation, and to sign a declaration confirming knowledge of the 1921 and 1944 health regulations. Personal records of the women's activities were kept on file with the Child and Morals Police, including such matters as length of stay on the island, address while staying in Curaçao, number of times in Curaçao (both in transit or for a longer period), and any debts that may have been incurred on the island. Photographs accompanied this personal record. Information about dates of arrival, initial registration, projected departure, actual departure, and removal from the register was kept in two other ledgers. Each new registrant was assigned a number, which was noted on all three records. In the period from June 1, 1944, to February 18, 1993, 15,235 different women had enrolled as prostitutes in the police register. Many had visited Campo more than once, bringing the total number of visits in that period to approximately 22,500.

In the 1990s, all the information was filed, updated, and supervised by a female police administrator. The two main ledgers were maintained as historical documents, while the personal files were destroyed after a period of time once a woman had been removed from the register, on the basis of a petition, death, old age, or retirement from prostitution. A second record was maintained by the Department of Public Health. All registered prostitutes were ordered to have in their possession a health card, commonly referred to as the pink card. If a woman failed to report for the weekly medical exam and to update the card, the doctors reported her tardiness to the police department, who in turn were supposed to track down the offender.

The pink card created some controversy over the years. It was stamped during the mandatory weekly visit to the government-appointed medical doctor and was a statement confirming the woman's compliance with government rules of abiding by the health regulation that stipulated that prostitutes had to be medically examined on a regular basis by appointed specialists. Most commonly, it was taken to signify a certificate of good health—a guarantee that the woman was not carrying any sexually transmitted diseases or infections. However, given that men's health conditions were not controlled or monitored, the possibility of a woman becoming infected by a male client directly after such a medical check rendered the pink card virtually invalid as a sign of good health. An illusion, rather than the practice of providing safe sex, had been not only created but also sustained by the system since 1944. The assumption of the prostitute as the vector of disease and threat to public health thus remained solidly in place, placing all the responsibility on sex workers to prevent the spread of disease and removing any from the broader public, particularly clients of sex workers.

Recruitment and Selection of Sex Workers

The administration of work permits for the brothel changed little between 1949 and the end of the twentieth century. Foreign women interested in work in Curaçao applied in writing to the director of the immigration department. The letters in turn were forwarded to the administrator at the police registration bureau, who screened them according to a number of criteria: (1) that Campo Alegre was mentioned in the letter, (2) the applicant was between the ages of twenty-one and forty, and (3) that a correspondence address was provided. The actual

character of the work at Campo did not have to be specified, and the
nature of the work was rarely stated in correspondence between the
Curaçaoan authorities or by the applicants. Once preselection criteria
had been met, the applicant's status was checked in the police and immigration department files, and permission granted to the woman to
travel to Curaçao once she was free of a criminal record or had not
worked at Campo during a certain period (formerly six months; in the
1990s, one year). A letter from the Child and Morals Police Department would then be sent to the applicant, in Spanish, instructing her
to arrive on the island around a certain date between Monday and
Thursday with a valid passport and visa (if necessary), a health report
(not more than one week old showing the results of chest x-ray,
syphilis test, and, in the 1990s, an HIV test), four photographs, and a
year-return airline ticket.

Some differences over the years are notable. Whereas, for example,
in the 1940s photographs sent with the woman's letter of application
were straightforward black-and-white passport snaps, in the 1990s,
larger color photographs were sent, in which the women often appeared full length, sometimes topless or skimpily dressed in bikinis or
underwear and in various semierotic poses. The actual numbers of
applications had also changed. While they continued to exceed the
number of places in the brothel, the total amount had decreased over
the years. Thus, while in the 1970s the bureau received as many as
sixty applications per day, in 1993 this number was approximately
sixty per week. Despite this decrease, there were still far more women
interested in working in Campo/Mirage than could be housed in the
brothel, and not all applications would be processed. "I divide the
permits between those who have worked before at Campo Alegre
and new applicants, because otherwise the newcomers would never
have a chance," explained the officer in charge of issuing the permits.
Within the selected group, a larger number of permits would be issued than were actually needed, given that not all of the applicants
would be able to travel to Curaçao at the appointed time. In the mid-
1990s, of the seven hundred to nine hundred permits sent out per
year, around 70 percent were actually used.

In the 1990s recruitment of women for work in Curaçao was more
explicit and was linked to a broader organized system of recruitment

for and travel to work in the brothel. Contact persons on the Campo/Mirage payroll were on site in the Dominican Republic to collect applications for processing by the Curaçaoan authorities. It was generally held that the contact men in the Dominican Republic merely facilitated the application process and acted as mediators between the women and the Curaçaoan authorities. Their role was described by various people in Curaçao as a necessity because of the weak postal and communications systems in the Dominican Republic and to ensure that the candidates arrived on the island with the required documents and tickets. However, others on the island were convinced that the middlemen explicitly recruited women for Campo/Mirage and made a first selection of candidates. The Curaçaoan authorities explicitly encouraged the participation of the middlemen as they thought it allowed the owners "an opportunity to organize their own business," to exercise more control over the brothel's affairs, and to reduce the government's role in the whole process.[32] Independent recruiting agents also operated elsewhere, particularly in Colombia; however, since this activity was not arranged through Campo/Mirage, these middlemen charged the women anywhere up to U.S.$100 for their services. From Suriname a woman who recruited Brazilian women for four clubs in Rotterdam in the Netherlands also selected women for the Curaçaoan sex industry. Rather than charging directly for her intermediary work, the costs were added on to the other expenses and debts owed by the women to the club owners in Paramaribo.[33] The police administrator in Curaçao reported that she advised women not to make use of independent middle persons and instead "to write directly to the 'Chefe de Immigracion' and to tell their friends they don't have to pay," as the services of the Curaçaoan police department were free of charge. The Curaçaoan police department in effect acted as the primary middleman or procurer for the state-legalized brothel, a role that over half a century had grown stronger rather than weaker.

While the brothel has been a fixed part of the Curaçaoan landscape since 1949, by 1997 its image had begun to decline. Conditions within the brothel had greatly deteriorated, and many clients preferred to go elsewhere, with both the women working in the brothel and their clients complaining and protesting against the poor

standards.[34] In an effort to regain business, the brothel owner reno-
vated the women's rooms, promoted live shows, and attempted to diversify the class and nationality of women who worked in the
brothel. Business recuperated, with a greater emphasis on entertainment for men than on prostitution. The new ten-year treaty between
the United States and the Dutch Kingdom that grants the U.S. Air
Force access to Aruba and Curaçao and their civilian airports, as
part of the U.S. Southern Command (SouthCom) web of military
facilities and functions in the region, may also mean a resurgence in
the twenty-first century of Campo as the place for R&R for the
stationed militaries.[35]

Violations

With the lifting of laws banning brothel keeping, trafficking, pimp-
ing, procuring, managing, and otherwise profiting as a third party
from prostitution in order to accommodate Campo/Mirage, the
colonial state has done little to enforce its laws in other parts of the
island. Between 1986 and 1994 two cases involving forced prostitution were brought to the attention of the Curaçaoan police. Raids on
suspected clandestine sex houses and prostitution locations had by
that time also ceased to take place. In interviews, police informants
reiterated the idea that it was difficult to prove that undocumented
sex work was taking place, even though it was common knowledge
that clandestine brothels and sex houses were in operation. In order
to produce any evidence, they argued, the police had to catch men
and women in the act. Furthermore, spokespersons for the department charged with policing and controlling sex work argued that the
department did not have the resources—neither finances nor person-
nel—to effectively carry out its responsibilities. In 1995, a renewed
effort was made to pay attention to the problem, although in this
case, working women, rather than pimps or brothel owners, were the
target. During the weekend of May 20–21, 1995, raids were carried
out in various places on the island. Sixty-three women were arrested
on the island without work or residency documents. The majority of
the women were reported to be from the Dominican Republic and
were to be deported by the Immigration Service.[36] In 1996 yet another

case made the news, this time involving five Colombian women who had been recruited to Curaçao under false pretenses and who ended up in a nightclub having to "entertain" guests against their will.[37] Even though the women took their case to court and won back payment of their salaries, no case was made against the persons who coerced and tricked them.

Pimps: The State and Others

The Curaçaoan context points to a system in which there are various levels of control and management of prostitution, implying several layers and levels of pimpage. At one level, the government regulates and facilitates sex work of Caribbean women, having taken upon itself the task of management and administration of prostitution through a police registration bureau, the Immigration Service, and the government health clinics, and through the licensing of the Campo Alegre/Mirage brothel. Furthermore, the government en-courages the recruitment of women for the sex trade and fully partic-ipates in the selection of candidates for the brothel. The colonial state is thus the primary organizer and regulator of prostitution on the island, and over a period of fifty-odd years its involvement as main "pimp" and "trafficker" has grown stronger rather than weaker. At a second level, the Campo/Mirage organization directly procures women for prostitution and draws profits from the rental of its "hotel" rooms to women. The third level consists of small-time hus-tlers, hotel owners, husbands, partners, and friends who directly or indirectly gain from the sexual labor of others. The government tolerates all activities in the name of servicing male sexual desires and for the protection of public health.

The situation on the island runs counter to international conven-tions concerning the ban on brothels and the abolition of the traffick-ing of women and minors for purposes of prostitution. It also explicitly violates the Curaçaoan penal code, which prohibits the facil-itation of sex work by a third party. Law enforcers in the country are quite aware of this awkward and contradictory situation in which they operate. Police spokespersons claim that prostitution is not legal on the island and insist on playing down the role of the police in regulating the activities. Nevertheless, they cannot completely hide their complicity. As the Chief of Police R. Ursula stated to a local journalist in 1990, "It's a bit strange—we regulate something which is forbidden by law."[38]

Nevertheless, despite all the attention to and scrutiny of the women's activities, as well as the overt control of their labor, neither the act of prostitution itself nor being a prostitute is mentioned or defined in the penal code or contagious disease regulations as a criminal offense or unlawful practice. Hence, women and men who engage independently in prostitution and who profit from their own sexual labor in Curaçao are not outside the law. Still, the complete lack of attention by government officials and the media to the demand side of the trade—the male clients, pimps, and procurers—places all the responsibility for sex work on the island on the women's shoulders. Men, as designers, implementers, and users of the regulationist system, have excluded themselves as actors in the scenario and thus deflected any attention away from their own participation. Male participation as clients is likewise taken for granted. Prostitution then remains defined and viewed in Curaçao as an inevitable social phenomenon to cater to male needs, and prostitutes as women who fall outside of the boundaries of normal female sexual life.

Construction of the SanDom

Within the context of a state-regulated system of prostitution on the island, a very specific category of the prostitute has emerged. Aside from the stated criteria for eligibility for work at the brothel, potential candidates are selected by the police administrator on the basis of gender and appearance. Being female is an unquestioned criterion in the heteropatriarchal framework, but it is the second criterion that requires greater attention here. The younger the women are, and the more they conform to the prevailing notion of what is attractive, the more likely they are to be considered as potential candidates. The woman in charge of the registration process in the mid-1990s put it in the following way: "If they look old, then they don't get a permit . . . or you have women who are not so attractive and when they come here they find it difficult to earn enough, so they fall behind in their rent payments and can't catch up. Then they have to leave."This police administrator viewed hundreds of photographs of young women and girls and, on the basis of what she understood to fit the Campo demand as communicated to her by the brothel director, made a selection. The majority of the applicants fit the image of the Caribbean "mulatto," often slender and light-skinned with straightened brown or bleached-blond hair. The selection process ensures that the majority of the prostitutes at Campo/Mirage fit neatly into the image of the hypersexual brown Caribbean woman, fit for illicit sexual relations but not for marriage, an image, as earlier chapters have pointed out, that has been present in various Caribbean territories for several centuries.

A change from the late 1940s to the 1990s in the composition of the Campo/Mirage prostitute population underscores this point. Although initially any foreign woman could work as a registered prostitute in the brothel, from the 1960s on women from the Dominican Republic and Colombia constituted almost 100 percent of the working population. In particular, women from Cuba, Haiti, and Venezuela were no longer represented in the group and were, from all accounts, banned from the brothel. A general explanation offered by the police was that the ban of women from these countries had been formalized through various intergovernmental agreements. However, I could find no documentation on such agreements. An interview with a spokesperson from the Venezuelan consulate in Curaçao in 1993 pointed out that the "ban" on Venezuelan women was the consequence of a diplomatic agreement between Curaçao and Venezuela to maintain good trade and business relations. Prostitution was presumed to sully these relations, and Venezuelan women were clearly not to be treated as prostitutes but as "respectable" women in Curaçao. The situation with Cuba is easily related to the clampdown on prostitution following the revolution within Cuba itself and the controlled migration patterns of Cubans since the 1960s. The exclusion of Haitian women is slightly more complex. On the one hand, it is related to the fact that prostitution in Haiti is not recognized by law and therefore falls outside any regulations or government agreements. On the other hand, negative stereotypes in Curaçao of Haitians define the women as "too black" and "unhygienic."[39] Haitian women do not fit into dominant ideals of beauty and therefore are not encouraged, recruited, or selected to stay at Campo/Mirage.

This hierarchy of color and nationality in association with notions of sexual attractiveness is repeated in other ways on the island and was visible at the time of my research in the 1990s through general observations. Haitian women, for example, were more occupied with trading activities than they were with prostitution. Other dark women, of whatever Caribbean nationality, if engaged in sex work, tended to be concentrated on the street or in run-down hotels and clubs. Light-skinned, often Latina, women were in greatest demand in the main nightclubs and brothels in town. A racialized male desire was at play, and men[40] were prepared to pay more for sex with a lighter-skinned woman than with a dark African Caribbean woman.[41] By the mid-1990s, the association between Latinas and prostitution was so pronounced in the national mind that any Spanish-speaking woman on the island was assumed by citizens to be a prostitute, and the label "SanDom" applied. National and racial/ethnic difference was coded as both sexually desirable and inferior to proper femininity. The reproduction of the classical Caribbean stereotype of the "good-time" brown-skinned "outside" woman was virtually complete.

Regulations designed to facilitate the sale of this racialized sexualized category of female labor to men are premised on a combination of assumptions about heteronormativity, the nature of gendered sexualities, the purity of national femininity, and the state's responsibility to protect public health. The regulations, from their inception, run counter to national and international laws and conventions regarding prostitution, while naturalizing migrant women as prostitutes. Heterosexuality is thoroughly inscribed in Curaçaoan social-sexual relations through the regulations, along with notions of the brown, exotic foreign woman as the quintessential sex provider. The colonial state regulations of sexuality in Curaçao, as illustrated through the regulation of prostitution, furthermore resulted in the creation, in law, of distinctive categories of women (good vs. sexual) and have located the SanDom outside of national boundaries, as a noncitizen and as contaminator of the nation. Simultaneously, access to this "Other" is granted to male populations—citizen and noncitizen alike—facilitating patterns of male promiscuity and heterosexuality for men. Heteropatriarchy has been fully institutionalized through the process, and a specific category of racialized female sexuality is the cornerstone for the development of prostitution. Evidence from other territories in the Dutch Caribbean, which I turn to in the following, suggests that a similar process has been at work, particularly since the mid-1950s, whereby women of select nations and color have been positioned as the most desirable sexual subjects.

Regulations in the Wider Dutch Caribbean

In Aruba, one of the six present-day Caribbean territories that remain a part of the kingdom of the Netherlands, the establishment of the Lago oil refinery in 1926 brought with it the need for a substantial labor force. Male labor was recruited from primarily English-speaking Caribbean islands and technicians brought in from the United States. The oil industry also meant a steady stream of oil tankers and ships that unloaded male sailors and crew members on the island. The large migratory single male population on the island was quickly deemed a threat by the local government to the local female population and the general morality of the island, and after consultations with Lago Oil Corporation executives, the colonial government agreed to import foreign women to sexually service the men. It was thought that this would protect its local female population from the migrant men and their "base" sexual instincts.[42] In 1944, the morals police and health departments were authorized by the colonial state to control and regulate prostitution, and bars and hotels were legalized for prostitution in and around the oil refinery town St. Nicholaas.[43] In 1950–1951, discussions among Aruban government officials raised the question of confining prostitution to one area, with some raising the idea of a centralized, state-regulated brothel akin to Campo Alegre.[44] The proposal met with fierce opposition from various sectors of civil society and was openly condemned by the Roman Catholic Women's League, the Commission of Protest on behalf of "women and mothers of the island of Aruba," and various clergy of Roman Catholic, Protestant, Anglican, and Methodist churches.[45] The government went no farther with its attempts to regulate prostitution on the island, and by 1952, it banned foreign sex workers from the island in an attempt to close down the

sex industry. The experiment to extirpate prostitution did not, however, achieve its goals and public pressure on the government grew.
Citizens felt increasingly threatened by a rise in number of rapes, illicit prostitution activities, and so-called bogus marriages. After
some police investigations into the matter, the colonial government
decided to reintroduce permits in 1957 for female foreign women to
work as "nightclub hostesses" in the sex industries. The new regulation allowed a bar or hotel owner to employ two to three non-
Aruban women legally, once the proprietor ensured that the women
were registered with the police department, stayed on the island no
longer than three months, and went for a weekly medical examination.[46] Prostitution remained tolerated by the colonial state for several decades under the shroud of "hostess work."

A study in the 1970s in Aruba revealed that prostitution was still
very much practiced and depended upon two main groups of women:
"imported" Colombians, who could stay for up to three months, and
"freelancers," women from the Dominican Republic who had
acquired resident status through marriage. The composition of the
sex worker population had changed since the 1930s, in part due to
broader political and economic concerns:

> When Lago first started . . . girls were brought in from Colombia,
> Venezuela, Cuba, Panama and Santo Domingo. After Castro, no more
> girls came from Cuba. Also for several years, since they got oil-rich, no
> more girls from Venezuela. Panama girls go to closer places . . . .[47]

Certain recruitment patterns were discernible. Marriages arranged
through brokers, which were commonly defined as bogus, facilitated
the arrival of women from the Dominican Republic, who could then
reside legally and work on the island. For women from Colombia, a
different system was at work:

> The process begins in a storefront agency in Bogota, where young
> women (mostly from rural areas) bring their photographs to be filed
> along with those hundreds of applicants for forwarding . . . several por-
> traits are sent periodically to the Chinese owners and operators of the
> fifteen crib-saloons and the one larger "brothel" that line the main
> streets in St. Nicholas. The owner indicates his choice to the recruiting

agent and, if the selected women is indigent, he will forward her passage money to the agency (which she will repay during her three-month stay).[48]

In 1978, the official police register in Aruba recorded 440 prostitutes: 287 from the Dominican Republic, 93 from Colombia, and 60 from other Dutch Antillean islands. By then, the clientele had changed from male migrant workers and seamen to local Aruban men.[49] Throughout this history, Aruban women were barred from work in this sector, a situation that clearly divided the female population on the island into "good" and "bad" women and that coincided with notions of the real or upstanding Dutch colonial female citizen (properly married and who didn't engage in prostitution) and the disruptive, immoral, foreign, predominantly Latina, sexual woman (who undermined the meaning of marriage and engaged in prostitution). The regulation under colonial state supervision thus helped to define national ideas of womanhood as compliant with heteropatriarchal norms of faithful and domesticated female sexuality, and legalized male heterosexual activity outside the home.

In St. Maarten the colonial Dutch penal code articles on prostitution, which included a ban on brothels, were upheld until 1960 when the lieutenant governor of the island legalized the *Japanese Club*.[50] The decision was rationalized by the government and publicly accepted as a direct response to a demand created by the establishment of a Japanese fishing industry and the presence of single foreign male fishermen who came with the industry. The men, it was assumed, needed sex, yet this need was seen as a threat to the purity of women of the nation. The government thus decided to recruit women from parts of the non-Dutch Caribbean to service the Japanese men. As reported in 1978:

> [T]o accommodate the sailors a House of Prostitution was officially opened. Rev. Moffett of the Methodist church along with some of the leaders protested strongly against it, but were told by the Lieutenant Governor of that time—Mr. Beaujon—that this place was opened for the Japanese sailors, and as a protection for the local girls and women. At that time everyone remained silent . . . feeling everything was under control, no one felt it a threat—not to the Health, Social or Religious areas . . . .[51]

The above-mentioned report also points out that many other "houses" and prostitution areas were known on the island, which were frequented by local men. These fell outside of the specific regulations set up for the Japanese Club and operated clandestinely. From the 1970s onward, male and female sex work grew and, by the 1990s, was intimately connected to the Free Trade Zone, a growing tourist industry, drug trafficking, and, since the mid-1990s, a home port for the U.S. navy.[52] In 1995, five clubs were known to exist on the island: the *Japanese Club*, *Chapotin*, *Petite Chapeau*, *Carmen Priest*, and *Last Stop*, "which also featured live nude shows."[53] In Jacqueline Martis's study of prostitution in the Dutch Antilles, she notes that "for a small island, St. Maarten has an impressive number of bars, snacks and striptease nightclubs."[54] The nightclubs operate under a hotel permit, may legally employ "dancers," are permitted to rent rooms to foreign migrant women workers, and can legally "bring in up to ten women at a time for up to a month."[55] The bar owners are required by law to apply for the women's work permits, paying over U.S.$400 for a permit for each "dancer." The women are not hired as prostitutes, and the practice of prostitution is generally ignored by the state. The arrangement in which foreign women (from Caribbean countries not part of the kingdom of the Netherlands) were permitted to legally work in the clubs in St. Maarten was intended to protect local womanhood from the "necessary evil" of prostitution, and created the idea that it was the Other woman who lacked in sexual morals and decency. As one presenter at a conference on prostitution in 1978 declared, "St. Maarten was invaded by prostitutes from foreign lands, such as Santo Domingo, Colombia and Haiti." It is the construction of the foreign woman as willfully disruptive and immoral that local citizens' organizations and groups have condemned and agitated against over the years.[56] Such sentiments serve to consolidate the treatment and ideological positioning of migrant/foreign women as hypersexualized and loose, and to maintain a notion of the good woman (decent, faithful, monogamous, sexual only for procreative purposes in marriage and for the family) as the ideal Dutch Antillian female subject.

For Suriname, the articles in the Dutch penal code were introduced as 306 and 307 of the local penal code, and even though the country gained political independence from the Netherlands in 1976, the laws have not changed; that is, the "promotion of female indecent behavior with obvious sexual provocation" continues to be prohibited by law, not prostitution itself.[57] With regards to the smaller islands of the Dutch Antilles—St. Eustatius, Saba, and Bonaire—little had been documented or written about the local government's dealings with prostitution. Nevertheless, while further research into the history and situation in each separate territory would be helpful to establish accuracy pertaining to the laws and present extent of the sex trade, a main trend runs across the Dutch Caribbean territories. The Dutch penal code of 1911 defined the broader context for prostitution laws and regulations in the colonies: brothels were banned throughout the kingdom and the active promotion of prostitution was criminalized. Nevertheless, prostitution was considered a necessary social evil, and sex work itself was not criminalized, allowing some forms of tolerance of sex work and the legal existence of the social category of the prostitute. Through this process in the colonies, categories of womanhood were produced that distinguished between decent, domesticated local women and loose, exotic, disruptive, hypersexual Others.

Public Protest and Resistance to Legal Sex Work

The situation in the Dutch Caribbean has produced various ideas and efforts to eradicate the state regulations of prostitution as well as prostitution itself. Politicians, women's organizations, and members of the Catholic Church have been the main proponents of abolitionism and have expressed their views in a variety of ways. In Aruba, as already described above, alliances between women's organizations and the Catholic Church in the early 1950s were successful in preventing the government from constructing a state-regulated system, with the consequence that prostitution continued to be tolerated yet occurred undercover. In Curaçao in 1949, several government ministers criticized the establishment of the Campo institution. Although their main concerns were framed around questions about the financing and management of the brothel, they were more fundamentally about whether the Curaçaoan state authorities were acting in accordance with the penal code and international conventions against the trafficking in women.[58] In July 1951 a petition signed by "2147 women from all ranks, standings and beliefs, from all parts of Curaçao" was sent to the governor in an attempt to hold the government responsible to its promise of reinvestigating the "problem" of prostitution on the island.[59] The petition demanded the abolition of Campo Alegre. Likewise, that same year, during a meeting of the government council, several council members argued against the existing government regulations and institutions for prostitution, including Campo Alegre. They were adamant that prostitution was "against laws of nature" and "against public moral health," that Campo was a "fiasco" and had exacerbated social problems.[60] A few years later, the chairman of the council raised the question of the legality of previous government decisions and regulations.[61] Moreover, in August 1955, community plans were made to press for the closure of Campo. From correspondence around this issue, although it remains unclear whether the action actually took place, it appears that not only was a petition drafted, but it was proposed that any action be spearheaded by women. Twenty reasons were given in the petition to the government for closing Campo, among them that the sex house represented:

> a public neglect of a Divine Order and thus, a gross insult to our religious sentiments, which we do not have to endure any longer; is against our Penal Code . . . , a violation of International Conventions and the Treaty of Geneva . . . , a permanent danger for families and children . . . , a center for trafficking and use of drugs . . . , an evil cancer-tumor, that smells far outside our borders . . . , a subversion of public morality and physical health . . . , an over-stimulation of sexual desires . . . [and is] not a blessing, but a curse for Curaçao.[62]

Such opposition to the state regulation of prostitution, with its sexually conservative and religious undertone, was echoed in newspaper reports.[63]

Surprisingly, although the Roman Catholic Church would seem to have been one of the most obvious agents of opposition to both prostitution and regulationism, as has already been described earlier, spokesmen of the Church during the 1940s and 1950s took another approach to the phenomenon. They defined prostitution as an immoral and unnatural "perversion," yet advocated regulation on the grounds that it was better to have some control over the "evil" than to allow it to spread wildly. Members of the Catholic Church also actively participated in the committee that recommended regulated prostitution on the island. Doubts nonetheless began to grow about this position. Father Brenneker, for example, recognized that his efforts to absolve Campo clients for their "adulterous" behaviors or "abnormal cravings," by either sending them away from the Church or dismissing the behavior summarily, did not seem to have an effect on the men's visits to sex houses. He feared that the Roman Catholic Church "played down the social evil and supported the government sanction."[64] Hence, he proposed that priests explain to men in detail about the nature of their actions and only offer absolution after a test period of three weeks of relaxation and prayer. Thus, in spite of the Church's official acceptance of the regulation of prostitution, not all the clergy seemed to fully support this development and attempts made on a day-to-day level to eradicate it.

A more recent development in the abolition movement was an attempt by several Dutch Antillian women's groups of predominantly Catholic leanings. Organized by the Curaçaoan arm of the Dutch Antillean women's umbrella organization, the Steering Committee, a conference on prostitution was held in Bonaire on June 22–26, 1978, with women attending from various Dutch-, Spanish-, and English-speaking Caribbean countries. The conference was the first of its kind in the region. Speakers presented perspectives on the state of prostitution in the Dutch Caribbean and the Dominican Republic, and an attempt was made to formulate a common position for the region by Caribbean women. In a closing statement, participants at the conference defined causes of prostitution and resolved to be active in the spheres of education and law They called for education about sexuality and gender relations "to aid in correcting the prevailing improper and immature attitudes that precluded development of healthy relationships between the sexes" and to "combat prostitution."[65] On the legal side, the conference resolved to pressure governments to enforce laws to hinder prostitution. Participants indicated their expectation that the Church play a key role in achieving these objectives. Finally, it was proposed that a regional committee of medical doctors, lawyers, clergy, and government representatives be set up to continue the direction, communication, and work laid out during the conference.[66] Religious persuasions and middle-class adherence to a conservative sexual ideology dominated the discourse. The Steering Committee articulated its view on prostitution as a violation of womanhood and an activity that led to a moral degeneracy in society. Poor women were to be "saved" from the degrading practice of prostitution.

Such a position toward sex work and sexual relations has persisted among Dutch Antillian middle-class women. In protest against the Lispcomb international telephone sex line in 1991, for example, two of Curaçao's most prominent women's organizations, the Steering Committee and Centro di Dama, along with the Council of Churches, Roman Catholic Church, Adventist Church, and several nongovernmental organizations, petitioned the government council of Curaçao. The letter expressed concerns of "The Committee for the Combating of Moral Decadence," which protested the establishment of the telephone sex line, demanding a parliamentary hearing on the subject.[67] Moreover, the pervasive stigma that was attached to women from the Dominican Republic—the SanDom—was reason for some Spanish-speaking women to publicly claim respectability and to distance themselves from the image of the prostitute. In the 1990s, for example, the UMLA (Union Mujeres Latinos Americanos), which established itself as an organization of professional Latin American women in Curaçao, held public events to celebrate its specific position and achievements, and to publicly claim another image of Latinas on the island.[68]

By defining sexual-economic relationships as immoral and prostitution as a social evil and inherently oppressive to women, movements that were predominantly mediated by Catholic-dominated women's organizations have sought to eliminate prostitution from Dutch Antillian society and to abolish any forms of legal sex work. However, through the struggles by professional, middle-class women citizens during the twentieth century to cleanse the nation of prostitution, a construction of female sexuality as monogamous, faithful to men, and procreative has been affirmed. Women who fail to adhere to this model are condemned, dismissed, or pitied. The exclusion of the SanDom from participation in the nation, evident through law, physical confinement, and control in brothels and sex houses, and the continued stigmatization they receive in middle-class women's discourses point to immense barriers that have been erected against women who do not fit into the hegemonic ideal, yet whose sexualized labor power and bodies have been defined as critical to the sustainability of island life. The SanDom remains at once needed and despised, and exists as a racialized disposable worker whose life and body are under immense control and surveillance.

5

FOR LOVE OR MONEY?
FANTASIES AND REALITIES
IN SEX TOURISM

I decided I wanted to go on vacation, but with that decision, there were
two things I had to consider: first, that I didn't have a lot of money to
spend on such things, two, that availability of sex was VERY important!! . . . the Caribbean made sense . . .[1]

One of the first mentions of sex tourism in the Caribbean was by
Frantz Fanon in the early 1960s, when he observed that the region was
becoming "the brothel of Europe" due to the neocolonial relationships
that were embedded in global tourism industry and the emergence of
prostitution in the industry. Since then, sex tourism, or tourist-ori-
ented prostitution, as it is sometimes named, has become an increasingly important topic of research and discussion due to the growing
reliance of national governments on income generated by tourism and
tourism-related activities. Tourism today constitutes one of the largest
global economic sectors, and for some Caribbean countries, it accounts
for up to 70 percent of the national income. It was promoted in the
1960s by the United Nations as a strategy to participate in the global
economy and was embraced by Caribbean governments as a way to diversify the local economies, to overcome postcolonial economic crises
that threatened to cripple the small nation-states, and to acquire foreign exchange. The largest tourism markets for the Caribbean are
North America and Western Europe—with the United States,
Canada, France, Britain, and Germany in the lead. The most popular
tourist destinations in the region are the Dominican Republic, the
Bahamas, Jamaica, Puerto Rico, the U.S. Virgin Islands, Cuba, and
St. Maarten, with Guyana and Suriname receiving the smallest number
of tourists.[2] The industry accounts for approximately 25 percent of all

formal employment in the region and is generally seen to be one of the fastest-growing sectors and one of the few ways in which the small nations can compete in the global economy. With the estimate that for every person in formal employment in tourism there is at least one other engaged in informal activities in the industry, predictions are that tourism in the Caribbean will continue to be an important source of livelihood for its working peoples.[3] Indeed, it has been argued that "there is probably no other region in the world in which tourism as a source of income, employment, hard currency, earnings, and economic growth has greater importance than for the Caribbean."[4] The centrality of tourism to social, political, and economic life in the region cannot be underestimated.

While tourism sustains large proportions of the working sector of the Caribbean, economic benefit for working people is limited. Foreign and transnationally connected Caribbean business elites dominate the industry, and the majority of the large tourist resorts and facilities are owned and controlled by transnational corporations.[5] The development of the all-inclusive tourist package in which flights, airport transfers, hotel accommodations, meals, drinks, entertainment, sports facilities, excursions, etc., are fully paid in advance, usually in the country of origin, means that few expenditures within such packages are made in the host country and a large proportion of the income generated from tourism remains outside the Caribbean. In addition, around 70 percent of foreign exchange that is eventually earned in the Caribbean from tourism by the state and local businesses pays for imported goods and services. In some countries this "leakage" can be as high as 90 percent.[6]

The local tourism economy is managed by Caribbean governments and local elites, although these remain little more than "managers of Western enterprise."[7] Attempts by Caribbean governments to diversify their economies or to delink from the global economy and to establish control over national production and resources have not necessarily been possible or desired. Since the 1980s, with the restructuring of the global economic system, most countries in the region have had their economies tied to global trade and markets through structural adjustment programs (SAPs) managed by the World Bank and International Monetary Fund (IMF), and more recently under the guidance of the World Trade Organization (WTO). SAPs plunged many Caribbean territories into poverty or even bankruptcy (as in the case of Guyana) and heightened unemployment among working peoples. Together these trends stimulated a search for new survival strategies at both the community and national levels. Restructuring and the new neoliberal trade agreements brought a shift from agricultural production to export processing, light manufacturing, information processing, and tourism, much of which is dependent upon corporate demands for cheap, flexible, undemanding, service-oriented, dexterous labor. Many Caribbean countries have become the home to export-processing zones, with tax-free incentives to foreign companies, exemptions from labor laws, special access to transportation and communications channels, etc., which remain highly profitable for the overseas corporations, but less so for the national governments or working peoples.[8] Strapped for alternatives, offshore banking, money laundering, drug trafficking, and informal commercial trading are a few of the activities that national governments have allowed or explicitly promoted to bring in foreign exchange to sustain their economies and to service their foreign debts.[9] Concomitantly, these activities allow many women and men to continue to provide for their households and families. In many instances, these alternative and informal industries and activities have become more lucrative and viable than attempts to compete with globally powerful corporations that control the regions' industries. Neoliberal trade agreements since the 1990s that further erode possibilities for small island and small nation-states to effectively participate in the global economy compound the difficulties for Caribbean governments to independently control and manage their own resources and industries, and to adequately provide employment, health and food security for their populations. In the late twentieth century foreign owners and transnational elites controlled not only the tourism industry, but also the majority of banks, oil and sugar refineries, mining operations, logging companies, manufacturing and assembly plants, and telecommunications industries, all of which drew upon the region for raw materials, labor power, and services. The Free Trade Agreement of the Americas (FTAA) promises to continue this trend in the twenty-first century.[10]

The Caribbean tourism product hinges on specific resources, particularly the year-round warm, sunny conditions and beaches, the tropical rain forests and coral reefs, and the region's music, such as reggae, calypso, and dance hall, and cultural events, such as carnival. The industry offers a variety of packages, including golf vacations, weddings and honeymoons, dive trips, and ecotours, with the sole raison d'etre of providing pleasure to the visitor. Caribbean women and men predominantly work in the industry at the lower echelons for meager wages in jobs such as barmen, waitresses, cooks, cleaners, maids, gardeners, and entertainers. Male and female labor constitutes a part of the package that is paid for and consumed by the tourist during the period in which she or he seeks to relax and enjoy—in the leisure time the tourist has set aside to recuperate and restore the mind and body in order to maintain a healthy and productive working life upon returning home.[11]

Sex Tourism

Sexual services in the tourism industry are today a part of a range of informal services that are solidly integrated in the tourism industry.[12] Sex tourism is thus a part of the informal package that is indirectly offered to the visitor, and sustains not only many women's households and lifestyles, but also those of men. Predominantly young women either explicitly or implicitly solicit men's attention at hotel bars, nightclubs attached to resorts, or on the beach. Caribbean men as sex providers to tourist women also became increasingly visible in the 1990s. As with women, sex work offers the men possibilities for meals, cash, clothes, or some commodity that enables them to better provide for themselves and their families, as well as ways to travel or go abroad and thus to be a full participant in the transnational, globalized world. Many of the relationships that occur within sex tourism can be likened to transactional relations, where "girlfriends" and "boyfriends" are the operative term for clients. It is a site where "romances" occur, and where some form of desire on the part of the Caribbean woman or man is expressed as part of the relationship. In this respect, sex tourism often represents that space where sexuality and economics converge in discreet ways. For many women and men, the encounters are not bound by monetary transactions, but flow from and into more general practices of hustling or making do, in countries where the informal economy is tightly interwoven with the formal, and sexuality with economics.

Sex tourism in the Caribbean for the most part settles around women as sex workers and men as sex tourists, yet despite their relatively small numbers, men as hustlers in sex tourism have commanded much attention. Not only does their participation as sex providers contravene traditional understandings of prostitution, but it raises questions about international race relations and male sexuality. The island of Barbados, one of the earliest mass tourism sites in the region, has been a primary focus for study of this subject. For that island, it was established in the late 1970s that sex tourism was an extension of informal and formal sector activities in which young Barbadian men were engaged—strategies to escape low-paying and demeaning occupations, and as a form or resistance to the existing social, economic, racial, and sexual order.[13] Later studies elaborated on some of these insights among "beachboys," drawing attention to the negotiations that took place between black Barbadian men and white women around their sexual, gender, and racial identities, as well as the way in which the relationships were shaped by the location of Barbados as a Third World nation locked into dependency within the global economy.[14] Some research equates the men's activities with a form of entrepreneurship.[15] More recently, heterosexual male sex work in the tourism sector has been studied elsewhere, such as in Jamaica, Cuba, and the Dominican Republic.[16] Bisexual and homosexual male sex work has also been noted in a number of the English- and Spanish-speaking territories and the Netherlands Antilles.[17]

Chris Ryan and Michael Hall, leading tourism studies' scholars whose main focus has been on Asia, argue that sex tourism is an interaction between two groups of equally positioned marginal peoples—tourists and prostitutes—based upon similarities between the two groups. They identify three main features common to tourists and sex workers: the power of dress, which involves a sensuality of undressing and an explicit display of the body; the formation of particular spatial communities; and a transitional state of existence.[18] The authors further argue that tourists and prostitutes both occupy a position of power and powerlessness, that "the working girl exercises the power to earn cash; the tourist exercises power due to the possession of money."[19] Due to the centrality of bodily pleasures to the practice of tourism, Ryan and Hall claim that the step from sensual experiences such as sunbathing to sexual activity is to be expected, explaining sex tourism as a logical or "natural" outcome of the tourist experience in a hot climate.

This formulation of sex tourism as an interaction between two sets of social equals and as a natural outcome between two marginal groups in a tropical context is one that has been produced in various other studies of prostitution and sex tourism, particularly in relationship to Asia.[20] It is, however, not an explanation that serves the Caribbean well. The tourist as a marginal person is a questionable notion in the Caribbean context, given the extreme dominance of tourism in the region and the kinds of preferential treatment that tourists receive. Caribbean governments are subservient to the global economy and the foreign exchange brought in by tourists, and a person holding a greenback or Euro commands service and deference. Thousands of tourists are off-loaded from tourist cruise ships on any given day of the week in ports and harbors of small islands, swarming the island's shops, beaches, restaurants, or nature resorts in hordes, while displacing local populations. Gigantic cruise ships tower over small towns, dwarfing the highest buildings and distorting the landscape. Prime beach locations are taken over by tourist resorts, with the hotels usually denying local residents access to the facilities. Tourists are protected by the police and are not apprehended, jailed, or brutalized if some misdemeanor occurs. Tourist hotels absorb much of the electrical and water resources of a town or village, busloads of tourists are given priority service at roadside snack bars, and prices at many restaurants, supermarkets, and craft shops are unaffordable for the average working-class Caribbean woman or man. Moreover, the overwhelming whiteness of tourists to the region places them automatically in a position of privilege in a region where the combination of light skin color and European or North American ethnic and cultural heritage has historically signified power and authority. Thus, short of reducing sex tourism to issues of social identities or to anxieties about transgressing boundaries of propriety and decency, it is difficult to conceptualize tourists in the Caribbean as marginal to the economy, landscape, or social life in the tourist destination, irrespective of whether they have sex with a local person. Most tourists arrive already assured of their position as "king." Ryan and Hall's perspective thus elides the relations of power that are embedded in the Caribbean tourism industry, including the dominance of tourists in the relationship with women and men who service them while on vacation. As celebrated author and novelist Jamaica Kincaid notes about the similarities and differences between the empowered tourist and dominated local resident:

> [E]very native of every place is a potential tourist and every tourist is a native of somewhere. Every native everywhere lives a life of overwhelming and crushing banality and boredom and desperation and depression, and every deed, good and bad, is an attempt to forget this. Every native would like to find a way out, every native would like a rest, every native would like a tour. But some natives—most natives in the world—cannot go anywhere. They are too poor. They are too poor to go anywhere. They are too poor to escape the reality of their lives; and they are too poor to live properly in the place where they live, which is the very place you, the tourist, want to go . . .[21]

Travel to the Caribbean, to become a tourist, to take a vacation, to indulge in a fantasy for a few days or weeks, to "do nothing" for a while and have others care and cater to every need and fancy, sets the tourist in a privileged position vis-à-vis the local working person. This is premised upon long-standing economic, gender, and racial relations of power between tourist and local, between wealthy and poor nations, between the haves and the have-nots, between those who participate as "white" and those defined as "black," which form the broader context within which Caribbean sex tourism takes place. Nevertheless, fantasies about the erotic and exotic nature of Caribbean sexuality and life prevail, masking inequalities between tourist and the Caribbean inhabitant, yet compounding the long-standing relationship of dependency of the Caribbean on the global North.

Master Fantasies

Characteristic of sex work related to the Caribbean tourism industry is the autonomy of the individual sex worker and the wide range of arrangements that exist between the tourist and sex worker, with an emphasis on longer-term, transactional relationships. These last in many instances for the period of stay of the tourist, sometimes extending into a situation where the tourist sustains the relationship through gifts, a ticket, and money after returning home, and occasionally results in marriage or a sustained partnership. Beaches, bars, casinos, discos, and nightclubs within and around tourist hotels and resorts are the main locations where tourists individually meet local women and men.

The emphasis that many Caribbean women and men place on their activities as something to do to get by—as work or hustling—is not always shared by tourists. For example, some visitors to the region express the idea that Caribbean women are not really hustling for money, and that they, the tourist, are not clients:

> You can have any girl you want. Just stop any one on the street and ask her to go with you and she will. That's because the average salary is about US $10 per month and they know that hanging out with a foreigner will bring them something if only a drink and dinner . . . Bring little gifts like panty hose and perfume and you'll be treated like a king.[22]

Moreover, men who would not necessarily practice prostitution at home are able to do so while on holiday abroad due to preconceptions that what occurs in Third World countries is "not really prostitution" and that the "girls" are "not really like prostitutes."[23] As described in chapter 2, the line between prostitution and other sexual-economic relations in the Caribbean is extremely blurred, and many sexual relations are premised upon economic imperatives and needs. In the tourism sector, work with a tourist can rest heavily on the idea of finding a caring foreign partner with enough financial security to assist the Caribbean woman or man in overcoming economic hardship, unemployment, and a bleak future, or of obtaining "La Gloria" in some Dominican women's words.[24] For some, this includes leaving their home countries to live with their lover, going abroad—going "a foreign" or "fuera" in local idioms. Being able to sport material symbols of development—designer clothes, shoes, U.S. dollars, and the like—is commonly the external trapping that accompanies this search. Caribbean women and men thus may seek to establish a "romance" that will provide them with some economic security or an escape from the hardship of poverty. Yet for tourists from cultures where in hegemonic discourse sexuality symbolizes love and desire, and is considered to be sullied by economic relations, especially for women, flirtations and solicitations from young women and men are easily read as signs of nonprostitution activities that approximate genuine interest and attraction.

In eighty-three letters written about the Caribbean publicly posted on a "World Sex Guide" website between November 1994 and July 1999,[25] most or all of the sex workers were described as "not real hookers." While acknowledging that women participated in prostitution due to financial need and a lack of other economic opportunities, the letters stressed that the men believed that the women genuinely enjoyed all types of sex with them, and that the women were particularly good at what they did:

> None of these are real hookers—most are part time girls who like sex and want to make some money for clothes . . .[26]

> Just how good are they sexually speaking? Pretty damn good for the most part . . . No dead fish here . . . They really are very uninhibited . . . .[27]

> Basically Marcia (not her real name) is not a real hooker, but a very attractive and horny girl who likes to make a bit of extra money (much needed in Jamaica). In return, if you treat her right, she'll give you a great time with no hassle. There's plenty of village girls like this around Negril and Montego Bays these days.[28]

> You never get the feeling that they are after your money, and they don't have a [sic] attitude of a whore . . . These chics have so much class its hard to believe they are prostitutes.[29]

The highly sexualized image of Caribbean women held by sex tourists rests on an assumption "that local girls are really hot for it," and the women's "highest ambition is to be the object of a Western man's desire," that after all, the women "are doing what just comes naturally" to them.[30] The women are not, in the imaginations of the men, prostitutes who are having sex for money, but are perceived as poor women who genuinely enjoy the sex. The idea that the young brown or black women are naturally sexy and desire to have sex with much older (sometimes quite senior and overweight) white men for pleasure enables tourists to deny any exploitative aspects of their relationship with the Caribbean. Indeed, male tourists sometimes venture to rationalize their visits to the Caribbean for sex as a way to benefit poor, oppressed women, presenting themselves as benefactors. Twenty-two letters in the sample presented some aspect of this idea. As one man stated:

> I much rather sponsor a Cuban family by renting a room in their house than giving the money directly to the Cuban government . . . I much rather give my money to a suffering Cuban . . .[31]

Sex tourism is defined in this way as a form of development for poor people in poor nations and as a way to "help" poor women and their families, masking the inequalities of power that are involved and allowing the sex tourist to perceive himself as benevolent and desirable. Furthermore, the idea that women in the Caribbean are hypersexual and are not professional prostitutes often results in the tourists presenting their encounters with the women as "romances" or "love":

> We spent the day together. Life was good! My American buddy just about married the girl he was with . . . Pamela took me to the airport early in the morning . . . . She cried. . . . I felt like shit. I wish I could have brought her home with me . . . If you are going to Santo Domingo be prepared to fall in love with these women. I'm going back again . . .[32]

> Girls are incredibly sexy and behave like real girlfriends.[33]

> Is she ever hot though! They just don't come that way back home . . . I'm in love. I'm pretty convinced she is too . . .[34]

Finding romance and love while on vacation in a hot climate has been written about by various male researchers and journalists, particularly in Asia. As one writer confirms:

> Men also look for "love" in a customer-prostitute relationship—thus their "disappointment" in the commercial approach to prostitution in Western societies . . . perhaps this is the reason for some men to engage in sex tourism with planned sexual behavior with prostitutes in developing countries where their money supposedly can buy not only more sex, but also more tenderness on the side of the prostitutes.[35]

A distinction that is sometimes made in the literature on sex tourism between romance and prostitution remains in such instances difficult to discern. Indeed, in the Caribbean, the academic discussion about the complex array of relationships in the tourism industry and the inadequacy of the binary—romance and sex tourism—to capture the distinctions has led some researchers to propose that a third category exists: companion tourism.[36]

Apart from the perception that the Caribbean is a region of the world where sex can be had that is fun, cheap, and undemanding, and allows for an adventure away from the mundane, Caribbean men and women alike are constructed in tourist imaginations as racial-sexual subjects/objects—typically, the hypersexual "black male stud" and the "hot" brown or black woman—whose main roles are to serve and please the visitor. In arrangements and representations of this aspect of the tourism industry, rearticulations of exoticism are evident. Over one-third of the letters posted to the website explicitly related racial and cultural differences to sexual desirability. For the authors of these letters, a hierarchy of beauty/attractiveness was associated with notions of race and culture. Comments about Puerto Rican Latinas, Cubanas, Dominican mulattos, and light-skinned Caribbean women prevailed and were highly positive.[37] Some of the recurring ideas about the erotic, hypersexual nature of the Caribbean and its women were represented as follows:

> The DR has wonderful possibilities. Prostitution jives fairly well with the culture, Dominican women are beautiful, prices are excellent, and you have a fair chance of being treated well . . . I find that watching a fine brown-sugar Dominican teenager take off her clothes and shake her ass like only Dominican chics can does wonders for clearing your mind and getting up your guts (not to mention you [sic] cock) for the bargaining process.[38]

Latin American, Spanish-speaking Caribbean cultures and "brown" femininities were represented in the letters as sexually attractive and available to the men. As one tourist described:

> Since I prefer Latinas and brunettes, for me Cuba is the closest thing to paradise I think I'll ever see. It's heavenly because many of these young Cubanas are "available."[39]

Or as others wrote:

> Aruba is the place where you go to get the knockout of your life. The Ladies are all from Colombia and Venezuela.[40]

> For $100 per night . . . one can find a gorgeous, light skinned and young latina to spend the night with.[41]

There were, however, some exceptions to this generalized pattern, with some authors expressing a specific appreciation for black women:

> By far the best place for sex in Jamaica is Negril. Sex is available and cheap, and for those of us who prefer black women, I can't think of anywhere that comes close.[42]

Yet there were also those comments that denigrated blackness (sometimes associated with Haitian nationality):

> I know beauty is in the eye of the beholder, but most of these women are truly not great lookers . . . This is not to say that there were not some attractive women available—but they are in the minority. In terms of race, most are black—about 70%—while the rest are more Latino looking— There were actually a number of nights that I went back to my hotel room alone because none of the women appealed to me (this would never happen in Brazil or Thailand!) . . . these are without a doubt some of the butt ugliest women I have ever come across. Unbelievably ugly. Most are Haitian and are old (at least in hooker years) and heavy.[43]

Viewing the "brown-skinned" woman as more desirable than the black woman in the contemporary tourism industry does not contradict the earlier described—European-American and Caribbean—exoticist ideologies and patterns. Instead, this serves to reinforce them. Comparisons between exotic Caribbean women and those in the North (the United States in particular), and the sensuality of the white (female) body, further consolidate these ideas. A delight with sexy, mixed-race, mulatto, sultry, tanned, Latin, brown-sugar Caribbean women is furthermore contrasted with notions of white women's sexuality as staid, cold, impersonal, or mundane:

> Another very noticeable thing was how friendly all the girls were. There was none of that "hard ass" attitude so commonly seen here in the States . . . Being with these girls was a thoroughly pleasant experience.[44]

> I went in and noticed that most of the girls were not Puerto Rican. Most looked like rejects out of an American (NY, LA, Dallas) strip bar. The show was pathetic. . . .[45]

> I love it here the table's [sic] are turned and the women were chasing me around. New York women are cold as fish, in comparison.[46]

Be warned: eurochicks will want a real romance from you, with all the related mind trips, they consider intercourse a mere byproduct of that . . . As usual, you will have to pay for their drinks and stay up late speaking about psychology and their childhood to get some, the day before you leave, once.[47]

The tourists construct Caribbean women both sexually and racially, in opposition to European women, whereby "White skin is devalued because it is connected to civility, or feminist discourse, and is thus less sexual."[48] Caribbean women are sexier than women in white, postindustrial, developed societies, and eroticism is thought to be found in the still natural, backwards, untamed world. The contemporary tourist industry enables male visitors to dabble in their exoticizing sexual fantasies while away from home.

Mistresses

As already noted, a reversal of traditional prostitution relations also takes place in Caribbean sex tourism. In such instances, the woman visitor is the sex tourist and the Caribbean man the sex worker. Similar to the ways in which some male tourists perceive sex in the Caribbean to be "not really prostitution," so too do tourist women often define their sexual encounters with black men as "romance." One of the best-known illustrations of the eroticized relationship between North American women travelers and Caribbean men is captured in Terry MacMillan's novel *How Stella Got Her Groove Back*. MacMillan's account has spurred the idea that "love" can be found by women vacationers to the Caribbean. As one young woman writes, under the heading "Want What Stella Had!":

My girlfriend and I are planning a JAMAICAN getaway in July/August, but don't know where to go. We want a place that's suitable for two 25 year-old (single) best friends . . . We're looking for our groove with the hope of getting it back like Stella did![49]

Likewise, relationships between women tourists to Ambergris Caye in Belize and Belizean men are described as "makoibi"—a "love sickness" in Belizean Creole—which is likened in intensity to a first love.[50]

In Jamaica and the Dominican Republic, less than 5 percent of the
women who were engaged in sex tourism defined their sexual encounters as purely physical or just about sex.[51] Most couched their sexual activities in terms of friendships and romances.

This distinction made by some observers and women visitors—
between sex tourism and romance tourism—can also be understood
in the context of definitions of female sexuality in the global North.
Hegemonic constructions of femininity and female heterosexuality
in North America and Western Europe locate women as passive sexual beings who value intimacy, tenderness, monogamy, and love over
sexual intercourse, stressing courtship, coddling, care, and affection.
In this construct, money and sexual desire for women are strictly sep-
arated—it is only "bad girls" who connect the two. Men, in Western
hegemonic constructions of masculinity, on the other hand, are the
sexual aggressors, straightforward in their sexual dealings, eternally
seeking to satisfy their physical urges, for whom sex is easily discon-
nected from love. Women tourists from the global North thus often
perceive themselves and are often perceived by others as seeking romance and love rather than sex, and thus can lay claim to being different from male sex tourists through pursuing a softer, more socially
acceptable, less "deviant" version of the male client-female prostitute
relation. However, a closer examination of the relationships dissolves
the rigid distinction between male and female sex tourism. Similar to
women who are oriented to working with male tourists, Caribbean
men who entertain women in the tourism industry stress the importance of money, status, or material goods in the sexual relationship.
Male hustlers in Barbados, for example, describe their encounters
with tourist women as highly dependent upon a woman's wealth: "I
like to get involved with executive ladies, with women with class,
women with cash" or "Technically speaking I love women who have
money. I can tell the one's who got money . . ."[52] Nothing is accidental
about their choice of "romance" partner. In a survey among 240
women tourists in the Dominican Republic and Jamaica it was found
that one-third of the sample admitted to having sex with one or more
local men during their vacation.[53] The researchers note that "almost all
the sexually active women surveyed stated that they had 'helped their
partner(s) out financially' by buying them meals, drinks, gifts or

giving them cash."[54] Thus, despite the fact that around 40 percent of the women described their encounters with local men as "holiday romances," with 12 percent believing it to be "real love," a majority of the women were providers of cash, gifts, meals, and drinks to their male sexual partners.

At Negril Beach in Jamaica the number of white, over-thirty large women in the company of slim, athletic black men in their early twenties was particularly striking. Although many of the women tourists were working class, were often strapped for cash, and rarely directly gave money to their sex partners, they offered the men various other material benefits, ranging from meals and drinks, to gifts for the men's children, to a trip to Europe or North America.[55] Clothes, a car, or a place to live could also be a part of what women "pay" for their romantic encounter while on vacation away from their family, husbands, and children. Other studies of female sex tourism in the Caribbean reveal that while romance relationships between tourist women and local men contribute to "breaking taboos and challenging tradition," this practice is not inherently or necessarily transformative of gender, racial, or economic relations.[56] Thus, while female sex tourism allows some married women to cross the monogamous boundary, to engage in random, fleeting sexual relationships with strangers, or to experiment with payment for sex, the exploitative relationship upon which tourism in the Caribbean is premised goes uncontested. Women simply become equal to their male counterparts in the consumption of Caribbean sexuality. Their position in the global economy, as citizens of wealthy nations who can afford to travel and pay for leisure time and activities in some exotic part of the world, is reinforced rather than disrupted. The definition by the women of these relationships as primarily "friendships" or "romance" serves to keep alive the myth that women are interested in sex only when it is attached to notions of love and intimacy, confirming hegemonic notions of gender difference, while it absolves women from the global North of any responsibility for global inequalities. Moreover, the relationships reproduce long-standing racist fascinations with black male sexuality and stereotypes of Caribbean culture. For example, tourist women in Negril expressed the view that they were able to "fall in love" with young black men who may be half their age and weight because "Jamaicans love big women." Jamaican culture, it is assumed, predisposes men to liking older, larger women. In Barbados and Jamaica, a man's physical appearance, particularly skin color, affects whether he will be attractive to women—the darker he is, the more able he is to secure a woman's attention. Notions about black men as sexually hyperaggressive abound. In Negril, some women complained about their trials and annoyances with Jamaican men, yet were ultimately accepting of pushy behavior or abrasive comments they received from the men. "Rudeness" is perceived as part of Jamaican masculinity, even though it verges on harassment and violence at times.[57] Black male sexuality is allowed, indeed expected, to be vulgar and out of control—rough, tough, and abusive. The women's definitions of their own behavior and motivations serve thus to elide, rather than to reveal, from themselves and others, the complexity of the relationships that are deeply informed by their own positions in the global economy and in racial and national hierarchies.

Male Hustlers

The term *rent-a-dread* was coined in the 1990s to name young male beachboys in Jamaica, due to the preponderance of dreadlocked hustlers and the marketability of the Bob Marley image to the rest of the world. By 2000, however, the Rasta style had made way for a Michael Jordan look. Men in their early twenties, with lean, lithe, muscled bodies and closely shorn heads, sporting low-slung, baggy, knee-length shorts and stylish dark sunglasses, worked the beach, immediately making contact with any new arrivals, insisting on becoming a companion. They were quick, smart, and to the point, and known locally as "rentals." Rastas and other dreadlocked men were not in evidence during the daytime hustle. A generation of men either had retired or no longer wished to publicly identify with the Bob Marley Rasta image. As one former rent-a-dread explained, after the age of forty, beach hustling "didn't work the same." Indeed, his hustle and that of other older dreadlocked men took place in a more discreet fashion: some sold tourist souvenirs and gifts on the beach, while others were ganga dealers, some were property caretakers, and yet others tourist guides. Many, however, were still on the lookout for a woman they could "romance."

In some instances former beach hustlers become gigolos, sepa-
rating themselves from the poorer, younger rentals through having
some of their own money or property, and receiving cars and presents
or overseas trips in return for their attentions. They are less dependent upon, or less desperate for, material rewards for their company.
As one Australian woman experienced, she got "caught up in the
romanticism of the island, the swinging palm trees, the white sand,
the azure ocean and the exotic men walking on the beach." She spent
"a fortune" on building a house on land owned by the family of her
"Rasta Gigolo," which he then claimed and continued to live in after
their relationship ended.[58] Some can afford to "kick back" and enjoy
what the beach resort town has to offer, often paying their own way
for meals, drinks, and entertainment. One Rasta in my study came
from a hotel-owning, solidly middle-class "brown" Jamaican family
and had immediate access to this class lifestyle, commanding deference from both his peers and the younger generation. He spent his
time selling ganga, hanging out at parties, coffee shops, and Ital
(Rasta food) places, and cruising around in the car provided by one of
his lovers. He used his family's hotel properties to entertain "his
women" and did not need to rely upon a woman paying for a hotel
room for sex. Another ran the day-to-day business of a small beach-
front hotel owned by a former girlfriend with whom he had a child.
The woman lived with their daughter in the United States, and she provided him with a place to live, some income, and an occasional trip
out of Jamaica. The Rasta served as the manager of her property and
she the absent landlord, visiting once a year. Yet another former rent-
a-dread I interviewed acted as a tourist guide. In one instance I came
across him in Kingston accompanying an American couple who had
promised a friend of his a job and future in the United States. The
couple had flown them all from Negril to Kingston to visit the U.S.
Embassy to secure a visa and, while waiting for the visa, toured
around Kingston. All expenses were paid by the couple, and the
Rasta was expected to be the local translator and tourist guide. He
was at the twenty-four-hour-per-day beck and call of the couple, the
tourists commanding his attention with offers of multiple return
trips to Kingston, elaborate meals, a stay in comfortable lodgings,
and visits to sites and events normally out of his range of activities.

A constant supply of ganga paid for by the tourists kept him mellow and seemed to ease any discomfort or pain.

In contrast to the laid back Rasta image, the new generation of rentals are quick, busy, and energetic. Some flit back and forth between clubs and hotels on the tourist coasts and their homes elsewhere on the island. They engage in direct hustle, open flattery of women's bodies, and constant references to the sexual pleasure they can give a woman, and operate with a conviction that the woman will pick up the tabs at the restaurant or bar. Many express outright an eagerness to travel abroad. The young men flaunt their bodies as their primary asset, exposing their well-muscled dark torsos at the slightest opportunity. Nighttime beach parties are crowded with such young men, often accompanying larger, older, white women. The couples are all body contact, exchanging few words, working themselves up for full sexual intercourse on the beach or in a hotel room.

Whether as native informants or as sex partners, rentals and rent-a-dreads live on the tourist dollar and the perks that tourism brings. The tourism centers are seductive, a chance to participate in the dreams and desires of a carefree, hedonistic moment, far removed from the squalor, toil, or stress of everyday Jamaican life. Pleasure for the men is claimed to be first and foremost in their minds, although without any material gain, it is questionable whether any would continue to pursue it through this avenue. Some men at Negril, for example, explained to me that young women who took their spring break vacation in Jamaica were uninteresting to beach hustlers, for the women were reputed to travel on extremely small budgets and were thought to have no extra money to entertain or provide for the men.[59] Likewise, in the Dominican Republic, men who hustle both male and female tourists claim that sex work with young women is not profitable enough.[60] More often than not, the hustlers are acutely aware that their sexuality is closely linked to economic and material benefit. As one Rasta aptly puts it: "There is no free love for the underprivileged. We will grant their wishes for free, but with an expectation of promises, which is usually that the future will be better."[61]

The encounter between women tourists and black male hustlers reveals another set of myths that are articulated by the men themselves. The men take great pride in their "hardness," which includes an aggression and force in pursuing a woman, a "vigorous" style of lovemaking, and the promise of complete sexual satisfaction that usually implies an eternally erect penis. It is an aspect of their masculinity that is thought to be matched only by a strong woman. Small, young women are seen by the men as too frail and delicate, thus easily hurt or bruised by the men's "natural" power. The larger the woman, the more "man" she can take, is the image. This is coupled with the notion that due to ideals of beauty, age, and attractiveness in North America and Europe, "oversize" women do not have the opportunity to engage frequently in sexual intercourse in their home places and are in need of sex. It is an idea that is heard in various ways in the beach town, and not just from men. One white American woman who had worked in Negril since the 1970s and knew the scene and the individual players well had come to the conclusion that there was a niche market for large white and black women over thirty who "don't get it at home." Older, larger women who infrequently engaged in sex were thought to be deprived of a natural heterosexual entitlement. This is coupled with the commonly held assumption in Jamaica that sex is a biological imperative—both for men and women—yet that frequent sex stretches a woman's vagina and that what men want (and apparently need for their own pleasure) is "tight pussy." A large woman who is thought to infrequently engage in sexual intercourse is thus constructed as an ideal sexual pleasure partner for black men who see themselves as strong and biologically wired with hyperactive libidos. A less frequently heard view, but one that nonetheless also circulates, is that women tourists visiting Negril explicitly seek out sexual encounters with Caribbean men while on vacation out of "sexual greed." It is an image of the Western woman as sexually loose and demanding, who strays well beyond the boundaries of decent (constrained) female sexuality. It invokes a notion of a rapacious sexuality of Western civilization that consumes the Caribbean to serve its own interests.

Irrespective of whether tourist women are perceived as sexually deprived or greedy, the Jamaican men see themselves, and are often seen by others, as the ones who can satisfy older, large, sexually needy women. They fashion themselves to accommodate the demand. Two of the hallmarks of hegemonic Caribbean masculinity—an insatiable

sexual desire and a large, ever-hard penis, both of which are continually in need of expression and can tirelessly sustain multiple sexual
partners—are continually evoked and paraded in the tourism industry. This image is reproduced endlessly in Negril through carvings,
drawings, and artifacts produced for tourist consumption that depict
men with large, erect penises—"the big bamboo"—that in the context
appears to complement the size of the white female tourists.[62]

Nevertheless, an exchange I was privy to between two men about
their sexual encounters with women tourists disrupts the monolithic
image of the Jamaican man as the ever-ready black stud. Both men
agreed that if women were heavy, it required from them a great deal
of physical energy and strength to engage in sexual intercourse, with
the younger, more lithe of the two men declaring that he refused to
"handle" such women because it was "too much hard wuk." This
other side of the story then suggests that the image of the robust,
powerful, and every-ready Jamaican man is as much myth as it is
reality. Not all the men desire to play the role of the indiscriminate
black male sex machine, even while they continue to find ways to
participate in the sexual-economic hustle of women tourists.

The Fantasy Industry

The tourism industry does little to curb the fantasies described
above. In fact, its survival rests heavily upon the perpetuation of the
myth of the hypersexual Caribbean. Postcards, travel brochures, and
airline and hotel advertisements make ample use of images of brown
and black women and men to market the region to the rest of the
world, appropriating the image of Caribbean sexuality to seduce and
entice potential clients. In these promotional materials, the women
are often scantily dressed and sensually posed, inviting the viewer to
"taste" the Caribbean. Black male sexuality is increasingly a part of
the explicit image that is beamed around the world. Black men as
masseurs of white, naked women in tourism advertisements on
North American television, or on tourism industry websites, sporting
knee-length penises, are now part of the promotion of the region.

The marketing of the region through notions of its sexually loose
and available women and men is not a trade secret and complements

the marketing image of the Caribbean as a place that is available for corporeal pleasures and sensual fun. While some islands, such as Antigua or Anguilla, still cater almost exclusively to the wealthy and rich, providing upscale resorts, hotels, dining, sports, and entertainment facilities, and where sex tourism is enacted very discreetly, mass tourism to other parts of the region, such as Jamaica, the Caribbean coast of Mexico, the Dominican Republic, Cuba, Aruba, Puerto Rico, Tobago, and Barbados, has engendered a more explicit selling of the erotic and the exotic. Spring Break, for example, is an important component of the tourism industry in Negril, Montego Bay, and Cancun, when thousands of college and university students from the United States and Canada are enticed to take a break from the "chore" of academic work to party for a week in a context free of parental supervision and rigid, puritanical restrictions on alcohol, drugs, and sex. Spring Break is thus, in a country such as Jamaica, an important part of the year, where the government sends representatives to greet the first arrivals, and whole sections of the daily national newspapers are dedicated to reporting on events that are staged for the young people, such as dance or beer-drinking competitions. Spring Break fills hotel rooms to bursting, keeps many a large and small eatery alive, and provides seasonal employment for domestic workers, cooks, waitresses, taxi and bus drivers, busboys, entertainment coordinators, artists, gardeners, and other service people. American televison and song artists are flown in to entertain the young people, while reggae, soca, salsa, and meringue artists are hired by resort after resort to bring a local, rootsy flavor to the vacation. Spring Break is positively heralded by the media as a time to allow the young tourists to indulge themselves in every conceivable pleasure of life, with police and entertainment coordinators standing by to protect them.[63] Despite the low budget of the individual spring breaker, their sheer numbers make this group of tourists economically attractive to the tourism industry. Particular events and facilities are thus geared to these hordes of young people, such as fleets of jet skis, late-night parties on the beach, sunset trips with "all-the-beer-you-can-drink," reggae music fests, happy hour at a bar that may have a water slide, and nightly discos. And while in any North American university or college, Spring Break is a week break from classes when students are provided time to catch up with reading and assignments, for the Caribbean it lasts several months, starting as early as February and ending in April. In a country such as Jamaica, Spring Break is one of the most important times of the tourism season, dominating the industry's resources and attention. The spring break allure, however, is not tied to the physical bodies of local women and men. Rather, it is the image of the exotic, unbridled, and uninhibited sexuality of the Caribbean that is abstractly drawn upon to attract the tourists. Sexual relations most likely occur among and between the spring breakers themselves, with few venturing into relationships with the locals. Caribbean men and women in this scenario are the animators, those who deliberately create an atmosphere for fun and complete sensual pleasure. They are the tour operators and hotel managers as well as entertainment coordinators, souvenir sellers, entertainers, and beachside hair braiders. Their mandate is to make the young people comfortable and relaxed. Feeling good about one's body and sexuality, a la Caribbean style, is part of the message. Easy, noncommitted sexual relations among spring breakers are then an expected part of the scenario.

Some all-inclusive "SuperClubs" offer a similar promise, albeit to an older crowd. In a visit to one of these resorts I had an opportunity to observe some of the operations firsthand and to interview visitors, workers, and managers. The hotel resort was located at the very far end of the town, isolated from everyday life, upscale in its appearance with well-tended grounds, a pool and jacuzzi, ample, comfortable airconditioned rooms, two beaches, referred to by hotel workers as the prude and the nude beaches, and large, overdecked common areas for dining, dancing, and partying. It contained 280 rooms and was regularly serviced by around 400 workers, with an increase during the high season. The concept of a hedonist SuperClub was launched in the mid-1970s by a Jamaican business family and, according to the manager, caters to guests who are "a bit more racy and amorous" than found in most other resorts. The guests are average, everyday professionals, mostly between the ages of forty and sixty, ranging from "cabdrivers to brain surgeons," who desire a relaxing and comfortable vacation. Some spring breakers and sex tourists are found among the guests, but they are few. While claiming that the resort caters to a variety of different tastes and groups, the manager insists that the determining factor for the guests is not age, but rather their "state of mind." Even though guests must have achieved a minimum age of eighteen, the resort is specifically designed and promoted for people "seeking pleasure as a way of life." It is an adult resort, and as one entertainment coordinator put it, it offers an opportunity to "run around in a Garden of Eden paradise." According to the manager, 40 percent of the clientele are "repeaters," with white Americans, Canadians, and Europeans, as well as richer or nonresident Jamaicans, making up the bulk of the guest population. I also came across Colombians and other Latin Americans, as well as several black American men at the resort. The main attraction is that the visitors can take their clothes off, perhaps meet someone else, and engage in as much sex as desired. As one performer spelled it out to the crowd during his show, lest anyone was unsure of the purpose of their stay: "you are here for sex."

Despite the location of the SuperClub and its promotion of nudity and unlimited sex, interaction between Jamaicans and tourists is minimal. The Caribbean setting merely provides an exotic setting, far away from home, where sexual desires, pleasures, and fantasies are lived out for a few days. Black Jamaican working women and men are not the primary object of desire, but rather, it is the image of the Caribbean as a place of sensuality that sustains its popularity. In the resort, entertainers, workers, and managers, who are predominantly black Jamaicans, are trained to do their jobs with discretion. They remain clothed even when working on the nude beach. During toga parties the entertainers, dressed in robes seductively draped to allow glimpses of naked breasts and torsos, stay on the stage and perform mechanically. While animating the crowd below them, they maintain a distance from the wildly clapping and jumping crowd that consists mostly of white overweight, over-forty men and women dressed in strips of white cotton, revealing as much of their butts and breasts as they dare, baring a lot of wobbly flesh in between. Despite ideas that Jamaica has a mystique, there is little interest among the visitors in learning about the country or people, and as one man assured me, he was quite content to stay in the compound. Some men hope, however, to meet a Jamaican woman while on vacation, although it is unclear, given the setting and their reluctance to venture outside of the resort, how this could be easily accomplished, other than approaching one of the hotel workers. Jamaicans who stay in the resort as guests mostly arrive in couples, who by their color, dress, and cars are obviously upper class. With rates starting at U.S.$140 per night, this is hardly a resort for the average working-class Jamaican person, although Jamaican residents from the area are sometimes permitted to join the pajama and beach night parties.

The SuperClub is surrounded by a myth of public sex orgies and wild nude parties and has become a celebrated success of the Jamaican tourism industry. For some, such as a man of Jamaican descent, resident in Canada, the resort affords anonymity: the secluded and closed nature of the resort allows guests to indulge in sexual fantasies without the wife or family ever having to know. Its deliberate separation from everyday Jamaican life and people, its almost taboo and secluded nature, yet its simultaneous location in Jamaica, allow tourists to visit and leave with the impression that the island is about forbidden sensuality and sex. The Caribbean as erotic and exotic is both a fabrication and a reality, fashioned by the tourist industry, sustained by the management and workers, and desired by tourists. The Caribbean as a place of sexual pleasure is confirmed in such an arrangement.

Gendered Identities and Power

Tourism in the Caribbean at the end of the twentieth century reproduces exoticizing tendencies present in the region since the sixteenth century, while new global hegemonies that rest upon an increasing economic gap between the postindustrial metropole and peripheral areas that provide cheap labor, natural resources, and playgrounds for the rich, extend its scope. Western European and North American women are increasingly participants in a form of tourism that demands sexual participation from the local population, and female sex tourism is a growing spectacle in countries such as Barbados, Jamaica, the Dominican Republic, Cuba, the Dutch Antilles, and Belize. Sex tourism also suggests that gender and sexuality for both men and women in the Caribbean are

constructed in the international context as part of a service provided by the global South to the North. As a playground for the
richer areas of the world to explore their fantasies of the exotic and
to indulge in some rest and relaxation, the labor, sexuality, and bodies of Caribbean women and men constitute primary resources that
local governments and the global tourism industry exploit and
commodify, to cater to, among other things, tourist desires and
needs. It is a site for European and North American men to reenact
colonial masculinity. For tourist women a sexual experimentation
with a racial Other, while retaining a sexualized femininity, occurs.
The black man is required to be the sexually aggressive and compe-
tent partner, allowing the tourist woman to combine economic
power and authority with traditional Western configurations of
femininity as sexually submissive and subordinate. On the flip side,
the Caribbean men who engage in heterosexual encounters do not
challenge this representation. Rather, through an appeal to hegemonic constructions of Caribbean masculinity, they keep up appearances and perform their role as the hypersexual, heterosexual
black man, acquiring some power and clout through their associations with foreigners. Sexuality is one of the means through which
they maintain their status as "real" men in society, and their role as
sexual companion to multiple women extends the widely accepted
practice of informal polygamy for Caribbean men. The ideological
delinking of sex tourism with the men's activities serves also to distance them from what is seen as a woman's terrain—prostitution—
an economically driven relationship. The myth of romance stresses
pleasure and desire and adds to the notion that Caribbean men are
driven by strong libidos that seek enjoyment and fulfillment. The
economic content of their relationship with tourist women is
buried under powerful gender constructions. Nevertheless, racial
and economic inequalities between North and South do not exempt these men from sharing a position similar to that of women
sex workers in the global tourism industry. Neither male nor female
Caribbean sexuality operates in the tourism sector on an equal
playing field with that of North American or Western European
sexuality. The bodies and sexual energies of Caribbean men and
women remain in the first instance platforms upon which the

reproduction of First World labor and a reshaping and retooling of gendered identity and power occur. Caribbean men and women, on the other hand, continue to make do in their individual struggles to keep their heads above water, to find "love," and to participate in the global economy. Their participation both confirms and challenges dominant notions of Caribbean sexuality and gender.

6

Trading Sex across Borders: Interregional and International Migration

Migration, both historically and contemporarily, is an important part of Caribbean livelihood strategies and social aspirations and is critical to the very existence and future of the region and its peoples.[1] To some scholars, the Caribbean itself is constituted through migration and diaspora formation and is home to one of the most transnationally connected and migratory peoples in the world.[2] While some of the migration relates to the movements of peoples from Europe, Africa, India, China, and the Middle East into the region, and from the region outward to Western Europe and North America, the Caribbean also has a long history of migration *within* the region and to Central and South America that is often overlooked but which is central to this study. Contemporary regional migrations follow a long history of interregional movement of Caribbean peoples. These include displacements due to political revolutions (for example, that which sent Haitians to other Caribbean countries); the movement of wage laborers from small islands in the region to sugar plantations in Guyana and Trinidad and Cuba after the emancipation of slavery; and early-twentieth-century labor migrations for the construction of the Panama Canal, banana and sugar industries in Central America, and oil-refining industries in Curaçao and Aruba. Since the 1980s, economic destablization and political crises have resulted in mass migrations between neighboring or nearby countries.[3] Migration further afield—to Europe and North America—has followed colonial ties, ranging from movements for higher education in the colonial mother countries to labor migrations and family reunifications. International migration has also been conditioned by political upheavals in Caribbean countries as well as specific immigration policies of the receiving countries, which are dictated by these countries' needs for labor but are simultaneously influenced by racist ideologies about migrants from the global South. The interregional and international migrations have resulted in large diasporas of Caribbean peoples who reside in countries other than their birth places yet who maintain strong links with their home communities through family ties, work, trading of goods, and financial remittances.

Regional Sex Work Movements

While male agricultural, industrial, and domestic labor and political migrations have commanded the most attention, various patterns of movement around the region during the last quarter of the twentieth century have discernibly involved sexual labor. In this context the most prominent sending country from the 1980s onward is the Dominican Republic, with women taking up temporary work in brothels, hotels, and bars in Haiti, Curaçao, Antigua, Panama, St. Maarten, and Suriname.[4] In 1996, for example, 50,000 Dominican women were estimated to be engaged in sex work outside the country, many of whom worked regionally.[5] Furthermore, Guyanese women were involved in sex work in Suriname, Trinidad, and Barbados; Trinidadian women traveled for sex work to Colombia and Barbados; and Haitian women moved into sex industries in the Dominican Republic, Curaçao, and Barbados. Conversely, several countries hosted foreign sex workers from South and Central America. Brazilian women crossed borders into Suriname and Guyana; Colombians went for sex work in Curaçao, Aruba, Trinidad, and Suriname; and women from Honduras, Guatemala, and El Salvador were located in the Belizean sex industry.[6]

While these regional migration patterns are heavily conditioned by heterosexual norms, through which women are sexual providers and men the serviced clients, men also move regionally to work in tourist resorts elsewhere, such as from Jamaica to the Dominican Republic or Cuba.[7] This latter scenario does not necessarily change or challenge the dominant construction of heterosexuality in the region.

To date, all reported regional sex trade migrations rest upon cross-gender sexual-economic exchanges, sustaining the image of Caribbean societies and prostitution as profoundly and rigidly heterosexual.

Poverty, under patriarchal conditions, is a primary reason, many argue, for women to migrate and work in the sex trade. However, the movements and migrations within the Caribbean are not only tied to these factors, and cannot be simply explained in this fashion. Racial ideologies also condition the migrations into the sex trade. For example, Haiti, with the third largest population in the region, is the poorest nation of the Americas, with a large number of women in desperate economic situations, yet Haitian women do not feature prominently in regional migrant sex work (nor in the international sex trade for that matter), despite being highly mobile and often engaged in regional informal commercial trading activities. Indeed, the long-standing racial hierarchy that is entangled with ideas of sexual desirability and the persisting association in the Caribbean of Haiti as a site of darkness and backwardness act as barriers to the incorporation of Haitian women into the regional sex trade. In the Dominican Republic, Haitian women confront prejudice and discrimination from the broader population as well as from local sex workers, which often lead to accusations about migrant Haitian sex workers undercutting prices that local Dominican women charge.[8] A common perception among Dominicans is that Haitians are diseased and dirty, and Dominican women, including sex workers, go to great lengths to distance themselves from blackness in order to not appear Haitian.[9] In some instances, Haitian women are forbidden by bar owners and managers from living in hotel brothels.[10] Throughout the region, black Haitian as well as many other dark-skinned women, if involved in migrant sex work, are concentrated in the lowest paid, least mobile areas of the sex trade.

Arrangements for legal migrant sex work in Curaçao confirm this racialized tendency in the regional sex trade. As described earlier, national patriarchal definitions of womanhood, which require Curaçaoan women to be chaste, pure, domesticated, married, and sexually monogamous, and which underpinned the establishment of the *Campo Alegre* brothel in the late 1940s, led to the creation of the

"SanDom" image of the ideal prostitute on the island—a migrant woman of light brown skin tone with a slender though shapely body and loosely curling hair. Women fitting this description are consciously selected for work at Campo, and outside of the state-regulated sector are highly represented in sex work in the nightclubs and brothels and at elite parties. Black women are not easily selected to work at the brothel. Outside Campo/Mirage, Haitian sex workers work in and around run-down hotels, bars, and brothels. This trend is repeated in Suriname, St. Maarten, and Antigua. A rejection of blackness, with a preference for the light-skinned woman as the migrant sex worker, exotic dancer, entertainer, or escort, is refracted in regional migrant sex work arrangements.

Regional Trade and Sex

Regional migrations often combine with other income-generating activities and are part of the activities of small entrepreneurs. In Curaçao, permits are issued for sex work in the legalized brothel for a maximum of three months, yet to maximize earnings or to cover any evidence of sex work from family members, many women who work in Campo Alegre buy goods in the Free Trade Zone or in duty-free stores for resale once at home. Those who do not work in the legal brothel enter the country on a fourteen-day tourist visa and may combine trading with sex work; they are formally known as small-scale entrepreneurs who "travel outside their country to purchase merchandise to sell in their home territory and/or in other countries"—as an extension of the higgler or trader known in the Caribbean for several centuries.[11] As noted by researchers in Jamaica, "in keeping with the traditional approach of the Jamaican woman, who devises strategies to cope with macro-economic developments that restrict her earnings, her response . . . was to become an Informal Commercial Importer, plying Venezuela, Panama and Curaçao and bringing into Jamaica imports that had become scarce due to the shortage of foreign exchange."[12] Clothing, shoes, textiles, cosmetics, and household goods constitute the bulk of the purchases made by the traders and their activities take them to places such as Panama, Miami, Puerto Rico, the Dominican Republic, Curaçao, and Haiti. In the early

1990s, traders who went to Curaçao made an average of 14.7 trips to Curaçao a year.[13] Once in Curaçao, the women were likely to stay at the smaller hotels and "pensions" in the Otrabanda and Punda areas of the capital, or with family. It was assumed by government authorities that if a woman stayed on the island longer than two or three days, she was engaged with prostitution activities.[14] Those who sold sex while on a visit did so at the small hotels and pensions where they lodged, or solicited from the street, at "bar dancings" (discotheques), or from any of the numerous "snacks" (small roadside snack counters and bars). On average, the traders spent U.S.$1,247 per trip in Curaçao, making approximately U.S.$683 profit per trip.[15] The women's entrepreneurial role in supporting the Curaçaoan economy, contributing to the family income at home, and supplying household and consumer goods throughout the region for affordable prices is substantial, even though the activities take place in the informal sector. In some instances, trading leads to a sustained engagement in sex work.[16]

Regional migrant sex work is often a temporary income-generating strategy, and it is not always from abject poverty that Caribbean women get involved. Rather, a woman may run into a specific financial problem, and the idea that she can accumulate a large sum of money in a relatively short period through sex work often underlies a move into the trade. In the case of Haitian traders in Curaçao, women often rely upon sex work to build up their initial capital in order to begin with a trading career in household goods or other items. They tend to leave sex work once this capital is accumulated.[17] Similarly, in Barbados, "For TJ, fare picking provided her with the opportunity to accumulate the money she needed to buy a home and to begin saving the money she needed to invest in a transportation industry in her native home, Guyana."[18] For another Guyanese woman in the same study, it also provided a bridge between trading and starting her own business. Among the sex workers I interviewed in Curaçao from the Dominican Republic and Colombia, the majority stated that they intended to save the money earned through prostitution in order to start a small business of their own. Part-time or temporary sex work in another country or territory also provides women with money to buy luxury goods, to pay for college fees for the children, to acquire jewelry and clothes promoted by the fashion industry, or to finish paying for an education for themselves. Migration to Campo Alegre in Curaçao, where one can legally be in sex work for up to three months, offers women an opportunity to earn this extra money within a short space of time on a temporary basis. Nightclubs and upscale tourist hotels in Suriname for Brazilian, Colombian, and Dominican women, in Barbados for Trinidadian and Guyanese women, in Curaçao and Aruba for women from other Dutch Antillean islands, in St. Maarten and Antigua for Dominican women, and in Cuba for Jamaican women offer similar possibilities, although generally for shorter periods and under unregulated conditions and in undocumented statuses.

The Stigma of Sex Work in the Region

Few women who engage in sex work in another Caribbean territory are sex workers at home. Migration provides a high degree of anonymity and, due to stigmas that surround the link between sex and economic transactions, allows a mother, wife, girlfriend, or daughter certain protection from discrimination at home while also protecting a family from being associated with a "loose" woman. Indeed, any form of migration for sex, whether to another area within the same country, to another territory within the same region, or internationally, is a strategy that many women around the world employ to avoid the "whore stigma": the mark of shame that is attached to any woman who is considered to operate outside socially defined norms of chastity, virginity, decency, and fidelity.[19] The whore stigma is a powerful discourse that both dishonors and controls, in particular but not exclusively, female sexuality, supporting laws that outlaw or prohibit "deviant" sexuality. As is the case in countries such as the Dominican Republic, where the laws are not so explicit, it creates a climate where certain forms of sex work are met with intense disapproval.

Even in places where prostitution is partially legalized, as in Curaçao, the stigma has a profound effect. During the course of my own fieldwork, when I visited brothels, nightclubs, and specific streets areas, only one girlfriend "dared" to accompany me. Most other women I knew were fearful of being seen in known prostitution areas by a friend or family member and of damaging their reputation. Similarly, a Curaçaoan woman who had spent several years in the Netherlands working on the issue of the trafficking of women returned to the island to focus on the sex trade on the island and met with a wall of disrespect. It soon became established in her community that she and her co-researchers were visiting and associating with sex workers, and they too were labeled "whore" or accused of defending prostitute's rights because their "mothers were whores." After leaving the island, the project she had initiated on the sex trade did not survive due to the limited number of women on the island who would willingly continue her work.[20] Similarly, the owner of an escort service that serviced mostly wealthy tourists and visiting businessmen at five-star hotels, expressed the view that it was fear of stigma and discrimination on the small island that prevented Curaçaoan women from applying to work for his agency. Few local women could be recruited to work for him, despite the demand for Antillean women by the clients and the greater profitability he could accrue from hiring women who represented the local culture. The sole Curaçaoan woman who did work for the agency at the time of the interview was based away from home, on another Dutch Caribbean island, Bonaire, due to her fear of detection and stigmatization. The other six escorts employed by the agency were migrants from the Netherlands and Venezuela.[21] In Curaçao, the whore stigma appeared to carry so much weight among middle-class professional women that among women whose lives would seem to be intimately connected to sex work, such as health practitioners and policy makers involved in AIDS education, or as "by-sides" or "sponsored" women, stigmas prevailed and a distance from sex workers was maintained. Few middle-class or elite women openly ventured anywhere near the known prostitution sites. Even the nurses who worked in the health clinic in the brothel Campo Alegre were adamant that they would never visit their workplace at night, not even in the case of a medical emergency, despite their acceptance of interacting and working with sex workers during the day.[22] Sex work was defined by many on the island as a "nasty business," from which "decent" women should stay far away. Similar stigmas around prostitution have been recorded in other Caribbean territories and have been discussed in various ways in earlier chapters.

Migration or Trafficking?

The trafficking of women is an issue that is commonly raised in connection with the movement of women across borders for the sex trade. It is a specific discourse that is quite distinct from attention to migration, but is not specific to the Caribbean. The notion of trafficking has an international history and reach, appearing first through the abolitionists' movement in Western Europe and the United States that drew from Christianity for its vision of a moral society. Shaped by the politics of anti-black slavery abolitionism and empowered by the women's suffrage movement in both Europe and the United States, the notion of trafficking emerged within the context of the institutionalization of the nuclear, heterosexual family, and ideologies about sex as a biological duty for reproductive purposes.

Trafficking was also firmly linked to the unregulated migration of women for "immoral" purposes and came to dominate international attention, leading to a series of international debates and conventions spearheaded by the League of Nations about the traffic in women and children for prostitution in the early twentieth century. While the issue of sexual morality underpinned much of the discourse about trafficking, the broader international concern gave rise to a plethora of nationally defined law enforcement and policing efforts to control and regulate immigration flows of human bodies and labor into the core capitalist regions of world. Commonly framed within racist and anticrime ideologies, the anti-white slavery crusade was also advocated through a Western European- and Anglo-dominated middle-class feminist reformist movement to abolish prostitution.[23]

In the immediate post-World War II era, trafficking continued to be framed as almost exclusively attached to activities in the global sex trade, with a focus on curtailing activities that arose around the deployment of Western military troops around the world, particularly in Third World countries, and produced the 1949 United Nations Convention for the Suppression of Traffick in Persons and the Exploitation of Prostitution of Others. While control of international organized crime remained an underlying premise for the international convention, this was cloaked in a discourse about the protection of women in non-Western countries from third parties (gangs and syndicates) who were seen to lure them into, pimp, and profit from prostitution.[24] It coincided with the restructuring of colonial relations, and the formation of the postcolonial Third World bloc, which, while a tumultuous period, was marked by national reconstruction and local demands for human labor power in the global South and by formal recruitment of semiskilled labor by former colonial powers and large corporations, from the colonies into booming postwar industries in Western Europe and North America. However, in this period the issue of trafficking subsided, as Western nations' demands for cheap labor easily absorbed new migrants and the recruitment and employment of the new populations were directly overseen and regulated by governmental agencies.

Trafficking reemerged in the global consciousness in the 1970s, foregrounded in the first instance by feminists concerned about the social impact of the reconstruction and development of the Southeast Asian region in the aftermath of the Vietnam War and the continued stationing and servicing of U.S. military troops in the region. Sex tourism, mail-order bride arrangements, militarized prostitution, and the coercions involved in the movement and employment of women from poorer to more affluent areas in the region and further abroad for work in leisure, relaxation, and sex industries were paramount in the early campaigns.[25] In the 1970s earlier feminist definitions of prostitution as expressions of patriarchy and male violence to women were recuperated and expanded by radical feminists. The term *female sexual slavery* was popularized to refer to "all situations where women and girls cannot change the immediate conditions of their existence; where regardless of how they got into those conditions they cannot get out; and where they are subject to sexual violence and exploitation."[26] Sexual slavery, it was determined by some feminist scholars, constituted the very essence of sexual and gender politics, with male dominance comprising the primary cause for this violence and oppression.

By 1985 the issue of trafficking was an integral part of the international women's movement, becoming a part of the UN Forums on

Women and of various women's networks and organizations around the world.[27] In 1996 the UN Special Rapporteur on Violence Against Women commissioned a worldwide research project on the issue to establish the parameters of the problem.[28] The report marked a shift in international feminist and UN definitions of prostitution. The research evidence and subsequent advice to the UN called for the disassociation of prostitution with criminality, and a view of sex work as a legitimate form of gendered labor that was criminalized under some national laws and subjected to hyperexploitation and coercion by third parties. At this international level, the definition of trafficking was taken a step farther when the Special Rapporteur on Violence Against Women advised the UN Commission on Human Rights that the phenomenon should be linked to forced labor and slavery-like practices more generally rather than exclusively to prostitution and sexual exploitation. This redefinition of trafficking reflects a more general trend in transnational feminist theorizing on the subject that conceptualizes trafficking for the global sex trade as produced through the intersection of the workings of state, capitalist, patriarchal, and race relations of power, as well as to the operation of women's agency and desire to shape their own lives and strategies for survival and livelihood.[29]

In the Caribbean region, while the narrow approach to trafficking—as prostitution and violence to women—was evident among women's organizations and feminists from the 1950s onward, my own and others' research during the 1990s began to shift this approach and pay attention to trafficking as a violation of sex workers' civil, labor, and human rights. The situation in Curaçao amply demonstrates the reasons for the difference in approach. In my interviews with women working in the Curaçaoan brothel, several elements of what was commonly defined as trafficking were apparent, yet these combined with a high degree of female agency and self-consciousness about their activities. First, for women who clearly knew they would be migrating to the island for three months to work in prostitution (around 50 percent of the sex workers at any given moment in the brothel) and who entered through the legal channels, it was the working conditions within the brothel that they described as intolerable and coercive, not the work itself. Second, there was little evidence that the women were enslaved or physically held against their wills, yet some freedoms and rights were curtailed and impinged upon and the women faced specific types of economic coercion. Women working in Campo Alegre had to be in the brothel boundaries after 6 P.M. for the rest of the night and could not leave without special permission. They were required to reside in and to pay daily for a small, non-air-conditioned room in which they also worked, and which could keep them in debt. They were not allowed to cook in their rooms, and thus were expected to eat at the restaurant in the brothel compound, where a meal for one person cost a minimum of Nag13 (U.S.$6.50) and where credit was prohibited.[30] Besides these expenses, the women paid Nag25 (U.S.$12) for the mandatory weekly medical examination, and for any transportation to and from the capital. They were expected to clean their rooms and to take care of their own laundry, although clean bed linen and towels were provided by the management three times per week. Prices for toiletries and sundries sold in the brothel compound ran far higher than normal. In order to meet her daily room and board, a sex worker needed to have at least two paying clients per day/night. Several interviewees expressed bitterness about the high prices they felt they were forced into paying just to stay at the brothel, while others complained about the sums of money that were demanded by guards and other men in Campo for small services and security. In addition to payoffs exacted by these men, a profitable business surrounded the provision of loans for the airfare and documents for the trip to Curaçao. Few women could afford to pay these costs on their own, and money was borrowed either in their country of origin or from the hotel manager in Curaçao in order to acquire a round-trip ticket to the island. As several women from Colombia and the Dominican Republic described, they borrowed from a middleman, sometimes mortgaging a house belonging to the family, and were expected to pay back the loan once in Curaçao. The initial period on the island was a struggle to ensure that this debt, with interest, was paid off. Extras for the trip also added up considerably, such as assistance with the application process, transport to and from airports, and costs for health certificates, visas, birth certificates, passports, and other papers, and the women could be indebted for large sums to men both at home and in Curaçao. These financial obligations and pressures en-sured that even though the majority of sex workers in Curaçao were technically self-employed and independent workers, their earnings were barely their own. Debts, obligations, the basic cost of living in the brothel, and bribes kept them in a dependent position vis-à-vis the hotel owner or individual men. One woman estimated that after a stint in Campo, all she could hope to take home was between U.S.$800 and $900, which she considered to be inconsequential for three months of hard work (that had also involved a bout of physical violence that incapacitated her for several days). Third, a number of women were captured by the idea of a short-term, well-paying job in Campo in Curaçao, often couched in terms of nightclub or enter-tainment work, and were deceived into sex work. Information about what Campo was—a brothel—was incorrectly transmitted in the networks into which they were linked, and hence they were not al-ways aware beforehand that they would have to engage in sex work. Once having arrived and discovered the nature of the job, few could freely leave due to the loans they would have to repay. While the po-lice officer at the prostitute registration office claimed that she had really only come across two cases of total misinformation in her twenty years of registering women for Campo, in none of the corre-spondence and information about the job at the brothel disseminated by her office or other government authorities was prostitution or sex work mentioned. The lack of clarity on the part of the Curaçaoan state served not only to obscure the nature of the job, but also to facilitate the recruitment of women to the brothel under false pre-tenses.

The entrapment, coercions, and indebtedness migrant women face in the legalized sector in Curaçao are illustrative of the elements of force that women face throughout the regional sex trade, although in many places these are exacerbated by the illegal or criminalized status of commercial sex work. In cases where a visa to legally enter the coun-try for sex work cannot be obtained (as is the situation in virtually every other territory other than Curaçao), working on the wrong side of the law on a tourist visa, staying on in a country after a tourist visa expires, or being smuggled into the country without the necessary pa-pers and permits is common. In 1985, for example, newspapers in the

Caribbean and Europe carried reports of the death of twenty-eight Dominican women who were found suffocated in a ship container that had arrived in St. Thomas. The reports related the deaths of the women to trafficking for prostitution, although how this was organized and by whom was never fully investigated or exposed.[31] For gold mines in Suriname Brazilian women are recruited and hired by the foreman of a mining operation to live for three months with one miner who in turn pays 10 percent of his total earnings to the foreman. The foreman sponsors the woman's travel from Manaus, Brazil, to the mining camp in southern Suriname, covers her lodging expenses, and pays her a fixed salary in gold. Living and domestic conditions in the gold mining areas, however, are extremely rough, yet the women are bound to work off their debt.[32] Situations of several Amerindian women in brothels in the Corentyne area in Guyana have been described in chapter three, where "hijacking" or kidnapping were not the issue, but instead, the women were harmed by the conditions under which they were recruited and retained.

In sum, while outright kidnapping and enslavement do not feature prominently in the regional sex trade, deceptions during a recruitment process for a job in another territory, debt bondage, and smuggling are integral to women's experiences in interregional migrant sex work, irrespective of whether this occurs in the formal or informal sector of local economies. Such conditions, which do not rely upon complete ignorance or physical violence in order for women to enter into sex work, have been recorded in many other developing countries and have led many researchers to question whether the older feminist trafficking paradigm, which seeks to abolish prostitution and views sex workers as passive victims of patriarchy, is a productive or even sufficient way to represent the Caribbean sex trade.[33]

Factors Facilitating International Movement into the Sex Trade

International migrations that involve sex work are as equally complex as regional migrations, and oftentimes intersect. Until the late 1980s, Curaçao functioned as a springboard for Dominicans and Colombians to enter the Netherlands from where they could move to other

parts of Western Europe. The status of the island as a political dependency enabled direct migration from the Caribbean, sometimes
facilitated through brokered marriages or adoptions. Alongside this
route, migration took place from the Dominican Republic to
Germany, Switzerland, Belgium, Greece, Spain, Lebanon, Tunisia,
Turkey, Italy, and the United States, and from Cuba to Portugal and
Spain, and for male sex workers, from Curaçao to the Netherlands
and from Jamaica to the United States and Western Europe.[34] Puerto
Rico was a transit place in the 1980s for Argentinians to make their
way into sex work in New York, and in the late 1990s, Suriname
acted as a transit point for Brazilian and Dominican women to enter
the Netherlands.[35]

A number of factors influence these international migration
routes. The direct political and economic dependency of countries
such as Puerto Rico on the United States and Curaçao on the
Netherlands has enabled the Caribbean colonies to function as transit points from the wider Caribbean and Latin America to the
"mother countries." Colonialism thus provides a context and route
for international migration into the sex trade. Second, linked to drug
trafficking, networks operate to recruit and assist the women into the
global sex trade. The particular case of the Belgian-Dutch organization "Bende van de Miljardaire" was given much publicity in the early
1990s due to an undercover report by a Belgian journalist that later
led to a BBC documentary on underground trafficking in drugs and
women.[36] Operations such as the "Bende" were often found to be
large-scale. One network, for example, took around five hundred
women for cabaret work into Belgium, the Netherlands, Luxembourg,
and France under the guise of "folk dance."[37] The European gangs
worked directly in consortium with men in the Caribbean and Latin
American countries connected to nightclubs and the local sex and
drug-trafficking industry.

Women recruited and moved into the European sex trade through
such networks shared a number of experiences.[38] Originally hearing
about work in the Netherlands, Greece, or Belgium as home help, in
a beauty salon, and more often as a dancer, women, particularly from
Colombia and the Dominican Republic, were drawn into a network
that sent them through the hands of many middle persons, both in

the Caribbean region and in Europe, and landed them in sex work once in Europe. In the process the women incurred large debts, were maltreated or raped, and often recruited under false promises. The women were lent money to pay for travel documents and airline tickets, and "show money" was given to them for purposes of getting through immigration procedures on arrival in a European country. Debts of up to U.S.$20,000 became a part of the migrant women's experiences, which then had to be paid back, most commonly though prostitution or other forms of sex work.

In the mid-1990s, the International Organization for Migration (IOM) documented that Dominican women were recruited into sex work in the European countries of Austria, Germany, Greece, Italy, the Netherlands, Spain, and Switzerland through similar channels and methods, noting that on arrival, the women were expected to begin work immediately, were threatened into silence, and, almost without exception, had their documents taken away. Furthermore:

> The working system varies according to the country. Women trafficked to Greece said that they had to work as dancers/prostitutes for the first three months without pay which meant incurring debts for accommodation, food, clothes, etc. Then, for the following three months they were allowed to keep 25–30 percent of what they earned from which their debts had to be settled.
>
> They were rotated every week to different cabarets and had one day off a week. All of them suffered physical violence by the traffickers and were told not to reject any client.
>
> Those arriving in Spain described a similar system of exploitation, with the relative advantage that the women knew the language and could talk with the traffickers and clients.
>
> Those who traveled to Switzerland also reported a frequent change of work places and an obliged excessive consumption of alcohol, paid by the customer, and contributing to the traffickers gain.
>
> All of them reported to have traveled with a contract as dancer, but in fact, upon arrival they had been informed that their duties included sex with customers.[39]

While much has been made of this trafficking of women, and it is commonly assumed that this process involves innocent women and girls who are virtually kidnapped and press-ganged into sexual slavery, the realities for women from the Caribbean are variable and do not always confirm a victim image of the "trafficked" woman. In the early 1990s in Dutch cities such as The Hague, Alkmaar, and Rotterdam, women from the Dominican Republic and Colombia comprised one of the largest groups of prostitutes, yet the majority declared being conscious of the fact that they were moving to Europe for sex work, having heard about the possibility of work via female friends and family.[40] Indeed, both aspects—the women's awareness of the type of work they would be involved in and their family's or friends' assistance in getting there—have been repeatedly cited as typical situations for women from the Dominican Republic, and both complement and support the recruitment efforts by the international networks and gangs, and locate the women as willing, yet bonded, workers.

Family and friends are important factors in the international migration into sex work. The IOM report notes that "All women interviewed responded that they had heard about the possibility of traveling through a friend who either knew someone who had traveled or knew a woman who organized trips,"[41] and according to a survey conducted by the Dominican organization COIN (Centro de Orientación e Investigación Integral), around 44 percent of the women who traveled abroad and worked in the sex trade were helped by either friends or relatives.[42] In some instances family reunification plays a role, where a family member invites a woman to migrate or a migrant family network is used to enter a country and to stay on in an undocumented status. Here the family from the homeland or abroad actively collaborates.[43] The location of family or friends in a particular country is therefore of particular influence in the route, yet the undocumented status positions the women in the informal and underground sector of the economy. Prostitution and other forms of sex work are often the more lucrative types of employment that the women can take up, requiring neither prior training nor advanced knowledge of the language of the host country.

International migration into the sex trade is also heavily conditioned by the demand for cheap sexualized labor and bodies in industries abroad. From the mid-1970s to the early 1990s, young "brown" women from Third World nations were sought to fill Western European sex markets, and "exotic" women from Southeast Asia, South America, and the Caribbean were recruited through various means for work in red-light districts and sex farms in rural areas. Since the mid-1990s, despite the continued overrepresentation of women of color in the global sex trade, this pattern in Western Europe has changed to some degree. The increasing closure of European borders to new migrants through the Schengen Agreement and the consolidation of the European Union (EU), along with the collapse of the Soviet Union and the economic instabilities in Central and Eastern European countries (CEEs) and the Newly Independent States (NISs) that displaced women from formal labor market sectors, has led to what has become known in the popular media as the "Natasha trade"—the movement of women from CEEs and NISs into sex industries in the EU.[44] While this new population of European sex workers commands international attention for being linked to the operation of criminal gangs, and produces various horror stories in the media regarding the conditions under which women are recruited and work once in Western European countries, legislation in the EU embraces "Natashas" to the exclusion of women from Asia, Africa, Latin America, and the Caribbean. A 1999 report issued by the Organization for Security and Co-operation in Europe and the Office for Democratic Institutions and Human Rights notes that the increasing numbers of women and girls who are entering the sex trade in Western Europe from CEEs and NISs are directly linked to their ability "to enter legally as tourists, often without the need to apply for visas" thus constituting the fastest growing source of migrant women in Western European sex industries.[45] Travel agreements between states within Europe privileges some women over others to enter the EU legally. In the Netherlands, where the state permits entrepreneurs legal access to its markets, this extends to include self-employed workers in legal sex businesses. On November 20, 2001, the European Court furthermore ruled that sex workers from Poland and the Czech Republic had the right to work in the Dutch sex industry provided they did so as self-employed entrepreneurs. Such laws exclude non-European women. As Jan Visser, researcher and coordinator of the Rode Draad, the sex workers organization in Amsterdam, explains, "Since October 2000, the prostitution industry is fully legal in the Netherlands. Prostitutes from EU countries are protected by labor law. A special decree under the Alien Labor Law forbids employment of non-EU persons in Dutch prostitution."[46] Women from Asia, Latin America, and the Caribbean are thus particularly subject to illegal means to enter the EU and often land in undocumented status once in the European Union; they thus stand a priori condemned to situations of extortion, debt bondage, and highly exploitative labor relations in sex industries. The situation reinscribes the racial hierarchy that dominates the global sex trade, where despite the exoticism and perceived eroticism of brown and black women, whiteness remains at the pinnacle of desirability and white women remain more privileged, in relation to access to higher wages, better working conditions, freedom of movement, and greater levels of self-determination, than those from other areas of the world. Sexual labor of women from Asia, Latin America, the Caribbean, and Africa is cheaper and, because of the women's undocumented worker status, offers greater profitability to sex industry managers. The reassertion of racial hierarchies around female sexuality in the European markets is echoed in North America, where the problem of smuggling and debt bondage of undocumented workers in sex and other industries is primarily linked to migrations from Asia, Latin America, the Caribbean, and CEEs and NISs, although far less has been researched and documented on this issue than in Europe.[47]

In short, the main factors that facilitate specific migration flows from the Caribbean into sex industries abroad are direct colonial ties, drug-trafficking routes and networks, family and friend connections, immigration and labor laws of receiving countries, and specific demands for labor in sex industries. The international situation mirrors the conditions, constraints, and possibilities described above for the interregional sex trade, although in a more organized fashion. Undoubtedly, geographical distance and the greater costs to travel internationally make such sex work migrations a far more planned and organized venture than local and interregional movements, through which the investments and debts are higher and risks greater. Return home is also much more difficult for the migrant. Furthermore, cultural distance is greater in international migration than in regional

migration, where familiarity with language, climate, work ethic, social norms, race and ethnic relations, or even sex work expectations
can be more easily bridged than in a completely foreign part of
the world.

Marriage and Migration

Migrant sex work is also to some extent conditioned by marriage. For
example, until 1986, marriage in Curaçao was a vehicle used by many
women of foreign origin to stay and work on the island as licensed
sex workers. Such marriages created some controversy on the island,
with rumors circulating that foreign women, particularly from the
Dominican Republic and Colombia, "robbed" Curaçaoan women
and families of their men. Still, sums of about Nag2,000 are known
to have been paid by a woman to secure a partner (an Antillean or
Dutchman) in order to obtain a Dutch passport and all the citizen
rights accompanying the status of a Dutch national. Referred to as
schijnhuwelijken (bogus marriages), these arrangements enabled a
woman to reside and work in both the Dutch Antilles—as colonies
of the Netherlands—and the Netherlands, and to make claim to any
state social and health benefits. Children of the women, if recognized
by the marriage partner, were also automatically entitled to Dutch
nationality and rights. In spite of the official statistics that showed
that in the period 1983–1988 25 percent of all marriages in Curaçao
were contracted between Dutch Antillean or Dutchmen and foreign
women, *schijnhuwelijken* could not be distinguished from a "real" marriage and could not be proven.[48] Perceptions of bogus marriages, however, leaned heavily on stereotypes and prejudices against women
from the Dominican Republic, reinforcing the SanDom stigma. With
changes in the Dutch nationality law in 1986, which included a three-
year waiting period before a foreign bride could obtain Dutch nationality, the number of these marriages decreased significantly.[49]

   While for some women migration takes them into sex work for the
first time, for others the opposite is the case. Some of the international
migrants are sex workers in their home country who enter marriage
or a steady romantic relationship with a foreigner and are able to exit
the sex trade through migration. This includes women working in

the tourist resort of Sosúa in the Dominican Republic, Jamaican rentals working at the beach in Negril, Cuban *jineteras* in Havana, Barbadian beachboys, and Curaçaoan SanDoms working in Campo/Mirage or outside. Marriage or romance with the "right" person can lead to moving abroad to an affluent, developed country with no further sex work obligations, either temporarily or permanently, and is often a goal for many young women and men in Caribbean tourist destinations. In Curaçao, marriage to a Dutch citizen can provide a stepping-stone toward better work opportunities, living conditions, and futures believed to be available in the Netherlands. Visions of romantic love and a long and happy partnership that are a part of the dominant Caribbean ideal of sexual partnering and family life often underpin this movement. Marriage to a European or American man is often perceived by women as a way to escape hustling and poverty-stricken conditions, and in Curaçao, relationships between *macambas* (whites) and SanDoms are often described within this context.[50] In one case a Dutch medical doctor, who was attached for several years to the office within the Department of Public Health charged with the care of prostitutes in Curaçao, struck up an intimate relationship with a Dominican sex worker in Campo, married her, enabled her to leave sex work, and took her to the Netherlands. The Dutchman in this case was the benevolent provider and protector who "rescued" the sex worker with promises of a better life and retirement from the sex trade. She, on the other hand, gained financial and marital security. For the Dominican Republic, marriage for a woman to a European or North American male foreigner can be an end goal in itself through which the woman hopes to fulfill her dream of living overseas "in a big apartment or house full of amenities and maybe even a car," with care and protection for her family or children.[51] A story told in Papiementu, of which the English summary is reproduced here in its entirety, sketches the complex relationship that romance, marriage, and migration represents for many women in the region:

> In the short story "Muhé di Bida" (A Woman of the Trade), Milagros Arena leaves her native country at the age of seventeen to live and work as a prostitute with her cousin Beatrix in Guyana. She leaves her two-year-old daughter behind in Colombia with her sister.

Her cousin marries an American and returns to Colombia. Milagros dislikes being alone in Guyana and working there as a prostitute, and after seven years she decides to try her luck somewhere else. She is devoted to the virgin Altagracia and is very thankful to the virgin when she finds a job as a maid for a Colombian family living in Venezuela. In her spare time she continues being a prostitute and makes friends with Lucretia. When she learns from Lucretia that it is possible to apply for a job as a prostitute in Curaçao she decides to go there for three months. During her stay she makes the acquaintance of a Dutch man, Willem de Jonge, who likes her very much. Then, what she could never have dreamed of happens: Willem asks her to marry him.

Now, Willem wants to live in Colombia, but Milagros doesn't want to go. She is afraid that the same will happen to her as happened to her cousin Beatrix. When Beatrix returned to Colombia it was not long before her husband had left her for another woman.

Up till now Willem has been faithful to Milagros in Curaçao, but during a holiday in Colombia he had been with another woman. Willem is determined to go, and Milagros knows that it will be very difficult to change his mind. But she is certain she will succeed.[52]

Love marriages, however, are not always the case, particularly for women. A deliberate use of sexuality can enable a woman to acquire another nationality or residency abroad, allowing travel and stay in Europe or North America without restrictions. "Amor por residencia"—establishing a relationship with a foreigner in order to obtain residency abroad through marriage—can be a calculated migration strategy among sex working women in tourist resorts in the Dominican Republic.[53] For others, even if once engaged in sex work in the Caribbean, international migration may bring them into, or keep them in, the sex trade. In the Curaçaoan context, marriage or an adoption enable a woman to acquire Dutch citizenship and travel to Europe without immigration restrictions. In 1993, the sum for an arranged marriage ran around Nag2000 to 3000 (approximately U.S.$1,000 to $1,500), including travel costs to the Netherlands, and was often brokered by a third party, not always with the woman's full consent. The arrangements were linked to the underground market of forged and false documents—birth certificates, travel permits,

passports, and health certificates—as well as to more organized recruitment of women from the Dominican Republic to Europe. Usually in such a case there is little intention for the couple to live
together; the marriage is merely one of convenience, allowing the
woman to be a documented worker in the Netherlands. In cases
where the woman is tricked into such a marriage for prostitution, she
may be able to buy back her freedom through paying costs for marriage, travel, documents, and so forth. Since these costs far exceed the
actual amounts, the debts keep her in sex work for a long time, paral-
leling a situation of debt bondage or indentureship. "Wives" and
"daughters" are known to have been forced to pay off their debts for
travel and documents through sex work once in Europe.

Most of the marriages, whether for love, money, or work, confirm
the heterosexual nature of the Caribbean, positioning young brown
women as available sexual romance partners for richer, wealthier men
in industrialized countries. It is a process that is not exclusive to
Caribbean women, but extends to include black men. The "romances"
among rent-a-dreads, rentals, or beachboys and women tourists function in similar ways, where the goal may be travel abroad and marriage, or more directly to gain access to overseas travel, a better job,
educational opportunities, or a vacation. While some migrate indefinitely, others return and maintain one or more relationships that allow
them several trips a year.[54] The rigidly heterosexual public sphere of the
Caribbean, and the oppression of homosexuality that permeates the
region, has also meant that there has been little evidence of interregional migration for homosexual sex work relations, although some
for international sex work. In Curaçao, the majority of gay and transgender sex workers who were registered with the police in the early
1980s had migrated to the Netherlands by the early 1990s, where
some were believed to have continued with sex work. In the Dominican
Republic, some young men who worked with foreign gay clientele in
the 1980s "were successfully adopted in Santo Domingo and taken to
North America and Europe as 'lovers.' For many sex workers the main
motivation was migration rather than emotional involvement. . . .
[W]hen they reached young adulthood, many adoptive 'sons-lovers'
did run away. Most stayed abroad illegally. . . ."[55] Conditions for these
young "adopted" men appear not to differ much from those of

"trafficked" women, being "frequently locked up in apartments" once abroad.[56]

Migrant Work

Migrations into underground or gray areas of the global economy by women and men who are not the world's poorest is an issue that has been noted in broader migration patterns. For example, the beginning of industrialization and the link between this process and an increase in personal and family wealth have been correlated to large-scale emigration during the twentieth century.[57] Those who struggle to cover subsistence needs, although perhaps desirous to migrate, do not have ready access to money or collateral to help pay for travel to another country, and are generally seen to stay close to home. Furthermore, data on interregional Caribbean migrations indicate two trends: (1) that regional and international migration usually follows a stage of internal rural-to-urban migration—that most commonly international migrants are urban based prior to migration—and (2) that young, well-educated, middle- and upper-class occupational groups are overrepresented in the migrant population.[58] The image of the unskilled "country bumpkin" is not one that can be easily applied to Caribbean migrants. Migration within and from the Caribbean sex trade confirms these patterns, suggesting that the Caribbean women are not from the least educated, unskilled, or peasant- or rural-class groups. As the police administrator who worked at the Curaçaoan prostitute registration bureau for over thirty years observed about the women applying for work on the island, "the very poor don't come here because they don't have money for a passport, for a ticket, and they stay in their own country—they can't afford to leave." The majority of the women I interviewed at Campo/Mirage confirmed this image—most had obtained a secondary level of education, were engaged in semiskilled occupations or businesses when not in sex work, and came from urban centers in the Dominican Republic and Colombia. Nevertheless, migration invariably places Caribbean men and women into lower occupations, performing tasks and jobs shunned by local populations due to the labor conditions and poor salary, thus concentrating them in seasonal agricultural, construction, and domestic work. Sex work is an additional job that fits into this general description of migrant labor.

Economies of Scale

The profits, benefits, and accumulations that rest upon regional and international migrant sexual labor cannot be calculated, given its clandestine nature in most of the world and the fact that some of the benefits are sensuous and nonmaterial in nature. Nevertheless, in relationship to the local and global economies, migrant female sexuality is crucial to informal and formal sectors. Migrant women, for example, send remittances home from sex work abroad. In this context, while it is impossible to even guesstimate the amounts remitted from sex work, it is important to note that the amounts sent home to relatives by Caribbean migrants constitute a large and important part of national incomes. In the Dominican Republic during the 1980s, for example, remittances amounted to about one-fourth of the country's foreign currency; for smaller islands such as St. Kitts-Nevis this could be as high as one-third of the gross national product. The notion of the "barrel economy" is popularly used to refer to the extent to which goods and money sent back by migrants (often in a barrel) have led to a shadow economy in countries where the formal economy can no longer support its population. In a comprehensive overview of Caribbean migration patterns and the regional impacts, Puerto Rican sociologist Jorge Duany concludes that "the livelihood of many Caribbean households literally depends on the continuous inflow of cash from migrant workers."[59] The remittances are used mainly for personal consumption, and secondly for savings and investments. Remittances from sex work constitute a part of this flow.

Migrant sex work also enables Caribbean women to participate in the trade, circulation, and consumption of luxury goods and items. Income derived from migrant sex work is sometimes used as seed capital to purchase goods that are then traded in informal markets once at home or in another country, or is used for the purchase of supplies for a small store or business that a woman may own or manage in her home community. In both instances, it provides an important source for local communities to gain access to material goods that may not be available in their country through formal trade relations, or are simply too expensive if bought through regular channels. It thus supports the heavily feminized sector of informal commercial trading that traverses the region and draws from the plantation tradition of the higgler or Madam Sara within the region, and that, since the latter part of the twentieth century, integrates the global economy and local cultural contexts in new ways due to new transnational linkages and flows.[60] On the flip side, migrant sex work exposes women and some men to new countries, lifestyles, or fashions and allows them to participate in new consumption and acquisition patterns. They can acquire for themselves goods deemed to be modern, gain access to property in a developed region of the world, or help to keep their families at home supplied with the latest in luxury goods and items. The status that goes with a house in North America or Western Europe, or the latest in electronic goods or fashionable clothes, cannot be underestimated for people living in a region that is bombarded with ideas about the importance of material wealth through global media, yet which only a tiny national elite can legally access or afford. Migrant sex work is, in this respect, a continuation of the "creative ingenuity" that Caribbean women are known for in finding sources of livelihood, and represents a part of that "tenacious independent spirit" that shapes Caribbean women's resistances to oppressive or discriminatory circumstances.[61]

Caribbean migrant women's sexuality is also acutely important for entertainment industries, hotel and restaurant businesses, and mining operations that are locally or transnationally owned, as well for keeping government officials, police, and hustlers in pocket. It is used by the tourism industry to lure tourists to the region as well as to entertain the guests, and thus indirectly to fill airplanes, hotel rooms, and restaurant and bar seats. It serves to keep mine workers and businessmen invested in the job at hand. Economic benefits to immigration and customs officials and members of the police through bribes or tips that are often demanded from women as undocumented workers in a criminalized sector cannot be calculated, although the incidence of reports by women in the sex trade of corrupt practices at these levels indicates ongoing underhanded economic transactions. The reliance of migrant sex workers on other informal sector operators to assist them in moving from one place to another, in obtaining documents to cross borders, or to protect them from police interference or client harassment, also usually involves some form of payment. While in some instances this may be in the form of sex, most commonly cash is demanded or offered. Migrant sex work—regionally and internationally—enables Caribbean women in particular to participate in the global economy and to simultaneously contribute to Caribbean development, helping to sustain household, community, regional, and transnational economies.

7

DYING FOR SEX: HIV/AIDS AND OTHER DANGERS

As an infection that is primarily sexually transmitted and that is yet to be controlled by the medical establishment, HIV/AIDS has assumed a central place in global discussions about sexuality since the 1980s. The HIV/AIDS pandemic has devastated populations in various countries around the world, in particular in sub-Saharan Africa, with the burden of the disease being carried by poor nations in the global South and poor communities of color in the North.[1] For 2001, the Joint United Nations Programme on HIV/AIDS (UNAIDS) concluded that in the Americas, the Caribbean was the hardest hit area, with an approximately 2.2 percent rate of infection among adults (compared with 0.5 percent in Latin America and 0.6 percent in North America), of which 50 percent were women.[2] By 2002, the Caribbean ranked as the second most affected region of the world, with an estimated five hundred thousand people living with HIV/AIDS in a regional population of 34 million, with Haiti accounting for approximately 50 percent of the cases.[3] Although first reported among men who had sex with men in Haiti, Jamaica, and Trinidad and Tobago in the early 1980s, and originally defined as a homosexual disease, HIV/AIDS transmission in the region was quickly acknowledged to be predominantly heterosexual in nature.[4] AIDS is now established as the leading cause of death in the Caribbean among twenty-five- to forty-five-year-olds irrespective of gender, and sexually active adolescents are the sector of the population that stands to be the most affected by high levels of HIV infection.

Estimates are that around 70 percent of all persons with HIV/AIDS in the Caribbean are between the ages of fifteen and forty-four years old.[5] Highest concentrations of HIV/AIDS infection have been found among migrant populations, such as male workers at bauxite and gold mining industries in the hinterland areas of Suriname and Guyana, and Haitian immigrants in the Dominican Republic; among sex workers, especially in the poorest countries of the region, Haiti and Guyana; and among men who cross heterosexual boundaries, particularly in tourism centers. The Caribbean as a major site of disease, with Haitians, "sexually deviant" men and women, migrants, and "promiscuous" youth perceived as the greatest threats to public health, is now a common image in international and regional discussions. HIV/AIDS places a great strain on Caribbean public health resources and on the national economy. With no immediate cure or vaccine for HIV/AIDS, and with a continuation of current rates of infection, direct and indirect costs of the pandemic in some parts of the Caribbean countries are estimated to reach between 2 and 5 percent of the GDP by 2010.[6] Furthermore, life expectancies in various territories have declined because of AIDS. In the Bahamas, for example, the expectancy has dropped from age eighty to seventy-one, and in Haiti from age fifty-seven to forty-nine.[7] Given that HIV/AIDS mainly affects the well-being and health of the most productive sector of the population it will undoubtedly have a long-lasting impact on economic productivity and development of the region as a whole, as well as on the future demographic structure of the Caribbean.

Risk Groups in the Caribbean

Sex workers, migrants, adolescents, and gay and bisexual men appear in numerous reports and initiatives around the region as important players in the transmission of HIV/AIDS.[8] Women whose sexual agency is neither attached to one man nor constrained to the home, men who move outside of the dominant norm of heterosexual polygyny, sexually active young people under the age of sixteen, and women and men who cross national and state borders in their search to survive economically are defined by the state, policy makers, and many researchers as "risk groups." Through the definition they are located as primary targets for surveillance, education, and behavioral change programs.

The foregrounding of sex workers and other sexually active women who operate beyond the boundaries of the socially proscribed roles of faithful, monogamous partner, mother, and caretaker of the home as potentially diseased or as engaged in risky behavior sustains long-standing negative images of women who engage in sexual relations with more than one partner as a *whore, jamet, matrass,* or *sketel.* Caribbean women who publically or deliberately engage in sexual transactions have thus been taken up in the medical discourses of the state as "vectors of disease" and have encountered a double stigmatization—as loose women and as disease carriers. In Puerto Rico, in the late nineteenth and early twentieth centuries, sex workers and other "poor, unattached, disorderly" women, in the view of the island's authorities, were segregated, medically tested and controlled, and at times jailed in campaigns to eradicate venereal disease.[9] As described earlier, during the 1940s and 1950s in Curaçao sex workers were defined as dangerous to public health in the context of the spread of venereal diseases such as syphilis, and various specific policies and programs were institutionalized to separate them from the rest of society, to make testing for syphillis and other sexually transmitted diseases mandatory for this specific sector of the population, and to have the police department oversee and control their activities. The designation of sexually active women as vectors of disease reemerged in the 1980s with the HIV/AIDS epidemic, as a study from Guyana indicates:

> Very early in the AIDS epidemic, female CSWs were identified as one of the high-risk groups for HIV. In addition to being at increased risk themselves, they can serve as a core group for the transmission of HIV into the general population. This is especially true in countries like Guyana where heterosexual contact is the primary mode of transmission of HIV. *The recognition that CSWs may serve as vectors for HIV spread into the general population* has prompted the development of targeted HIV education programs for CSWs [emphasis mine].[10]

The contemporary focus has produced the notion of the CSW—commercial sex worker—in medical discourses in the region, whose lives are thought to be intimately associated with HIV/AIDS.

Men who are sexually involved with other men and who may also be bisexual—designated MSM (men who have sex with men) in Caribbean health and medical discourses—are also the subject of intensive scrutiny and investigation and research, and they too are posited as vectors of disease in regional HIV/AIDS research and prevention strategies. However, unlike the sex worker population, the men have been treated with some caution. Same-gender sexual relations are more often described in association with the desires of foreign gay tourists or as consequences of the tourism industry where beachboys have sex with tourist men for money.[11] Indeed, the initial problem of the HIV/AIDS epidemic in the Caribbean is traced to gay sex tourism.[12] Discussions about Caribbean male same-gender sexual practices that are not connected to sex tourism remain muted, despite the important insights and data that health research among gay and bisexual male populations in the Caribbean has produced.[13] Men who have sex with men thus remain in dominant discourse as a group suspected of being corrupted by the Yankee dollar and non-Caribbean sexual norms, desires, and behaviors. The focus on this group by health planners and practitioners, while important for raising awareness and knowledge about male sexual relations in the Caribbean, has not dispelled the stigma and discrimination toward men who practice sex that does not conform to the standard Caribbean sexual script. It has, however, carefully raised the issue that homosexuality or gayness is not an uncommon feature of Caribbean societies—that Caribbean men engage in a variety of sexual activities with other men as well as women. These findings, taken together with widespread practices of informal polygyny and transactional sex, have led to analyses of complex sexual networks through which multiple men and women are seen to be sexually connected.[14] Attempting to map such networks, however, remains a difficult task due to the stigmatization and criminalization of homosexuality, bisexuality, and prostitution, and the persistent ideal of heterosexual monogamy that is reinforced through many civil and state institutions.

Adolescents are another subsector of the population who are considered sexually risky, and young people are commonly assumed to be wrong if engaging in sexual activity at an early age. Where the line between early and appropriate falls, however, is unclear. In many places the "proper" and ideal time for first sexual intercourse is defined as after marriage and at least after the age of eighteen. However, in most countries the legal age of sexual consent is sixteen, and marriage under customary laws is allowed at a younger age. Young people are thus permitted by law to be sexually active in their midteens, and in some instances their early teens, yet are condemned for doing so if it falls outside of marriage. The taboo that exists around speaking about adolescent sexuality maintains the double standards and contributes to the misinformation that young people are dealt, by their parents, the Church, and the educational system.[15] In my study of adolescent sexuality in Jamaica, I drew the conclusion that by simply delivering to schoolgirls and schoolboys messages about the necessity to delay sexual intercourse until they are older, or by simply giving boys the message that they must take care to use a condom and "be safe," little guarantee could be made that the youth would follow this information. Young people may aspire to behave socially correctly and to wait until marriage, until they have their own house, or until they are deemed by adults to be ready, but in practice there are many variables that propel them into sexual activity at the age of fourteen or fifteen. The study found that pressure from peers to be "big" (mature/adult) was one of the most important factors for both boys and girls, within the broader context where sexual activity is privileged in the construction of Caribbean masculinity and poverty rules. "Battery" (gang rape) of girls among adolescent boys was viewed as normal. Incest and the demand for sex by boys and men in exchange for a meal, gifts, money, or a drive in a flashy car were forced upon many adolescent girls. The girls' sexual activity could also be sparked by their need or interest to obtain money or to secure popularity among their peers. However, apart from these obvious variables was the fact that the Jamaican youth developed a sexual curiosity at ages well below eighteen or even sixteen. Together, the factors in the study indicated that it may be extremely difficult for adolescents to live up to the dominant social ideals about sexual relations, irrespective of how hard they are convinced that these are right. Furthermore, while many young people in the study expressed an awareness of dangers of sexual activity in their early teens, such as greater vulnerability to HIV/AIDS infection or an unwanted pregnancy, few had a sense that their rights as adolescents were violated through early sexual activity. Sexual intercourse was seen by young people from age ten onward as something that was to be experimented with, that could be fun and enjoyable, but also as a natural urge that required satisfaction. Despite the repeated reports of sexual abuse, forced sex, or incest, particularly by young women, few adolescent boys or girls were likely to view sex among family members as violations of the law, and only some named forced sex an illegal act.[16] Men and boys were often presumed to be exercising their sexual rights. The arena within which Caribbean adolescents negotiate and develop sexual relations, identities, and desires is thus fraught with tensions, misinformation, secrecy, discriminations, and violence. HIV/AIDS compounds this complex arena for the young people, and because of their sexual and social vulnerability, they are in danger of becoming infected, particularly by older men. Without specific attention to the conditions and pressures young people face in developing healthy sexual practices, and for the role of adults in infecting this sector of the population, the identification of the youth as a risk group runs the danger of stigmatizing and blaming the young people as irresponsible members of society.

Migrants are defined as a fourth major risk group in the Caribbean. Men and women who cross borders as hucksters or informal commercial traders, mine and agricultural workers, or sex workers emerge as a category of vectors who engage in risky behavior. As one research report states, "Although tourism, war and commercial travel have all played a substantial role in the dissemination of HIV, the migration of the young, rural poor, both on a seasonal and long-term basis, has probably been of greater importance in developing countries." This particular report goes on to note that "bateyes" in the Dominican Republic—sugarcane plantation communities that are comprised predominantly of Haitian immigrants—are sites where the highest incidence of HIV/AIDS has been recorded in the country, although the researchers are careful to point out that "social disruption inherent in the migratory cycle fueled by poverty, and the resulting strategies for economic survival" are primary culprits for the high incidence. *Mobility*—a term usually reserved for movements that improve class standing—is used to capture the migrations of poor, often undocumented people from one Caribbean territory to another. This mobility, involving poor, invariably black sectors of Caribbean societies, is strongly associated with a lack of attachment to a single sexual partner. Lone migrants are seen to enter into multiple sexual relations once across a border—women primarily to keep themselves economically afloat, and men out of an assumed male right to regular sexual intercourse. The idea of infection through such mobile populations sustains discriminatory immigration and workplace policies that require health testing prior to acceptance into a job or country, such as that which occurs for women going to Campo/Mirage (described in detail in chapter three), as well as images of poor immigrant communities as pools of disease. Mobility easily then becomes a metaphor for unregulated cross-border movements of poor, semiliterate, black working sectors of Caribbean societies who pose a health threat to local, stable populations.

Undisciplined Sexuality

The highlighting of specific sectors of the Caribbean population for the spread of life-threatening diseases and infections within Caribbean HIV/AIDS studies and interventions is not unproblematic. On the one hand, research among risk groups is a necessary part of tracking the epidemic, for designing interventions to prevent further spread of disease and for being able to identify those in need of treatment. It remains an important part of the war on the HIV/AIDS pandemic. On the other hand, the approach reproduces ideas that certain populations are more of a threat to the general public health and are less responsible in their sexual behavior than other members of society, and are to blame for the epidemic. An emphasis on marginalized social groups as vectors of disease reconfirms rather than dispels notions of sexually active women and men who have sex with men as abnormal, undisciplined, or corrupted by Western values, and it produces an image of teenage sex outside of marriage as unacceptable and immoral. The construction of particular sectors of the Caribbean population as in danger of transmitting diseases, and thus as groups that are to be closely monitored and controlled, moreover reinforces the dominant sexual regime in the region.

The definition of socially vulnerable, marginalized, and economically powerless groups as the vectors of disease in Caribbean societies due to their sexual "looseness" has also led to a panic about sex itself and to trends that seek to resurrect the sexually faithful, nuclear two-parent family. Monogamy, and co-residency of sexual partners, is commonly viewed as the solution to the problem of HIV/AIDS in the Caribbean, with multiple partnering condemned as irresponsible and risky and negatively associated with drug use, sexual activity in adolescence, and immorality. Single parenting, particularly by a man, may be viewed as leading to increased risk of HIV/AIDS infection.[17] Abstinence (particularly in the case of adolescents) is another favored answer to the problem, exhorted through the Christian Church and the educational system. HIV/AIDS prevention programs for the youth thus "tend to begin with abstinence and often focus on mutual monogamy."[18] Researchers and health planners tend to stress a need for stable, monogamous relationships between Caribbean men and women and the eradication of looseness or sexual indiscipline in Caribbean society. This emphasis echoes trends in earlier social studies that called for the establishment of the Western-style two-parent, monogamous "New World Negro" family. It also invokes the image of a libido as an autonomous force that can behave according to its own will, requiring spiritual or rational control. The image of a natural sexual instinct or urge that requires discipline and control that seeps into discourses on HIV/AIDS compounds the image of the poor, black, and marginalized as out-of-control social groups incapable of taking charge of their own lives and destinies.

Moreover, the focus on these populations obscures sexual activities and responsibilities of the socially, politically, and economically powerful groups in Caribbean societies. It elides hegemonic heterosexual patriarchal arrangements and interests that not only tolerate, but also legitimize informal polygyny and multiple sexual partnering by heterosexual men. Sex working women, sexually active teens, and bisexual or gay men are made visible as "bad" sectors of society, and efforts are directed toward correcting their behavior and lifestyles, while "upstanding" and "decent" men (and women) are ignored by and large and left unhindered to engage in multiple sexual relations. Sugar Daddies and Mommies, sex tourists, and male prostitute clients are not the primary social groups that are identified as part of the problem, nor are they the social groups that are targeted to carry much responsibility for halting the transmission of the disease. Rather, the onus for controlling and preventing the spread of disease is placed in the hands of the poorest and most vulnerable in society. For example, acknowledging that an exchange of sex for money and material things "is substantial in the general population" leads public health institutions to stress that it is commercial sex transactions and activities of CSWs that are to be placed under strict surveillance.[18] Thus, although great strides have been made in the Caribbean around acknowledging HIV/AIDS as heterosexually transmitted and as connected to the general population, this knowledge has not yet translated into an approach in which the entire society is called upon to take responsibility for curbing the spread of infection.

The narrow attention for the designated risk groups also obscures other factors that complicate HIV transmission. Although HIV/AIDS transmission correlates with sexual intercourse and is thought to be directly related to the absolute number of sexual partners one has, and thus to the risk group one belongs to, there are important intervening factors. As the first sex worker in the English-speaking region to publicly announce her HIV-positive status relates, she acquired HIV not through sex work but because her steady, live-in male partner was infected. "Love" and "marriage" were more risky in her situation than sex work, and the behavior of her steady male partner was of greater danger to her than her activities as a sex worker. Research from Haiti introduces another critical factor. Among HIV-positive and uninfected women, the number of sexual partners proved to less significant than the *professions* of the women's sexual partners, that "the HIV-positive women were much more likely to have had relationships with truck drivers or soldiers."[19]

Thus, while HIV/AIDS is sexually transmitted, and it is well established that multiple sexual contacts enhance the likelihood of contracting infection, the occupations or class of clients and dominant ideals about marriage as "safe" come to the fore as critical factors in the Caribbean region. Male sexuality and men who are not MSM or beachboys feature prominently as "risky" factors. Nevertheless, the lives, professions, and activities of clients, sugar daddies, and other male sexual partners are rarely taken into account in research on

HIV/AIDS, whereby the overriding idea persists that promiscuity of certain social groups, particularly those who do not adhere to the hegemonic masculine model of sexuality, is the principal cause of the pandemic. Caroline Allen, a sociologist whose work on gender and HIV/AIDS is pathbreaking in the region, concludes that what is needed is more data on the powerful in society, i.e., on men.[20] Gendered relations of power are critical for understanding the HIV/AIDS epidemic. Furthermore, the panic about aberrant sexual behavior of socially vulnerable groups does little to challenge the rigid sexual scripts that maintain the epidemic. As noted above, monogamy is touted as the ultimate solution to the problem, yet informal polygyny, as I have traced in earlier chapters in this book, is the social norm and is firmly embedded in Caribbean societies. And while abstinence may sound like a perfect solution to well-meaning adults, young Caribbean people themselves do not necessarily wish to have one model imposed upon them, and instead express desires to have greater sexual rights and freedoms.[21] Sexual abstinence and celibacy until a later age could be one way forward, but it is not the only scenario, they argue. However, despite the information and impulses that suggest otherwise, "sexual excess" and "sexual indiscipline" of sex workers, gay and bisexual men, and the youth are made analogous to the spread of disease through many of the HIV/AIDS programs. In order to combat the epidemic, a narrow expression of sexuality—as monogamous, limited, and contained—is promoted. Indeed, one of the greatest misconceptions that circulates internationally about HIV, as noted by researchers attached to the Institute for Health and Social Justice in the United States, is that to stop the epidemic "people simply need to give up promiscuous sex, drug use and other dangerous behaviors."[22]

The Epidemiological Problem

Some scholars, researchers, and activists who have been long engaged with the question of HIV/AIDS in the international context have raised a number of recurring problems with research and interventions that are promoted by large sectors of the medical community and that inform many state policies and programs. One important weakness is that an exclusive focus on epidemiological scientific questions about HIV/AIDS fuels ignorance about other factors that shape human intercourse and how they influence the transmission and spread of sexually transmitted disease.[23] Cindy Patton, who has been active around AIDS issues for several years, explains that part of this weakness stems from foundational ideas upon which epidemiological science and knowledge rest, that epidemiological thinking developed from a concern "not so much with detailing or treating the diseases that befell the European body in a place, but with visualizing—often with graphs—the march of bodies that made visible the temporal sequence called 'epidemic.'"[24] Thus, the task of epidemiology was first and foremost to describe the spread of disease and to identify the bodies most likely to be the vectors—those that harbored and transported disease. This premise has led to the constitution of the risk group and the policing of its boundaries for purposes of containing the disease, spreading cures, or eliminating the vectors, and today lies at the heart of the epidemiological scientific endeavor.[25] The construction of risky populations has thus become key to the control of HIV/AIDS from an epidemiological perspective, and efforts to describe and map routes and vectors of transmission often reproduce stigmas and discriminations against specific sectors of a population. In addition, a tropical medicine gaze has entered into the mapping of the epidemic around the world. Whereas the United States and gay sexual practices were first identified as the site of HIV/AIDS, its emergence as a heterosexual epidemic shifted the focus from the global North to the South, with an emphasis on sub-Saharan Africa. AIDS became defined primarily as a tropical infection, and black sexual choices and lifestyles viewed as the core of the problem.[26] In the Americas, Haiti—the poorest, most racially stigmatized country in the region—became the hemispheric scapegoat. Science once again pathologized blackness and black mating patterns. The combination of the epidemiological approach with a racist construction of disease has not only shifted the geographical and social group focus, but also elides "the extent to which people may be constrained by factors they cannot effectively control" and implies a tendency "to see people living with HIV/AIDS as the authors of their own misery—individuals who have acted hedonistically or recklessly and are now suffering the consequences."[27] It serves to obscure underlying factors that cause the epidemic. Poverty, inequality in the distribution of wealth and social power, racism, gender and class inequalities, violence against women, and wars and other forms of armed conflict remain fundamentally unaddressed in much of the research and attention for HIV/AIDS.

Work in the Caribbean closely follows this international scientific trend. The Caribbean Epidemiological Centre (CAREC) defines early sexual intercourse, multiple sexual partnering, frequent sexual contacts, and male dominance during sexual intercourse (grouped together as "sociocultural patterns") and "repression of same sex preference, low appreciation of condom use and prohibition of commercial sex work" (under the umbrella of "legal and religious taboos") as causes of the HIV/AIDS epidemic.[28] High rates of internal and external migration are identified as exacerbating factors. The organization furthermore stresses surveillance, mapping, tracking, and behavioral change as critical for the eradication of HIV/AIDS. It advocates control of social groups defined as risky, through annual surveys, indepth research, and testing; it creates models, graphs, and charts of the spread of HIV/AIDS in the region; and it provides detailed guidelines for health practitioners and planners on how to carry out surveys among risk groups. Its overall aims and objectives are to create "a comprehensive HIV/AIDS/STI surveillance system . . . which collects analyses and publishes accurate and timely epidemiological behavioral and care information" that will "provide health planners and decision-makers with appropriate information, which is used to reduce spread, morbidity, and mortality from HIV-infection and other STI."[29]

The epidemiological thrust that views sociocultural sexual norms and behaviors as the primary causes of the epidemic does not necessarily get to the root of the matter for the Caribbean context. As noted above, in Haiti it has been clearly established that poverty and class inequalities stand at the heart of the problem, rather than actual number of sex partners.[30] Gender relations of power are also crucial to understanding the epidemic. In addition, the power that women have to insist on safe sex practices is heavily compromised by an imperative for immediate cash to feed children or themselves. Economic insecurity is, after all, an important reason for a majority of sexual transactions in the Caribbean, yet male power and control leaves women in a weak negotiating position to insist upon safe sexual practices. The criminalization of much sexual behavior that is practiced in the Caribbean is also a leading cause, as it pushes sexual activities underground and into clandestinity. The fact that prostitution, same-gender sexual activity, polygamy, and sex with a minor are codified as illegal acts furthermore contributes to a fear among certain populations of detection by the police or other state authorities, an underaccessing of public health services, and a reluctance to claim responsibility for many sexual acts. As long as certain sexual acts are made illegal by the state, "illegal" sex will continue to take place, placing anyone who engages in informal polygyny, transactional sex with an adolescent, prostitution, or same-gender intercourse at risk. Stigmas about loose women, "battymen," and irresponsible adolescents keep in place taboos and silence about common sexual practices and add to the risk.

Alison Murray and Tess Robinson, two critics of the HIV/AIDS epidemiological paradigm, argue that it has led to a contradictory situation for the risk groups, especially sex workers.[31] From research in Australia and Asia, the authors point out that many sex workers who are trained as peer educators in HIV/AIDS prevention projects framed within the epidemiological perspective face a double bind: On the one hand, they are valued and seen as socially useful for the outreach work they can conduct and for making sex safe for the wider society. On the other, they are trained to monitor and control sex workers based on assumptions about the social deviancy of female prostitution. Sex workers are thus recruited and trained to police and discipline themselves within a framework that places the blame and hence the responsibility for preventing the disease on their own social group. Furthermore, the authors found that the sex work peer educators are rarely provided with the tools to question and challenge wider economic, social, and political relations of power that keep prostitution or the epidemiological approach in place. They conclude: "The threat of HIV/AIDS is used as a justification for reinforced control, and in their recruitment as 'peer educators,' sex workers are being engaged to undertake their own surveillance."[32]

Injustices and Inequalities

Equally pernicious as the blaming and control that occurs through the incorporation of the epidemiological perspective in HIV/AIDS interventions and research is the use of vulnerable groups in developing countries for experimentation in the name of advancing scientific research and knowledge. In some instances, information about test subjects' health status is withheld. Health care is differentially provided by the state to different social groups, with often the poor and minority groups being denied adequate care. Bioethicist Annette Dula uses the term *medical violence* to name such medical practices, which, in particular, have grave effects on the lives of (poor) people of color. She explains that medical violence is "intentional" and "race-based, affecting the disenfranchised, oppressed and exploited and otherwise vulnerable and marginalized people," and "is performed by the state, by health care providers and by medical researchers."[33] The forty-year-long Tuskegee experiment in which four hundred syphilitic black men were part of a U.S. public health study but were not told the results of the tests carried out upon them and left un-treated is cited by Dula as a primary example of medical violence. Other cases she cites include the forced sterilization of women of color in the mid-twentieth century (where, for example, one-third of women in Puerto Rico were sterilized by 1965) and the screening of Latina and African American women workers at a government laboratory in California for syphilis, sickle-cell anemia, and pregnancy without their consent or knowledge. Testing and experimentation were carried out on the bodies of marginalized populations defined in dominant discourses as disposable social groups, and thus unworthy of information, treatment, and health care. In the case of HIV/AIDS research, poor communities in sub-Saharan Africa, in particular, but also in other places in the global South have been targeted for experiments and tests to both determine the nature of the disease and develop drugs and vaccines against HIV/AIDS. The epidemiological focus on analyzing transmission and rates of infection has resulted in situations where African sex workers, under the knowing gaze of international scientists, have been tested and tracked for a number of years while being repeatedly exposed to the HIV virus.[34] In other instances, sex workers in the global South have been tested anonymously and results of the tests regarding the women's individual health status not offered to them.[35] The knowledge gathered through such projects, while providing the researchers with details about the epidemic, is withheld from the tested women, and the information gathered by scientists does not automatically translate into direct interventions that protect the women involved in the studies from infection or death. Moreover, while it is widely claimed that testing and experimentation are critical for the development of vaccines or drugs to either eradicate or contain the epidemic, it is publicly and internationally recognized that the main beneficiaries are wealthy, white, gay populations in the global North who can afford to pay for antiretroviral drugs. The available medications, while not offering a cure for HIV/AIDS, have been widely recognized as causing "important changes in the morbidity and mortality profiles for HIV/AIDS."[36] The limited access to such drugs by populations in the global South has been the subject for much anger, criticism, and distrust of the global medical establishment and drug manufacturers and corporations. "Many countries, particularly those of sub-Saharan Africa, are being ravaged by the AIDS epidemic. This could have been curbed, perhaps defeated had massive and expensive worldwide support been put into public health measures, availability of medications, and more research into vaccines and drugs," notes one specialist.[37] Activists who participated in the 2000 HIV/AIDS conference in Durban, South Africa, concur:

> Terribly high levels of HIV infection and death due to AIDS are now a reality (rather than merely a projection) in poor communities worldwide. More than half of all these infections occur among women. AIDS is causing widespread devastation in Africa and Asia especially. THIS WAS AVOIDABLE. It is the consequence of negligence, particularly on the part of 'first world' governments whose resources could have been mobilized to come to the practical assistance of poor nations many years ago. Political authorities have preferred to neglect public health,

taking for granted the exorbitant cost of treatment, refusing to imple-
ment measures necessary for the strengthening of health systems, and pro-
hibiting countries from setting up local medication production or from
importing treatments essential for the survival of their populations.[38]

At the 2002 UNAIDS conference in Barcelona the issue of differential treatment of the rich and the poor continued to be at the forefront of many discussions. "Medicines Keep Victims in Rich Nations
Alive While Millions of Africans Are Dying" were newspaper headlines about the conference, with reports stating that "a vast gulf still
exists between those who will die in the absence of treatment and
those whose lives can be indefinitely prolonged by modern medicine."[39] The prohibitive costs that the multinational pharmaceutical
industries have placed on the drugs and the inability for most governments and individuals in the global South to afford them leave
many poor people living with HIV/AIDS in great danger. Despite
some new efforts by the companies to make drugs more affordable and
accessible to governments in the global South and to poor people
everywhere, experiments to find suitable medical tests, drugs, and
treatment for people with HIV/AIDS continue to benefit primarily
the white and the wealthy. Medicine Sans Frontier/Doctors Without
Borders publicizes the fact that most of the research about and profit
from drugs goes to the developing world. According to this organization, only 10 percent of research goes toward the 90 percent of the
"disease burden" that is found in the developing world.[40] Poor (black)
women and men, despite their usefulness for furthering knowledge
about the epidemic and possible preventions or cures, are still over-
whelmingly left to fend for themselves or to simply perish. Global
inequities of class and race are, as many HIV/AIDS activists and
medical practitioners recognize today, pernicious barriers against developing interventions and treatments that will take care of the
world's population in a justiciable manner.

The biases, violence, and stigmas embedded in the dominant epidemiological approach to HIV/AIDS are not completely absent from the
Caribbean landscape. Research framed in this paradigm has underpinned many activities and studies among sex workers, men who
have sex with men, youth, and, more recently, migrants. Much of the

attention in the region remains couched in medical scientific concerns about HIV/AIDS and reinforces notions of these populations as inherently risky and sexually out of control. Some of the most vulnerable sectors of Caribbean society thus remain targeted as the vectors of disease, as the populations responsible for behavioral change and the prevention of HIV/AIDS, and as test subjects. Their sexuality remains subjected to continual surveillance and control. Furthermore, despite many good intentions or policies of governments, health planners, and agencies to tackle AIDS, funds for treatment in the Caribbean are extremely limited. Standard treatments applied in the global North that keep many people alive and well do not apply to most of the region. Rather, antiretroviral drug use "is usually done on an individual basis with clients whose financial status is such that they can afford the exorbitant costs of these medicines."[41] Laws that discriminate against particular sexual populations remain in place, stigmas about certain sexual practices proliferate, and political will or ability to attack the structural causes of the pandemic is weak. Epidemiological research that tracks the pandemic is funded by international and North American health agencies, while programs run by local governments or nongovernmental organizations to provide care and treatment are poorly supported. Treatment is not a main focus of the interventions.

In a review of the gaps in policy and programs in Jamaica, which in particular impact young people, Aziza Ahmed identifies a number of problems.[42] Fear of being seen to be sexually active by service providers, she notes, is widespread and often hinders youth from seeking health tests or care. The stigma of youth promiscuity thus weighs heavily. This is coupled with the laws that define anal sex (sodomy/"buggery" laws), prostitution, and sex with a person under the age of sixteen as illegal. If young people or children are in breach of these laws, as many are if they are engaged in transactional sex, are sexually abused at a young age by older family members or "big men," or are sexually curious, they may be denied health care services and treated as criminals. The laws are great disincentives to young people for being tested or seeking treatment for HIV/AIDS and other sexually transmitted infections (STIs), as well as avenues through which judgmental attitudes about adolescent sexuality are legitimized. Ahmed also points out that the lack of attention for sexual violence in transactional sexual activities, incest and family sexual abuse, and adolescent involvement in sex tourism, as well as the inability of existing sexuality education programs to meet the needs of young people creates barriers in attempts to address the HIV/AIDS epidemic in Jamaica.

Recommendations that emerge from critical research on HIV/AIDS point to a need for Caribbean governments and health agencies to conduct wide-scale retraining programs of service providers, teachers, and police to reduce stigmas about sexuality; for governments to lift the laws that outlaw certain sexual acts and that serve to maintain stigmas and secrecy; for the health care system to create adequate and sensitive services, particularly for women and youth; and for there to be a widespread media and education campaign to foster a climate in which all people, especially youth, feel they can honestly and openly communicate their sexual needs, fears, and desires. Strongly recommended is that the climate of sexual openness and honesty include parents, the family, and the Church, and that greater tolerance of sexual difference be promoted throughout society. In addition, a demand for the decriminalization of prostitution and homosexuality is gaining ground among HIV/AIDS researchers and planners in the region.[43] Community-based health care projects in Haiti, which have been in operation since the mid-1980s, further advocate a holistic, low-cost approach, one that strengthens local knowledge and expertise in dealing with deadly infections and disease and makes testing, care, and medicines affordable to the poor. The universal availability of antiretroviral drugs for treatment is of overriding concern for scientists, health planners, and activists who wish to go beyond studies of the epidemic and to empower poor populations to be able to take their own health care matters into their own hands.

From "Vectors of Disease" to Empowered Women

Resistances to stigmatizations, discriminatory treatment, and genocidal attempts have been mounted in various ways, and not only from critical researchers and community organizers. In various countries in the Caribbean some sex workers have collectively asserted control over their own lives and destinies. They have established projects and organizations for their own empowerment and self-determination and demanded attention for tolerance of sexual diversity. At the beginning of the twenty-first century, two sex worker organizations existed in the region—one in Suriname, the other in the Dominican Republic—with a third initiative taking shape in Guyana. Each project/group is unique and deals with the specific cultural and economic context of its own country, although a number of similarities bind them together as part of a broader global sex workers' movement that articulates the particular politics of sex worker resistance and sexual agency.[44]

To begin with, the organizations and projects were initially developed from national concerns about public health and the spread of AIDS and HIV. In the Dominican Republic steps were taken by the government health department in 1985 to reach and educate sex workers about STIs. Surveys were held to assess the population in the capital, Santo Domingo, a peer outreach group was established for preventative health care work among sex workers, and doctors and nurses in fifteen hospitals in four different cities were trained. The activities rapidly grew under the auspices of the National AIDS Program. However, in 1987 the peer outreach program disengaged from the government agency and established itself as the nongovernmental organization COIN (Centro de Orientación e Investigación Integral). The organization developed its own intervention models with a focus on preventative health care work, support for HIV-positive and AIDS patients, finding alternative work for sex workers, and distributing condoms. The peer workers were christened *mensajeras de salud* (messengers of health) and their work extended to various cities and tourist centers. By 1994 the network of "messengers" consisted of 24 paid team leaders and 387 volunteers. The organization attempted to create a less stigmatizing image of the prostitute in Dominican society, to provide information about the risks and dangers associated with unsafe sex, and to break the silence and shame surrounding sex work among the wider public and among sex workers themselves. Despite COIN's valuable contribution to and perspective on sex workers' empowerment, an autonomous sex workers' organization was established in 1996. Named *Movimiento de Mujeres Unidas*, MODEMU (the Movement of United Women), its objectives are to promote the independent organization of Dominican sex workers, to raise the self-esteem and awareness of sex worker rights as women, citizens, and workers, and to advocate for broader economic options for poor women. MODEMU asserts itself as the voice of the Dominican sex workers. It set out to create mechanisms of solidarity and mutual support among sex workers to fight against violence, to prevent sexually transmitted diseases and AIDS, to promote the creation of health services, to provide legal and psychological assistance to victimized members, to train women to find other jobs, and to protect their children against stigmatization.

Developments in Suriname are similar to those in the Dominican Republic. In 1988, the Ministry of Health established a National AIDS Program and conducted various needs assessment studies among sex workers as one of the groups perceived to be risky due to the high levels of heterosexual infection and transmission in the country.[45] Street-based sex workers as well as over four hundred women operating in licensed and unlicensed nightclubs were targeted for research, education, and interventions. Holding weekly workshops in the main languages spoken in the country, as well as by foreign, migrant sex workers, in Sranan Tongo, Dutch, Spanish, Portuguese, and English, the projects covered a wide range of health, medical, and other issues. Workshops were also held for club owners. Nevertheless, such initiatives were short-lived and unsustained by the National AIDS Programme (NAPs), and in 1993, the Stichting Maxi Linder Association (SMLA) was established to address sex workers' needs in a less project-oriented, less epidemiological perspective, embracing a more holistic and woman-centered approach. While also distributing condoms free of charge and thus insisting on safe sexual practices, SMLA centered itself on the well-being and empowerment of women, moving away from the stereotypical HIV/AIDS intervention approach that viewed sex workers as health threats to society.

Guyana is the third place where a sex worker empowerment initiative was under way. In the early 1990s the Pan American Health Organization sponsored the Guyana Ministry of Health to undertake an HIV/AIDS study among sex workers in the capital,

Georgetown, out of which grew a sex workers' project under the supervision of the National AIDS Programme.[46] In addition, a baseline survey was conducted in Georgetown in 1997 to collect data on
sex workers and health, "recording demographic characteristics,
knowledge and beliefs relating to HIV/AIDS, condom utilization,
sex worker and client attitudes to condoms, contraceptive use, experiences of having an STI and use of drugs and alcohol."[47] The
initial projects remained within the epidemiological approach to
sex work and received limited support and funding; thus they were
contained and limited in their scope and effectiveness. However,
independent of these above-described initiatives, sex work began to
be taken up as part of the activities of the Red Thread Women's
Development Programme, an organization officially founded in
1986 aimed at creating income-generating opportunities for
women in Guyana while simultaneously challenging power structures defined around the axes of race, class, political affiliation,
and the undervaluation of women's work.[48] While Red Thread
had over the years developed a great number of projects and
worked in multiple urban, rural, and indigenous communities
across the country, in 1996 it first explicitly identified sex workers
as a category of low-income women that had not been included in
its outreach and mobilization activities and about whom little was
known by the organization. Participating in the regional sex trade
action research project, Red Thread started its first investigations
into the specificities and conditions in the sex trade in Guyana,
making contacts with sex working women primarily in Georgetown.[49]
A key bridge person in the educational, research, and outreach
work between the government AIDS program and the women's
organization was Dusilley Cannings, a former sex worker, peer
educator, and counselor with the sex workers' association in
Suriname. Through the Red Thread research other sex workers
became acquainted with the organization and became involved in
activities. In 2000, the organization was approached and funded
to conduct a survey with the aims of gathering and assessing information about the HIV prevalence among sex workers in
Georgetown, toward the preparation of a larger project to cover
sites outside of the capital.[50] Despite the emphasis by the funding

agencies on HIV/AIDS, the Red Thread team concluded from its studies that some sex workers desired a specific sex worker organization or project that would help them find alternative work if they wished to exit the sex trade, and through which they could fight for the legalization of sex work and against the discrimination they faced.[51] It was found that apart from the stronger connections that had been formed between Red Thread members and sex workers, and among sex workers themselves, the majority expressed an interest "for on-going meetings, and an organization that would cater to, and meet, their specific situations and needs."[52] They specified "the development of literacy and other skills," "the desire to organize in their own self-defense, mainly against physical injury by clients and the police," and "increased safety and protection (from HIV/AIDS)" as priorities.[53] In striving to address this interest and demand, Red Thread proposed to "develop and consolidate an organization for sex worker's empowerment in Guyana," with the objectives of increasing income-generating options for sex workers, improving access to reproductive health information, reducing the stigma attached to sex work, building the confidence and negotiating power of sex workers, enabling sex working women to guide future research on sex work in Guyana, and building alliances between sex workers and other working women in Guyana and elsewhere. The Red Thread organization would facilitate the development of such an organization through its center in Georgetown. The proposal was based on the growing identification by sex workers of the openness of the Red Thread women's organization to the issues of sex work and the support sex workers found at the Red Thread Center. Strong bonds had been established, and Red Thread was seen as a place where women could meet, discuss, and find respect above and beyond their work as agents to prevent and control HIV/AIDS. A crucial and important difference between the developments in Guyana and those in the Dominican Republic and Suriname is that the empowerment of sex workers occurs in collaboration with an established women's organization and explicitly makes the links between sex work and other income-generating activities. Sex work itself is not seen separate from the entirety of working women's lives and the strategies poor women engage in to sustain themselves and their households in a Third World context.

Other Dangers

In their work, organized Caribbean sex workers have pointed out that the link between HIV transmission and sex work, while very real, is not a problem that can be placed solely on their shoulders, and that they do not have to accept the stigmas and mistreatment because they are defined by dominant discourse as promiscuous, unruly, or disorderly women. A demonstration in 1993 on National AIDS Day on the streets of Paramaribo by sex workers and allies, under the slogan "No Condom, No Pussy," was, for example, a moment where sex workers made a public stand against such stigmatization and demanded that they be seen and heard as political sexual subjects. The public demonstration also claimed sex work as an activity about which women could take pride. Moreover, the sex workers presented a direct challenge to the broader Suriname population to take responsibility for its sexual behavior, reflecting as well ideas that sex workers could take control of their own health situations and could refuse to participate in sexual interactions with irresponsible clients. The multiple messages that were sent by the demonstrators sought to dislodge ideologies about sex workers as irresponsible, diseased, desperate, depraved sexual beings, and to express the idea that HIV/AIDS was a much larger problem that required attention and action from the entire population.[54]

With the Caribbean region being also plagued by dengue fever, gastroenteritis (a leading cause of death of children under the age of five), malaria (particularly in hinterland areas), and influenza, HIV/AIDS is not the only life-threatening dimension in sex workers' lives.[55] Malaria for women who live or work around gold mining camps in Suriname and Guyana is, for example, as great a concern as HIV infection, as is access to hygienic and sanitary working conditions, potable water, and health care services for protection, prevention, and treatment of a wide range of infections—sexually and nonsexually transmitted. Moreover, physical violence by clients, brothel owners, family members, or the police is a serious threat to the physical and mental health of women and men who step outside the dominant heterosexual, polygynous norm. Malnutrition and hunger in poor communities in the Caribbean are also important causes of ill health. In short, HIV/AIDS is one, but certainly not the only, health risk faced by persons engaged in commercial or transactional sex. In circumstances of poverty, in countries strapped by neoliberal structural adjustment programs and policies that reduce state social and economic assistance to the poor, and where domestic, street, community, police, and medical violence are everyday practices, women and men who transgress sexual boundaries know their lives are endangered on many fronts. Thus, HIV/AIDS is not the only problem to be contended with, and an overemphasis on sex workers' roles in the transmission and prevention of infection creates a false sense of security for the rest of the population, while deepening the hostilities, violence, and stigmas aimed at sex workers.

Nevertheless, awareness of HIV/AIDS among sex workers has led to a growing empowerment of a socially vulnerable, criminalized, and marginalized social group, and has enabled poor Caribbean women to begin to speak out about the hypocrisies, competing ideas about, and multitude of practices that make Caribbean sexuality a reality. Organizations of sex workers in the Caribbean are then an important part of the groundswell for critical campaigns that expose the conditions and double standards under which sexuality is shaped that seek to dismantle laws that criminalize sexual-economic transactional sex, and that demand nondiscriminatory, holistic, affordable, community health care. The Caribbean sex worker campaigns augment initiatives in the region, such as in Haiti, that fight for community, especially poor black women's, empowerment. They also mirror and connect with those of other sex worker empowerment organizations and AIDS activists elsewhere in the world who fight for greater freedom and security for all.

8

RESISTANCE, REBELLION, AND FUTURES

Sexual-economic transactions have been foregrounded in the foregoing chapters as a prism through which Caribbean sexuality is organized, regulated, and experienced. The transactions rest upon embodied resources that are used strategically for material gain and are highly mobile, temporary, and often part-time. In economic transactions, sexuality is commonly self-organized but may also be organized by and through third parties. Sexual-economic transactions and relations, however, do not necessarily produce a social identity of sex worker or prostitute; only some women and a handful of men publicly self-identify as such, but rather a number of activities are interwoven in people's lives. Sexuality is strongly linked to survival strategies of making do, as well as to consumption, which in itself is often seen as a prerequisite for survival. It is not always conflated with intimacy or love, nor necessarily, when economically organized, seen to violate boundaries between the public and private. Moreover, although many sexual-economic transactions reconfirm the dominant ideology of the Caribbean as a heterosexualized place, sexuality is not always cross-gender oriented. Same-gender and bisexual practices are everyday practices in the region. We have also seen throughout this study that sexual agents transgress boundaries of what is considered decent womanhood or respectability in many Caribbean countries and contest dominant constructions of female sexuality that support the hegemonic heteropatriarchal regime. Similarly, configurations of sex work often confirm racializing and exoticizing ideas about the hypersexual nature of the Caribbean, while they transform racialized, exoticized bodies into resources for freedom, betterment, and economic development.

In viewing the Caribbean sexualized, racialized body simultaneously as an actor and the stage, as self-actualizing and acted upon,
and as a producer and reproducer of variable meanings of sexuality, a
persistent theme in this book is about how the embodied subject
shapes and is shaped by sexual practices. Nancy Hartsock reminds us
that "We need to engage in the historical, political and theoretical
process of constituting ourselves as subjects as well as objects of history. We need to recognize that we can be the makers of history as
well as the objects of those who have made history."[1] As I started this
book, my interest in this theme was not only about the making of the
Caribbean sexual subject, but also the questioning of whether sexual
agents constitute a "rebelling pillar" in Caribbean society. To explore
this required not just an assumption of subjectivity and agency, but
also opposition to dominant modes and regimes of sexuality, and two
terms are significant to this exploration in this final chapter: resistance and rebellion. Resistance I take to mean politics and practices
that are lodged in material conditions of everyday life that work to
subvert, contest, or transform relations of dominance. While resistance may be highly organized and become part of an underground
movement, it may also simply inhere in the very "gasps, fissures and
silences" of relations of dominance, lodged in minute, day-to-day
practices and struggles of the colonized and oppressed.[2] Rebellion I
define as individual or collective acts that overtly defy and disobey
the established order, standards, or authority. Rebellions are thus radical, visible, articulated acts of resistance that seek to dislodge a prevailing system, using any means necessary. And following in Chandra
Talpade Mohanty's footsteps, rather than assuming resistance and
rebellion to emanate from an identity politics that simply draws from
positionalities within a web of relations of power around race, gender, sexuality, class, etc. ("I am, therefore I resist"), I take these types
of contestations to mean actions that are grounded in struggles for
change.

I propose here that it is through everyday acts of embodied subjects in their racialized, gendered, and economic specificity against
dominant sexual regimes and norms that it is possible to speak of
sexual resistance and rebellion in the region. These oppositions, however, are not always visible to the indiscriminate observer, but require

interpretation through a lens that takes sexuality as a central category of analysis. This may mean a rereading of history. So, for example, although no extensive study has been made of precolonial and pre-Columbian Caribbean Amerindian sexuality, there are some reinterpretations of whatever little research and evidence we do have that some Amerindian women went against the grain of heteropatriarchy and carved out a space that secured their sexual autonomy and freedom.[3] The fiercely independent women-only communities of Amazons that appear in various myths, legends, and stories, but perhaps also in actual community lifestyles of Amerindians, symbolize this rejection of heterosexist, patriarchal norms and authority—a collective, concerted effort by women to create their own universe according to their own principles. The "rebel woman" under slavery has also been named, claimed, and widely disseminated through work by historians Lucille Mathurin Mair and Hilary Beckles, and has been attached to the legend of Nanny, leader of a Maroon band in Jamaica. The rebel woman was, from all accounts, resistant to racialized, gendered, and sexual orders. Other scholars have produced insights into the subject of contemporary female heterosexual agency as resistant to dominant modes of feminine sexuality that prescribe procreation, faithfulness, and docility. Among African-Jamaican women who participate in dance hall music and culture, Carolyn Cooper notes that a redefinition of "slackness" occurs, where slackness is an oppositional stance to hegemonic standards of decency and piety.[4] Here, female slackness represents femininity that resists and escapes from male control encoded in "respectable" relationships—i.e., marriage— and becomes "a politics of subversion . . . a metaphorical revolt against law and order."[5] Women's independent participation in dance hall culture, exhibited through "uninhibited solo *wainin* on the dance floor," signals to Cooper a potentially subversive and transformative character of female sexuality in popular culture. Female sexuality in the dance hall is then "in part a radical underground confrontation with the patriarchal gender ideology and the pious morality of fundamentalist Jamaica society," and it is in the feminization of slackness in the dance hall that "women lay proper claim to the control of their own bodies."[6] However, slackness is not always a break with the dominant construction of heterosexuality, but rather a transgression of existing boundaries that are placed on female sexuality. Although female sexual prowess is, then, an "essential element" of the women's performances, female sexuality is, according to Cooper, imagined in terms of the male gaze.[7] Women are thought to claim their sexuality on masculine terms.

This ambiguity embodied in Jamaican dance hall culture emphasizes the constraints posed by and for female constructions of heterosexuality and some of the limitations to claiming all transgressions as resistances or rebellions. A similar theme runs through other cultural analyses of women's public dance and music performances. Questioning whether the explicit sexual gyrations ("wining") of female players in the Trinidadian carnival signifies women's sexual independence, as is claimed and applauded by some male observers, Natasha Barnes concludes that this revelry and celebration by women during the carnival must be read in different ways: that the performances at once produce an image of the sexually liberated woman and reaffirm the deeply heterosexist character of gender relations in this Caribbean society. Barnes notes that "by re-enacting and embodying patriarchal stereotypes that depict women as sexually available, women consent to, rather than critique their own subjugation." She adds that where women's sexual self-representation as free and uninhibited is linked to economic and status benefits, such "individual attempts at self-commodification are never truly emancipatory, because they cannot ultimately transform capitalist practices."[8]

Such reflections on women's sexual agency signal some of the contradictions embedded in analyses of cultural praxis. They raise questions about whether heterosexuality is always and already oppressive to women, and whether it is possible for women to express heterosexual subjectivity and desire without confirming the male gaze. Are, for example, Caribbean women simply "buying into" their own oppression when they claim heterosexual agency, or is it possible to ask whether we can imagine a heterosexuality that can be free of the existing norms, constraints, and boundaries? These analyses also raise questions about the relationship between sexual resistance strategies and struggles against hegemonic racial and economic orders. Is the transformation of capitalism, for example, as Barnes suggests, a precondition for women's sexual liberation? Or it is possible to conceive that sexual freedom may be an integral part of broader liberation struggles?

Caribbean Indian women's sexuality is one of the few arenas that takes heterosexuality as a site of rebellion. In an analysis of colonial constructions and national discourses that locate indentured Indian women as "harlots of Empire," Tejaswini Niranjana observes that the specific constructions of Indian womanhood opened up different possibilities of self-representation for generations of East Indian women. Women's contemporary involvement in *chutney soca*, she argues, while facing a patriarchal backlash from the middle-class and elite Indian community, provides a space for women's self-assertion, while signaling "patriarchy in crisis."[9] Rawwida Baksh-Soodeen is one of the few Caribbean feminists who claims sexuality as a site of revolutionary action. In her analysis of women's ritual dancing practices during the *maticore* and *laawa* ceremonies of Trinidad Hindu weddings that center on "a portrayal of the man-woman sexual act through folk dance," she writes that it is "here that the sexual education of Hindu girls begins" and that it is here that among women "open discussions about sexuality" take place.[10] She observes that these ceremonies are some of the spaces within Hinduism for Indian women (primarily working class) to express their sexuality freely, without fear of rebukes from or control by the men in their lives. Moreover, she argues, while the dancing could be simply dismissed as a form of wining, as represented in the Afro-Caribbean constructed carnival performances, it cannot be reduced to this, for it contains very specific elements that are lodged in Indian history, movements, and rhythms and that extend into the public sphere through chutney music. Wider societal attempts to police the "lewd" and "vulgar" expressions of female sexuality in chutney music are, she concludes, a hysterical response to the growing independence of Indian women. Instead, at chutney festivals women "state emphatically that 'my body and sexuality belong to me, and nobody (not my man, father, brother, son or the larger community) has the power to prevent my expression through dance.'"[11] Defining this expression as "revolutionary" "(and yes, it is revolutionary since it challenges one of the most fundamental forms of control of Indian women by Indian men),"[12] the case is made for an appreciation of women's heterosexuality that is fiercely resistant and publicly oppositional to male control and domination, powerful, and a source of change in its own right.

Baksh-Soodeen's writings are the most explicit we can find in Caribbean studies about the ways in which alternative understandings are produced through women's heterosexual agency. However, similar ideas pulse through recent studies of "unruly and disorderly women," which describe instances of female sexual agency and self-determination that subvert women-oppressive constructions of heterosexuality.[13] The *Pisenlit*—the figure of the "unruly woman" played during the nineteenth-century carnival in Trinidad—that coincides with the image of the *jamet* woman (lower-class "loose" woman) is one example that is posited as a challenge to the hegemonic sexual and gendered order.[14] Due to harsh discriminatory and stigmatizing treatment of *jamet* women, the carnival figure of the *Pisenlit* was "protesting the state's derogatory image of Afro-Creole women and the related violations of their very private aspects of their lives— blood, internal examinations and sex" and is viewed as a celebration of such women's "self-protection, reclamation and survival."[15] Together with the Stickfighter—the cross-dressing "warrior" woman who was evident in the same period—it is argued that such manifestations are also representations of Afro-Trinidadian women's solidarity, agency, and subjectivity that collectively and consistently "protested against injustice and inequality."[16]

Toward New Knowledge about Caribbean Sexuality

Sexual agency in the Caribbean is significant for exploring alternate frames and possibilities for transforming sexual relations, identities, and desires in the Caribbean. Building upon the premise that dominated groups develop their own situated knowledge from experiences of domination, and that "the experience of domination may provide the possibility of important new understandings of social life,"[17] alternate, counterhegemonic understandings, perspectives, and visions about sexuality are made visible in the region. As Hartsock states about situated knowledges:

[T]he extent that these knowledges become self-conscious about their assumptions, they make available new epistemological options. The struggles they represent and express, if made self-conscious, can go beyond efforts at survival in order to recognize the centrality of systematic power relations. They can become knowledges that are accountable and engaged.[18]

The extent that sexuality is the material for social and political action and produces specific consciousness and knowledge needs to be taken into account. While everyday practices may embody or be read as resistance, it is the collectivized and organized struggles by sexual agents that more readily reveal self-conscious efforts to address systematic relations of power, and it is through the articulations of collectives that organize around sexuality in the Caribbean that new knowledge and counterdiscourses become visible. The politics of sex worker organizations in the Caribbean allow us access to some of that alternative knowledge.[19] The sex worker movement illustrates a resistance, indeed an organized rebellion, that does not require from us a subtextual reading or reinterpretation of historical documents or studies, as it is public, collective, visible, loud, contemporary, and articulate, and likely to grow stronger (and more diverse) in the coming decades.

Sex Worker Politics

From the mid-1990s to the present day, Caribbean sex workers have stood at the forefront in the organized rejection of the hegemonic construction of female sexuality, and in claiming a politics of female sexual agency and self-determination. The self-organizations, such as the Stichting Maxi Linder Association (SMLA) in Suriname and MODEMU (*Movimiento de Mujeres Unidas*—the Movement of United Women) in the Dominican Republic, as described in chapter seven, emerged through public health concerns and the identification of sex workers as "vectors of disease" and a "risk group." The organizations embody a politics of working Caribbean women that contests specific hegemonic images of racialized, class-based sexualities and represents not just strategies of individual women, but collective struggles and identifications that are shared, materialized in everyday practices and activities of many women, and embodied in flesh and blood.

The organizations champion the empowerment and rights of sex workers in different cultural and linguistic territories in the Caribbean. They demand that the states meet the specific needs of their populations, and they organize to fight against a politics of stigmatization, stereotyping, blame, and surveillance. Even though the organizations continue to prioritize health education among their constituencies, they also organize to address a far broader range of issues. The most prominent are the laws that push women who are engaged in sexual-economic transactions into criminality and that sustain stigmas, discriminations, and prejudices against women who transgress the hegemonic notion of "decent" female sexual behavior and identity. In their activities, these organizations are a political voice for making sexuality a national and regional issue.

Examples of the public/political activities are varied. For instance, the theater group Avancemos, designed by the messenger-of-health sex worker peer educators in the Dominican Republic, performs and holds training sessions in sex work venues for workers, customers, and sex business owners about safe sex practices. A newsletter *La Nueva Historia: Periodico de la Noche*—a bulletin created by and directed at Dominican sex workers—is published monthly by COIN (Centro de Orientación e Investigación Integral), with approximately 5,000 bulletins distributed monthly in different parts of the country. Moreover, in May 1995 the first congress on prostitution and sex work in the Dominican Republic was held. The aim of the congress was to make the Dominican state and society attentive to the economic and social conditions that determine prostitution or sex work, and to the diversity of issues affecting women that practice the trade.[20] The sex workers' organization MODEMU, which was officially born out of the congress, placed its primary focus on raising political consciousness in the Dominican Republic about the situation in the country that pushes women and girls into sex work. Murray reports that "they affirm that the weak Dominican economy combined with the culture that heavily favors men and allows for their sexual promiscuity, creates an atmosphere where sex work is one of the few job options for poor women, and needs to be respected as work."[21] MODEMU continues to publicize its position and analysis and is active in the public arena in the fight against the marginalization and discrimination of sex workers in the country.[22] It also continues to conduct outreach in various sex work sites—in both the capital and tourist resorts—trying to organize and mobilize women to stand up for their human, social, and workers' rights.

Combining research, empowerment work, and political consciousness raising, the Maxi Linder Association in Suriname has also been active on many fronts. The organization proudly named itself after one of Suriname's most prominent prostitutes—Maxi Linder—not to simply state its focus on prostitution, but to publicly declare its identification with and support for women in sex work. Its goals are to "optimize the social, economic, mental and physical health and well-being of female commercial sex workers in Suriname" through "providing education, information, and skills training, support and advice on social, legal, and health matters; raising social awareness, and encouraging a positive self-image and solidarity, and offering protection against violence and abuse."[23] The organization also attempts to provide alternative job training and schooling for women who desire to leave the sex trade, as well as a safe haven for those who stay within it. Since 1994 the organization resides in a large downtown building that functions as a center for various workshops and training, child day care, health care consultations, and counseling for sex workers, as well as a drop-in center. In 1998 the organization secured a piece of land from the government outside of the city where women attached to the organization could grow garden vegetables for either their own consumption or sale. Other self-supporting and income-generating activities, such as making handicrafts and sewing, have been introduced, in order to create other economic options apart from sex work. Sex workers have also trained as peer educators and researchers, and undertake paid outreach work and research among female, male, and transgender sex workers on the streets, in brothels, bars, and clubs, and in gold mining areas. Following a harm reduction model, SMLA campaigns for the destigmatization and regulation of sex work "in order to reduce the vulnerability and lack of rights of women working in the sector and to ensure access to health care, social services and insurance."[24] The organization has furthermore participated in a number of regional initiatives, among them the 1996 project on trafficking in women in Latin America and the Caribbean, spearheaded by the Global Alliance in Trafficking in Women, and in follow-up workshops designed to develop guidelines for nongovernmental organizations for addressing the issue of trafficking regionally and in their own home territories.[25] Members of the organization also participated in the 1997–1998 regional study of the Caribbean sex trade, with the specific aim of researching and conducting outreach work among sex workers in the gold mining areas of Suriname, producing some of the first insights in the Caribbean into this phenomenon.[26] In 1996, it produced an educational video about the organization and its goals, emphasizing health care and HIV/AIDS prevention. More recently, it has expanded its reach to include sex workers of different ethnic groups, other than Afro-Surinamese women, as well as male and transgender sex workers. It is an organization that works publicly and confidently, advocating women's sexual rights and demanding public accountability for social conditions that make prostitution a reality and a danger for many women and men.

Both organizations insist upon bringing prostitution out of the dark and making sexual-economic relationships a public issue, while at the same time exposing male privilege and dominance and the oppression of Caribbean working women.[27] In so doing, they also articulate a particular definition of working-class Caribbean female sexuality. That the women are predominantly African Caribbean and from the poor and working classes also indicates a fierce articulation of black working-class female sexuality in the region, although the politics should not be considered exclusive to this racial group—women of mixed and Indo-Caribbean descent also participate in sex work and in sex worker organizations. Sexuality, through these organizations, is constituted as profoundly and intimately connected to economic transactions and income-generating processes. It claims to be promiscuous and polygamous if it desires, heterosexual without being oppressed, bi-, trans-, or same-gendered, and racially proud in its blackness or brownness. This sexuality demands to be appreciated as proactive and public, respected even when not tied to procreation, and controlled by women themselves.

The explicit and unapologetic connections that are made between sexuality and work and sexuality and the economy in sex worker politics have implications for a wider politics of sexuality. The claiming of "sex work" in the region embeds racialized sexuality into the economy as a long-standing practice that shapes and sustains the household, family, and nation, and as a viable means for self-employment. However, in situations where self-generated economic activity is the norm for women (such as involvement in informal commercial trading, marketing, domestic work, etc.), and in contexts where economic self-determination is a wider social and political goal, self-employment does not automatically translate into women's control over their sexuality or to sexual resistance. As we have seen in the previous chapters, self-employed sex work runs the gamut between practices that are highly exploitative (i.e., where a woman, out of desperation, sells sex on the streets for the price of daily bread) and situations where young lower- and middle-class women and men deliberately engage in transactional sexual-economic relationships to acquire a cell phone, to be invited for a drive in a flashy car, to travel to the United States or Western Europe, or to find a friend or marriage partner. However, self-employed sex work is the foundation for an explicit articulation by working women of their control over their own sexuality in its economic manifestations, constituting an important dimension of sex worker politics in the region. Being driven simply by necessity and need into self-employed sex work can be a survival strategy. Claiming a right to be engaged in sex work is a political stance, where prostitution or transactional sex is equated with other incoming-generating activities, such as trading, domestic work, or tourism service work, laying the basis for collective action and strategies of resistance.

Putting sexuality, as defined through everyday Caribbean practice, on the public agenda, as the sex worker organizations and initiatives do, makes not just prostitution, but broader sexual-economic relations in the region visible, for it speaks not only about overt transactions but also about the ways in which sexualities have been fashioned and refashioned through very particularly social, political, and cultural histories that began with the emergence of global capitalism. The politics is representative of a far wider experience of sexuality that has been deeply structured in Caribbean life, as a modus vivendi for many people. The experience of sex work or transactional sex is, as I have argued throughout this book, sedimented in everyday practices, people's psyches, and institutions in the forms of concubinage, prostitution, "the outside woman," visiting unions, sponsoring, sex tourism, and possibly (although weakly explored here) marriage. It is not an isolated experience of a few unruly, indecent, or loose women, but rather is an integral part of social patterns of sexuality. Sexual-economic transactions, as we have seen, exist in various arrangements and as a lived reality for large sections of Caribbean populations, not just for the few who claim a sex worker identity and politics. The image of female heterosexuality that is projected through sex worker politics exposes the double standard around male and female sexuality that shrouds the region, where men are encouraged to be promiscuous and women faithful. The image claims the right for women to exercise their sexuality in multiple relationships, outside the bounds of marriage bonds and dominant, restricting notions of love or romance. This claim of sexuality also redefines intimacy as not inherently tied to penetrative sexual intercourse but as attached to other parts of the body and acts, where the traditional "vanilla" or missionary-like heterosexual act is not necessarily the ultimate expression of pleasure, sexual desire, or love. As with many (although certainly not all) sex workers around the world, Caribbean women and men involved in explicit sexual-economic transactions do not necessarily define the absence of love in sexual intercourse as the root of the problem, nor do they always experience sex acts in the absence of intimacy as a violation of their human rights. Rather, organized Caribbean sex workers tend to identify the problems they encounter as lodged in the harsh economic conditions of their countries, laws that criminalize their lives, stigmas and prejudices that they and their children endure, and the violence and harassment they face from the state (i.e., police and immigration laws). These are defined as key oppressive elements. The extensive misogyny and violent tendencies of some of their male clients, dishonesty and corruption of "managers" and "boyfriends," and links between the global sex trade and underground criminal activity are also of primary concern. Furthermore, the discrimination sex workers face from health and social workers, the constant worry about contract-ing STIs from clients, and the often unhygenic conditions in which they work, compound the problems they face on a day-to-day basis.

It has been argued that a separation between sex and intimacy sig-nals alienation and degradation under capitalism and a dehumaniza-tion of women, and that this is one of the areas that makes sex work unlike other forms of labor. Yet, in the light of sex worker claims and definitions as described in this study, we must wonder whether such a universal claim about sexuality is helpful for thinking about sexuality and intimacy in the Caribbean, or for attempting to transform Caribbean sexual relations in the region. Sex work, as described here and as articulated through Caribbean sex worker organizations, is a response to intense exploitations, oppressions, discriminations, and violations that have been visited upon women in a world dominated by money, capitalist profit making, racialized desires, and masculine definitions and needs. Within this context, it also offers some alter-natives to participate in local, regional, and transnational economies and global patterns of consumption. Caribbean sex worker politics is then a rebellion against the hypocrisy and double standards that sur-round working women's lives and activities—an attempt not for the sake of claiming an identity, but for bringing to light and visibility a part of Caribbean life upon which family, nation, and development are constructed. Denial of this social reality and efforts to quash such expression serve to reinforce existing patterns of Caribbean heteropa-triarchy where the sexuality of poor black and brown women is disci-plined, policed, and kept within parameters defined by the state, the Church, and the elite, yet profoundly relied upon to service "naturally" promiscuous men and to prop up various national industries.

Futures

So where does this lead us? What does the resistance and rebellion of sexuality, which is making its presence felt through sex worker orga-nizations and which is insisting upon a public space and voice to name itself, say for the future? Will it transform broader meanings of sexuality in the Caribbean? Can this rebellion of sexuality aid in the abolition of sexual violence, exploitation, and poverty? Or does it serve to inflict more pain and humiliation upon poor women of color? There are many dimensions that remain open here and that argue against a predictable outcome. I have sought, however, to show in this study that the Caribbean has a long history of the commodification of sexuality under capitalist, heteropatriarchal relations of power that is deeply implicated with racialized processes and hierarchies. I have also argued that the conscious employment of sexuality has a long history, as an avenue of freedom from slavery and independence from control of the master, as an alternative to the constraining and constrictive elitist European-derived, Creolized, and indigenized nationalist models of marriage and the family, as a subversion or transgression of hegemonic masculine definitions of female sexuality, and as a way to participate in a globalized, transnationally connected world. Sexuality, as we have seen, is the cornerstone of gendered identities, household arrangements, and nation building, and is fundamentally connected to development enterprises, such as the tourism and gold mining industries, as well as to the informal trade of goods and commercial products. It is at once constraining and enabling, oppressive and liberatory. Yet, should sexuality continue to be kept in the dark, in the subterraneous cultures of dance hall or chutney soca, in brothels and nightclubs and bedrooms, or only be allowed on display once a year during carnival? Must it continually be oppressed by master narratives and arrangements that worship monogamy, heterosexism, and patriarchy? What if we were to embrace and appreciate Caribbean sexuality in its various and diverse configurations, and redefine Caribbean sexuality according to praxis?

Any answer to such questions must take on critical issues about the future of broader Caribbean social, political, and economic developments and the possibilities for people in the region to exercise control over their own intellectual, social, and economic resources. The Caribbean has for so long been dominated by and made reliant upon global capitalist interests, and the region's nation-states so heavily conditioned by the world system, that it is commonly accepted that massive decomposition and restructuring of the region must take place in order for there to be a change.[28] Where sexuality figures into this future scenario remains a question. Let it suffice to say, sexual resistance and rebellions may force a broader recognition of sexuality as linked to the global/local political economy, and as a potentially transformational dimension of the region. Experiences and struggles of sex workers, and those of other marginalized racially sexed bodies and subjectivities in the region, could then help to move the Caribbean forward.

Notes

Chapter 1: Introduction: Thinking about the Caribbean

1. Jose Piedra, "Loving Columbus," in *Amerindian Images and the Legacy of Columbus*, vol. 9, *Hispanic Issues*, ed. Rene Jara and Nicholas Spadaccini (Minneapolis: University of Minnesota Press, 1992), 252.
2. Frantz Fanon, *Black Skin, White Masks*, trans. Charles Lam Markmann (New York: Grove Press, 1967).
3. Piedra, "Loving Columbus," 252.
4. Stuart Hall, for example, claims the Caribbean as "the first, the original and the purest diaspora." See Stuart Hall, "Negotiating Caribbean Identities," in *New Caribbean Thought*, ed. Brian Meeks and Folke Lindahl (Kingston: University of the West Indies Press, 2001), 28. The region has also been theorized as the quintessential expression of Creolization. For a recent review and critique of the notion of the Caribbean as master symbol of Creole society, see Aisha Khan, "Journey to the Center of the Earth: The Caribbean as Master Symbol," *Cultural Anthropology* 16, no. 3 (2001), 271–302.
5. It is the crucible for an articulate anticolonial and antiracist political consciousness, visible in the life and works of such people and movements as the Maroons, Marcus Garvey and the UNIA, C. L. R. James, Frantz Fanon, Aime Cesaire, Rastafari, Walter Rodney, and Sistren.
6. Norman Girvan, "Reinterpreting the Caribbean," in *New Caribbean Thought*, ed. Brian Meeks and Folke Lindahl (Kingston: University of the West Indies Press, 2001), 3–23.

7.   See, for example, Patricia Mohammed, "Towards Indigenous Feminist Theorizing in the Caribbean," *Feminist Review* 59 (1998), 22–48.

8.   Hall, "Negotiating Caribbean Identities."

9.   See Edward K. Braithwaite, *The Development of Creole Society in Jamaica, 1770–1820* (Oxford: Clarendon Press, 1971).

10.   Jean-Pierre Jean, "The 10th Department," *NACLA Report on the Americas*, January/February 1994.

11.   I wholeheartedly concur with Murray, who, in speaking about Martinique, notes, "There is too much diversity of individual experience and too many intersections of discourses produced elsewhere—America, the rest of the Caribbean, Europe, Africa . . . to be able to claim that any singular cultural foundation or 'ethos' exists." See David A. B. Murray, *Opacity: Gender, Sexuality, Race, and the 'Problem' of Identity in Martinique* (New York: Peter Lang, 2002).

12.   This concept was made significant for the region by M. Jacqui Alexander in "Erotic Autonomy as a Politics of Decolonization: An Anatomy of Feminist and State Practice in the Bahamas Tourist Economy," in *Feminist Genealogies, Colonial Legacies, Democratic Futures*, ed. M. Jacqui Alexander and Chandra Talpade Mohanty (New York: Routledge, 1997), 63–100.

13.   See, for example, Brackette Williams, *Stains on My Name, War in My Veins: Guyana and the Politics of Cultural Struggle* (Durham, NC: Duke University Press, 1991); Aisha Khan, "What Is 'a Spanish'? Ambiguity and 'Mixed' Ethnicity in Trinidad," in *Trinidad Ethnicity*, ed. Kevin A. Yelvington (Knoxville: University of Tennesee Press, 1993), 180–207; Rhoda Reddock, "Douglarization and the Politics of Gender in Trinidad and Tobago," in *Contemporary Issues in Social Science: A Caribbean Perspective*, ed. D. Deosaran, R. Reddock, and N. Mustapha (St. Augustine: University of the West Indies, Department of Sociology, 1994. Reprinted in C. Barrow & R. Reddock *Caribbean Sociology: Introductory Readings* Kingston: Ian Randle Publishers, 2001, 320–333.); David Howard, *Coloring the Nation: Race and Ethnicity in the Dominican Republic* (Boulder: Lynne Rienner Publishers; Oxford: Signal Books, 2001); Claudette M. Williams, *Charcoal and Cinnamon: The Politics of Color in Spanish Caribbean Literature* (Gainesville: University Press of Florida, 2001).

14.   See Pierre Bourdieu, *Outline of a Theory of Practice* (Cambridge: Cambridge University Press, 1977); Pierre Bourdieu, "First Lecture: Social Space and Symbolic Space: Introduction to Japanese Reading of Distinction," *Poetics Today*, no. 14 (1991), 627–653; and Lois J. D. Wacquant, "Toward a Social Praxeology: The Structure and Logic of Bourdieu's Sociology," in *An Invitation to Reflexive Sociology*, ed. Lois J. D. Wacquant (Chicago: University of Chicago Press, 1992), 1–59.

15.   Bourdieu, *Outline of a Theory of Practice*, 3.

16.   Mohanty argues that Third World feminism is, in part, constituted through "the common context of struggle against racist, sexist and imperialist structures." See Chandra Talpade Mohanty, "Cartographies of Struggle: Third World Women and the Politics of Feminism,"

in *Third World Women and the Politics of Feminism*, ed. Chandra Talpade Mohanty, Ann Russo, and Lourdes Torres (Bloomington: Indiana University Press, 1991), 7. Or as Bannerji writes: "we non-white women who seek not only to express but to end our oppression need reliable knowledge which allows us to be actors in history. This knowledge cannot be produced in the context of ruling but only in conscious resistance to it. It must retain the integrity of our concrete subject positions within its very project and its present day method of investigation, in so far as it searches the history and social relations to trace the reasons for and forms of our oppression." See Himani Bannerji, "But Who Speaks for Us? Experience and Agency in Conventional Feminist Paradigms," in *Unsettling Relations: The University as a Site of Feminist Struggles*, ed. Himani Bannerji et al. (Boston: South End Press, 1992), 93.

17. See Kamala Kempadoo, "Exotic Colonies: Caribbean Women in the Dutch Sex Trade" (Ph.D. diss., University of Colorado, 1994).

18. This resulted in a book I co-wrote and edited with sex worker rights' activist Jo Doezema: *Global Sex Workers: Rights, Resistance, and Redefinition*, (New York: Routledge, 1998).

19. The steering committee was composed of myself, Gladys Acosta Vargas (ILSA), who was replaced by Cynthia Mellon, Jacquie Burgess of CAFRA, and Elena Diaz of FLACSO–Cuba. The main researchers were Christel Antonius-Smits and the Maxi Linder Association (Suriname), Shirley Campbell, Althea Perkins and Patricia Mohammed (Jamaica), Amalia L. Cabezas (the Dominican Republic), Joan Phillips (Barbados), Laura Mayorga and Pilar Velasquez (Colombia), Kathleen Ragsdale and Jessica Anders (Belize), and Jacqueline Martis (the Netherlands Antilles). The project also involved, among others, Yamila Azize Vargas of the Gender Studies Program at the University of Puerto Rico; Francisca Ferreira and Ana Jimenez of COIN and Martha Guzman of MODEMU in the Dominican Republic; Dusilley Cannings in Guyana; Juanita Altenberg, Teersa Burleson, and Tania Codrington of the Stichting Maxi Linder Association in Suriname; Michelle de la Rosa of Kamaria in Puerto Rico; Sulma Manco of Cormujer in Colombia; Karen de Souza, Cora Belle, Shirley Goodman, Halima Khan, Chandra Persaud, and Vanessa Ross of the Red Thread Women's Development Programme in Guyana; and Imani Tafari-Ama, who worked with the Center for Gender and Development Studies at the University of the West Indies at Mona, Jamaica, to make the conference possible.

20. Kamala Kempadoo and Cynthia Mellon, "The Sex Trade in the Caribbean" (Boulder: University of Colorado, CAFRA and ILSA, 1998); Kamala Kempadoo, ed., *Sun, Sex, and Gold: Tourism and Sex Work in the Caribbean* (Lanham: Rowman and Littlefield, 1999). Additional chapters to the original research project results were contributed by Julia O'Connell Davidson and Jacqueline Sanchez Taylor; Beverly Mullings and Nadine Fernandez.

21.   In Spring 2001, I supervised research by an American exchange
        student, Giovanna Torchio, on sex tourism in Jamaica. Giovanna
        subsequently developed her research into an Honors thesis at Con-
        necticut College, focusing on female sex tourists. During Giovanna's
        fieldwork stay in Negril, I joined her and carried out informal inter-
        views and observations among Rastas and rentals and with man-
        agers, entertainment coordinators, and visitors at the resort
        Hedonism. This research complemented other periods of observa-
        tions I had conducted at Negril and Montego Bay between October
        2000 and July 2001. I am also particularly grateful to Anne Marie
        Campbell and Peggy Campbell, who at the time were conducting
        research on HIV/AIDS and sex work in Jamaica through the
        Ministry of Health, and Pauline Pennant of FAMPLAN Jamaica
        for openly discussing their work with me.
22.   See Kamala Kempadoo, "Adolescent Sex: A Study in Three Commu-
        nities in Jamaica" (Kingston: UNICEF and UNFPA, Jamaica, 2001).

Chapter 2: Past Studies, New Directions: Constructions and Reconstructions of Caribbean Sexuality

1.   Christine Barrow, *Family in the Caribbean: Themes and Perspectives*
       (Kingston: Ian Randle; Oxford: James Currey, 1996).
2.   Ibid.; Also Raymond T. Smith, *The Matrifocal Family: Power,
       Pluralism and Politics* (New York: Routledge, 1996).
3.   Frazier, for example, argued that "when the Negro was liberated from
       the customary and traditional forms of control, individual impulses
       were released. Theft and licentiousness . . . were the natural conse-
       quences of this crisis . . . . Even in those cases where the family disci-
       pline had been well established, the lack of authority on the part of
       the master to enforce obedience to the husband's or parents' will
       meant a breakdown of family life." Frazier, E. Franklin, *The Negro
       Family in Chicago* (Chicago: University of Chicago Press, 1932),
       32–33. Frazier's work supported a broader movement in both the
       United States and Britain that sought to address "the Negro problem"
       both at home and in the colonies. In the British Caribbean, the
       Moyne Commission (the West India Royal Commission of
       1938–1939) collected information about "mating" and family life
       among working-class Afro-Caribbean people in order to identify the
       problems and to construct social polices and programs. The work of
       the commission highlighted the Afro-Caribbean family and sexuality
       as socially deviant and immoral and prompted the development of var-
       ious policies and interventions to integrate "lower-class Negroes" into
       "proper" family and sexual habits. The Mass Marriage Movement in
       Jamaica that was initiated in response to the Moyne Commission's

demand for "an organized campaign against the social, moral and economic evils of promiscuity" was a striking example of a localized attempt to inculcate and institutionalize these dominant ideas, and to regulate Afro-Caribbean sexual behavior. For an extensive discussion, see Barrow, *Family in the Caribbean*, Part I, 3–240.

4.   This includes Melville J. Herskovits, *Rebel Destiny: Among the Bush Negroes of Dutch Guiana* (New York: McGraw-Hill, 1934); Melville J. Herskovits, *Suriname Folk-Lore* (New York: Columbia University Press, 1936); Melville J. Herskovits, *Life in a Haitian Village* (New York: Octagon Books, 1964 [ca. 1937]); Melville J. Herskovits and Frances S. Herskovits, *Trinidad Village* (New York: Alfred A. Knopf, 1947); and Melville J. Herskovits, *The Myth of the Negro Past* (Boston: Beacon Press, 1958).

5.   Keeping relations, also known as "visiting relations" in other Caribbean family studies, is used to describe a steady relationship between two adults yet where the partners live in separate households. The women-only households are often composed of several generations of related women and have also been termed "grandmother households."

6.   Herskovits and Herskovits, *Trinidad Village*, 6.

7.   These include but are not limited to Fernando Henriques, *Family and Color in Jamaica* (London: Eyre and Spottiswoode, 1953); Fernando Henriques, *Prostitution and Society: Primitive, Classical and Oriental*, vol. I (London: MacGibbon and Kee, 1962); Fernando Henriques, *Prostitution in Europe and the New World*, vol. II (London: MacGibbon and Kee, 1963); and Fernando Henriques, *Children of Caliban: Miscegenation* (London: Secker and Warburg, 1974).

8.   See, for example, Raymond T. Smith, *The Negro Family in British Guiana: Family Structure and Social Status in the Villages* (London: Routledge and Kegan Paul, in association with the Institute of Social and Economic Research, University College of the West Indies, Jamaica, 1956); M. G. Smith, *West Indian Family Structure* (Seattle: University of Washington Press, 1962); Smith, *The Matrifocal Family*; Henriques, *Family and Color in Jamaica*; Edith Clarke, *My Mother Who Fathered Me: A Study of the Families in Three Selected Communities of Jamaica* (Kingston: University Press of the West Indies, 1999 [ca. 1957]).

9.   Henriques, *Family and Color in Jamaica*.

10.   Henriques, *Prostitution and Society*, 419.

11.   Smith, *West Indian Family Structure*, 255.

12.   Ibid., 254.

13.   Ibid.

14.   Linden Lewis, "Nationalism and Caribbean Masculinity," in *Gender Ironies of Nationalism*, ed. Tamar Mayer (New York: Routledge, 2000), 274.

15.   Errol Miller, *Men at Risk* (Kingston: Jamaica Publishing House, 1991).

16.   For an extensive discussion of Miller's male marginalization thesis, see Keisha Lindsay, "Is the Caribbean Male an Endangered

Species?" in *Gendered Realities: Essays in Caribbean Feminist Thought*, ed. Patricia Mohammed (Kingston: University of the West Indies Press, 2002), 56–82.

17.   Graham Dann, *The Barbadian Male: Sexual Attitudes and Practice* (London: Macmillan Caribbean, 1987), 1.

18.   Ibid., 3.

19.   Including Barry Chevannes, "Sexual Attitudes and Behavior of Jamaican Men" (Kingston: Jamaican Family Planning Association, 1986); Claudia Chambers and Barry Chevannes, "Report on Six Focus Group Discussions: Sexual Decision-Making Project" (Kingston: ISER-UCLA, University of the West Indies, 1994); Barry Chevannes, "Sexual Behavior of Jamaicans: A Literature Review," *Social and Economic Studies* 42, no. 1 (1993), 1–45; Janet Brown and Barry Chevannes, "'Why Man Stay So': Tie the Heifer, Loose the Bull. An Examination of Gender Socialization in the Caribbean" (Kingston: University of the West Indies, 1998); Barry Chevannes and Herbert Gayle, "Adolescent and Young Male Sexual and Reproductive Health Study, Jamaica: Report to the Pan American Health Organization" (Kingston: University of the West Indies, 2000); Barry Chevannes, *Learning to Be a Man: Culture, Socialization and Gender Identity in Five Caribbean Communities* (Kingston: The University of the West Indies Press, 2001).

20.   Chevannes, *Learning to Be a Man*, 216–17.

21.   Ibid.

22.   Clarke, *My Mother Who Fathered Me*, 72.

23.   Ibid.

24.   Ibid., 66.

25.   Olive Senior, *Working Miracles: Women's Lives in the English-Speaking Caribbean* (Cave Hill: ISER; London: James Currey; Bloomington: Indiana Press, 1991).

26.   Ibid.

27.   Ibid., 178.

28.   Barrow, *Family in the Caribbean*, 181.

29.   Patricia Mohammed and Althea Perkins, *Caribbean Women at the Crossroads: The Paradox of Motherhood among Women of Barbados, St. Lucia and Dominica* (Kingston: Canoe Press, University of the West Indies, 1999), 110–11.

30.   Eudine Barriteau, *The Political Economy of Gender in the Twentieth Century Caribbean* (New York: Palgrave, 2001), 26.

31.   See, for example, Chevannes, *Learning to Be a Man*, 14.

32.   Linda Peake and Alissa D. Trotz, *Gender, Ethnicity and Place: Women and Identities in Guyana*, Routledge Studies in Development and Society (New York: Routledge, 1999), 127.

33.   Patricia Mohammed, "A Symbiotic Visiting Relationship: Caribbean Feminist Historiography and Caribbean Feminist Theory," in *Confronting Power, Theorizing Gender: Interdisciplinary Perspectives in the Caribbean*, ed. Eudine Barriteau (Cave Hill: University of the West Indies Press, 2003), 101–125. See also Rhoda Reddock,

Women, Labor and Politics in Trinidad and Tobago (London: Zed Books, 1994).

34. Barriteau, *The Political Economy of Gender in the Twentieth Century Caribbean*, 26.

35. Butler, Judith *Bodies That Matter: On the Discursive Limits of Sex*. (New York: Routledge, 1993), 238.

36. Patricia Mohammed, "Writing Gender into History: The Negotiation of Gender Relations among Indian Men and Women in Post-Indenture Trinidad Society 1917–47," in *Engendering History: Caribbean Women in Historical Perspective*, ed. Verene A. Shepherd, Bridget Brereton, and Barbara Bailey (New York: St. Martin's Press, 1995), 25.

37. See, for example, Gayle Rubin, "Thinking Sex: Notes for a Radical Theory of the Politics of Sexuality," in *Pleasure and Danger: Exploring Female Sexuality*, ed. Carol S. Vance (London: Pandora Press, 1988), 267–319.

38. Mohammed, "Writing Gender into History," 25.

39. Evelyn M. Hammonds, "Toward a Genealogy of Black Female Sexuality: The Problematic of Silence," in *Feminist Genealogies, Colonial Legacies, Democratic Futures*, ed. M. Jacqui Alexander and Chandra Talpade Mohanty (New York: Routledge, 1997), 177.

40. Gloria Wekker, "'I Am Gold Money' (I Pass through All Hands, but I Do Not Lose My Value): The Construction of Selves, Gender and Sexualities in a Female, Working Class, Afro-Surinamese Setting" (Ph.D. diss., University of California, Los Angeles, 1992), 36. For the definition of *mati work*, see also Gloria Wekker, "Of Mimic Men and Unruly Women: Exploring Sexuality and Gender in Surinamese Family Systems" (paper presented at Caribbean Feminisms, University of the West Indies, Cave Hill Campus, 2002).

41. M. Jacqui Alexander, "Redrafting Morality: The Postcolonial State and the Sexual Offences Bill of Trinidad and Tobago," in *Third World Women and the Politics of Feminism*, ed. Chandra Talpade Mohanty, Ann Russo, and Lourdes Torres (Bloomington: Indiana University Press, 1991), 147.

42. Alexander, "Erotic Autonomy as a Politics of Decolonization," 65.

43. See, for example, Antonio E. de Moya and Rafael Garcia, "Three Decades of Male Sex Work in Santo Domingo," in *Men Who Sell Sex: International Perspectives on Male Prostitution and HIV/AIDS*, ed. Peter Aggleton (Philadelphia: Temple University Press, 1999), 127–139; Marvin Leiner, *Sexual Politics in Cuba: Machismo, Homosexuality, and AIDS* (Boulder: Westview Press, 1994); and Ian Lumsden, *Machos, Maricones, and Gays: Cuba and Homosexuality* (Philadelphia: Temple University Press, 1996).

44. Denise E. Brennan, "Everything Is for Sale Here: Sex Tourism in Sosúa, the Dominican Republic" (Ph.D. diss., Yale University, 1998), 81.

45. Kevin A. Yelvington, *Producing Power: Ethnicity, Gender and Class in a Caribbean Workplace* (Philadelphia: Temple University Press, 1995), 26.

46. Peake and Trotz, *Gender, Ethnicity and Place*, 143.

47.   Carole S. Vance, "Pleasure and Danger: Towards a Politics of Sexuality,"
       in *Pleasure and Danger: Exploring Female Sexuality*, ed. Carole S.
       Vance (London: Pandora Press, 1988), 9.

48.   Andrew Parker, Regina Maria Barbosa, and Peter Aggleton, eds.,
       *Framing the Sexual Subject: The Politics of Gender, Sexuality, and
       Power* (Berkeley: University of California Press, 2000), 7–8.

49.   Ibid., 9.

50.   For general discussions of sexuality, race, and colonialism, see Ziaud-
       din Sardar, Ashis Nandy, and Merryl Wyn Davies, *Barbaric Others:
       A Manifesto on Western Racism* (London: Pluto Press, 1993); Anne
       McClintock, *Imperial Leather: Race, Gender and Sexuality in the
       Colonial Contest* (New York: Routledge, 1995); Sander L. Gilman,
       "Black Bodies, White Bodies: Toward an Iconography of Female
       Sexuality in Late Nineteenth-Century Art, Medicine, and Litera-
       ture," in *Race, Writing, and Difference*, ed. Henry Louis Gates Jr.
       (Chicago: University of Chicago Press, 1986), 223–261.

51.   See also T. Denean Sharpley-Whiting, *Black Venus: Sexualized Sav-
       ages, Primal Fears, and Primitive Narratives in French* (Durham, NC:
       Duke University Press, 1999).

52.   F. R. Augier and Shirley C. Gordon, *Sources of West Indian History*
       (London: Longman Caribbean, 1960), 1.

53.   Hulme notes that there are four main sources through which
       Amerindian life has been written: "'first-hand' reports of colonists,
       missionaries and travelers from Columbus onwards, who have writ-
       ten accounts of the native Caribbean inevitably colored by their own
       perceptions and predispositions"; "histories of the European nations
       in the Caribbean which . . . rely on the official documents and reports
       lodged in European archives, where the native cultures tend to exist,
       at best, in the margins"; "a developing but relatively small-scale
       Caribbean archeology"; and "an anthropology which, in the virtual
       absence of native societies to use for comparative purposes, has to
       rely on an interpretation of accounts of the native Caribbean written
       exclusively by Europeans." See Peter Hulme, *Colonial Encounters:
       Europe and the Native Caribbean 1492–1797* (London: Routledge,
       1992), 45–46. See also Ricardo Alegria, "The Study of Aboriginal
       Peoples: Multiple Ways of Knowing," in *The Indigenous People of the
       Caribbean*, ed. Samuel M. Wilson (Gainesville: University Press of
       Florida, 1997), 9–19; and Jara and Spadaccini, *Amerindian Images
       and the Legacy of Columbus*.

54.   There is an ongoing debate about these terms, their etiology, and
       appropriateness for identifying and describing various culture and
       language groups encountered in the Caribbean in the fifteenth and
       sixteenth centuries. See, for example, Louis Allaire, "Visions of
       Cannibals: Distant Islands and Distance Lands in Taino World
       Image," in *The Lesser Antilles in the Age of European Expansion*, ed.
       Robert L. Paquette and Stanley L. Engerman (Gainesville: University
       Press of Florida, 1996), 33–49; and Samuel M. Wilson, ed., *The In-
       digenous People of the Caribbean* (Gainesville: University Press of

Florida, 1997). It appears to be generally accepted that the name *Arawak*, unlike *Carib*, was never a self-ascription but rather a Columbian invention.

55. See Hulme, *Colonial Encounters*; Allaire, "Visions of Cannibals"; Verene A. Shepherd, *Women in Caribbean History: The British Colonised Territories* (Kingston: Ian Randle; Oxford: James Currey; Princeton: Markus Wiener, 1999); Allaire, "Visions of Cannibals," and William F. Keegan, "Columbus Was a Cannibal: Myth and the First Encounters," in Paquette and Engerman, *The Lesser Antilles in the Age of European Expansion*.

56. Comments about the women's activities were sometimes associated with a notion of a lack of femininity. Columbus, for example, in reporting on his first voyage, identified an island, Matinino, which he described as inhabited exclusively by women "in which there is not a man." The women he stated "engage in no feminine occupation, but use bows and arrows of cane . . . and they arm and protect themselves with plates of copper" (The Letter of Columbus, reproduced in Peter Hulme and Neil L. Whitehead, eds., *Wild Majesty: Encounters with Caribs from Columbus to the Present Day* [Oxford: Clarendon Press, 1992], 15). Comments about Amerindian men included "wearing their hair long like women" and sitting around "idle"— talking and drinking, while the women did most of the work. The practice of "couvade"—where men share in the birthing of children through fasting and confinement, sometimes even experiencing labor pains themselves—has been a phenomenon consistently remarked upon by missionaries and anthropologists, presumably because of its striking difference from European masculine behavior (Jacques Meunier and A. M. Savarin, *The Amazonian Chronicles*, trans. Carol Christensen [San Francisco: Mercury House, 1991], 85). See also Shepherd, *Women in Caribbean History* , 11.

57. Jara and Spadaccini, *Amerindian Images and the Legacy of Columbus*, 20–21. Boucher adds that "what good traits Amerindians might possess . . . were snuffed out by Satan-induced vices such as incest, sodomy, adultery and . . . cannibalism." See Philip P. Boucher, *Cannibal Encounters: Europeans and Island Caribs, 1492–1763* (Baltimore: Johns Hopkins University Press, 1992), 27. "Bad" sexual practices were more commonly associated with Caribs, who were a priori constituted in the European imagination as savage, man-eating, "one-eyed dogs," and it is also primarily through discussions and accounts about Island Carib and European contact that images of "transgendered," "third-gendered," and same-sex relations among Amerindians emerge. (See also, Piedra, "Loving Columbus" Trexler, "Sex and Conquest.)

58. See Barbara Bush, *Slave Women in Caribbean Society: 1650–1838* (Bloomington: Indiana University Press, 1990). Also Williams, *Charcoal and Cinnamon*.

59. See Vera M. Kutzinski, *Sugar's Secrets: Race and the Erotics of Cuban Nationalism* (Charlottesville: University Press of Virginia, 1993);

Marietta Morrissey, *Slave Women in the New World: Gender Stratification in the Caribbean* (Lawrence: University Press of Kansas, 1989); Bush, *Slave Women in Caribbean Society*; and Reddock, *Women, Labor and Politics in Trinidad and Tobago*.

60. Morrissey, *Slave Women in the New World*, 147.

61. Hilary Beckles, *Natural Rebels: A Social History of Enslaved Black Women in Barbados* (London: Zed Books, 1989), 141.

62. Henriques notes: "In time no European male in the Caribbean, who could afford it, was without his colored mistress, either a freedwoman or slave" (Henriques, *Prostitution in Europe and the New World*, 195). Bush, Morrissey, and Henriques also point out that this power was not only exerted by the colonial elite and planter class, but extended to include white men of lower classes due to the racial hegemony that existed of white over black. Even the European bond servant, who stood at the margins of white society in an almost comparable position to that of slave, was seen to have "augmented the process of their masters" through engaging in clandestine sexual affairs with slave women, due to the privilege that their whiteness conferred upon them (Henriques, *Prostitution in Europe and the New World*, 201).

63. It needs to be noted that while my attention here is on issues of race, working-class sexualities have been an equally important focus of attention. The prostitute and lesbian were, for example, defined in European nineteenth-century science, art, and medicine as examples of degenerates, whose deviancy was seen to lodge in their genitalia and sexual behaviors. See Gilman, "Black Bodies, White Bodies."

64. Mohanty, "Cartographies of Struggle," 17.

65. Gilman, "Black Bodies, White Bodies," 250.

66. Robert J. C. Young, *Colonial Desire: Hybridity in Theory, Culture and Race* (London: Routledge, 1995), 181.

67. Norman Whitten and Rachel Corr, "Contesting the Images of Oppression: Indigenous Views of Blackness in the Americas," *NACLA Report on the Americas*, May/June 2001, 25.

68. Nevertheless, the positioning of the mestizo/a as a racially more cultured social group in countries such as Cuba, the adherence to the view of a people descended from Indios as opposed to Africans in the Dominican Republic, and the esteem given to Spanish in Trinidad who are claimed to be descendants of both early Spanish invaders and Amerindians on the island suggest that racial/cultural mixing through sexual intercourse between Amerindian and Europeans created a social category that occupied the middle echelons of the racial/civilized hierarchy. For further discussion, see Khan, "What Is 'a Spanish'?"; and Howard, *Coloring the Nation*.

69. Gilman, "Black Bodies, White Bodies," 256.

70. Barbara Bush, *Slave Women in Caribbean Society*; Richard C. Trexler, *Sex and Conquest: Gendered Violence, Political Order, and the European Conquest of the Americas* (Ithaca, N.Y.: Cornell University Press, 1993); Bartolomé de las Casas, *The Devastation of the Indies: A Brief Account*, trans. Herman Briffault (New York: Seabury Press, 1974); Fernando Henriques, *Children of Caliban*.

71. Fanon, *Black Skin, White Masks*, 63.
72. Ibid., 47.
73. Eileen J. Suarez Findlay, *Imposing Decency: The Politics of Sexuality in Puerto Rico, 1870–1920* (Durham, NC: Duke University Press, 1999), 9.
74. See, for example, Edward Said, *Orientalism* (New York: Vintage Books, 1979); Malek Alloula, *The Colonial Harem* (Minneapolis: University of Minnesota Press, 1986); Rana Kabbani, *Europe's Myths of Orient* (London: Pandora Press, 1986); G. S. Rousseau and Roy Porter, eds., *Exoticism in the Enlightenment* (Manchester: Manchester University Press, 1990); Reina Lewis, *Gendering Orientalism: Race, Femininity and Representation* (London: Routledge, 1996); Meyda Yegenoglu, *Colonial Fantasies: Towards a Feminist Reading of Orientalism* (Cambridge: Cambridge University Press, 1998); Micaela di Leonardo, *Exotics at Home: Anthropology, Others, American Modernity* (Chicago: University of Chicago Press, 1998).
75. In Rousseau and Porter, *Exoticism in the Enlightenment*, 6–7.
76. Hulme, *Colonial Encounters*.
77. The case of Sarah (Saartje) Bartmann, known in Europe as the "Hottentot Venus," illustrates the character of white European male perceptions and treatment of African womanhood at the beginning of the nineteenth century. Taken to Europe in 1810 from her South African homeland, Sarah Bartmann was exhibited naked, as a rare and curious object, for five years in various European cities, both in museums and at private parties. "Scientists" and "scholars" were interested in demonstrating the association between skin color, physiology, and sexuality and fixed on the size of her genitalia and buttocks for examination. Her nude body was the source of much excitement and fascination as well as repulsion. Considered a symbol of beauty in several South African communities, in Europe her elongated labia (the "Hottentot Apron") and pronounced buttocks ("Steatopygia") were seen by scientists as proof of the natural, primitive, pathological sexuality of Africans and signifiers of extreme difference between European and Africans. See, for example, Gilman, "Black Bodies, White Bodies"; Sharpley-Whiting, *Black Venus*; and Deborah Willis and Carla Williams, *The Black Female Body: A Photographic History* (Philadelphia: Temple University Press, 2002).
78. Roy Porter, "The Exotic as Erotic: Captain Cook in Tahiti," in Rousseau and Porter, *Exoticism in the Enlightenment*, 118.
79. Sharpley-Whiting, *Black Venus*, 86.
80. Henriques, *Children of Caliban*, 110.
81. Beckles, *Natural Rebels*, 146, in reference to a statement made in 1820 in the British colony of Barbados.
82. J. A. Rogers, *Sex and Race: A History of White, Negro and Indian Miscegenation in the Two Americas: The New World*, 6th ed., vol. III (New York: Helga M. Rogers, 1972), 146.
83. Kutzinski, *Sugar's Secrets*, 75.
84. See Kamala Kempadoo, "'SanDom's' and Other Exotic Women: Prostitution and Race in the Caribbean," *Race and Reason: Journal of the*

Institute for African-American Studies, Columbia University (1996), 48–54; and Patricia Mohammed, "'But Most of All Mi Love Mi Browning': The Emergence in Eighteenth and Nineteenth Century Jamaica of the Mulatto Woman as the Desired," *Feminist Review*, no. 65 (2000), 22–48.

85.   See, for example, Daryl Cumber Dance, "Matriarchs, Doves and Nymphos: Prevalent Images of Black, Indian and White Women in Caribbean Literature," *Studies in Literary Imagination*, no. 26 (1993), 21–31; Ramabai Espinet, "Representation and the Indo-Caribbean Woman in Trinidad and Tobago," in *Indo-Caribbean Resistance*, ed. Frank Birbalsingh (Toronto: TSAR, 1993), 42–61; and Jeremy Poynting, "East Indian Women in the Caribbean: Experience and Voice," in *India in the Caribbean*, ed. David Dabydeen and Brinsley Samaroo (London: Hansib/University of Warwick, 1987), 231–264.

86.   See Basdeo Mangru, "The Sex Ratio Disparity and Its Consequences under the Indenture in British Guiana," in Dabydeen and Samaroo, *India in the Caribbean*, 211–230; Rhoda Reddock, "Freedom Denied: Indian Women and Indentureship in Trinidad and Tobago, 1845–1917," *Economic and Political Weekly*, no. 20 (1985), 79–87; Verene A. Shepherd, "Gender, Migration and Settlement: The Indentureship and Post-Indentureship Experiences of Indian Females in Jamaica, 1845–1943," in Shepherd, Brereton, and Bailey, *Engendering History*, 233–57; and Dale Bisnauth, *The Settlement of Indians in Guyana 1890–1930* (London: Peepal Tree Press, 2000).

87.   Mohammed Orfry, CO 571/4 WI22518 (1916), quoted in Reddock, "Freedom Denied," 84.

88.   Young, *Colonial Desire*, 182.

89.   Bush, *Slave Women in Caribbean Society*; Beckles, *Natural Rebels*.

90.   Alison M. Jaggar and Susan R. Bordo, eds., *Gender/Body/Knowledge* (New Brunswick: Rutgers University Press, 1989), 4.

91.   Margrit Shildrick and Janet Price, "Openings on the Body: a Critical Introduction," in *Feminist Theory and the Body: A Reader*, ed. Janet Price and Margrit Shildrick (New York: Routledge, 1999), 4–5.

92.   See Lynda Birke, "Bodies and Biology," in Price and Schildrick, *Feminist Theory and the Body*, 47. Also see Banu Subramanian, "The Aliens Have Landed! Reflections on the Rhetoric of Biological Invasion," *Meridians* 2, no. 1 (2001): 27.

93.   Birke, "Bodies and Biology," 45.

94.   Sharpley-Whiting, *Black Venus*, 86.

95.   Frederick Engels, *The Origin of the Family, Private Property, and the State* (Peking: Foreign Language Press, 1978 [ca. 1884]).

96.   Eva Illouz, *Consuming the Romantic Utopia: Love and the Cultural Contradictions of Capitalism* (Berkeley: University of California Press, 1997).

97.   Barbara O. de Zalduondo and Jean Maxius Bernard, "Meanings and Consequences of Sexual-Economic Exchange: Gender, Poverty and Sexual Risk Behavior in Urban Haiti," in *Conceiving Sexuality: Approaches to Sex Research in a Postmodern World*, ed. Richard G. Parker and John H. Gagnon (New York: Routledge, 1995), 167.

98. See, for example, Leith L. Dunn, "Jamaica: Situation of Children in Prostitution: A Rapid Assessment" (Geneva: International Labor Organization/International Programme on the Elimination of Child Labor, 2001).
99. Wekker, "I am Gold Money".
100. de Moya and Garcia, "Three Decades of Male Sex Work in Santo Domingo," 152.
101. It was the island of Matinino in the Eastern Caribbean that was claimed by Columbus to be inhabited exclusively by women and that produced the image of the "Wild Woman" or Amazon of the Caribbean. This was a construct for women who defied European gender roles and challenged patriarchy both militarily and sexually. The Amazons of the Eastern Caribbean are said to have ventured off their island once a year, demanding sexual intercourse with men in order to become pregnant and secure reproduction of their own tribe. After the birth of the child they were believed to nurture girls and kill, eat, or send away the male children. (See The Letter of Columbus.) Although the Amazons appear to have been fictitious, Queen Isabella took the matter seriously and offered rewards to her explorers for discovering Amazons in the New World. "Many capitalists also put the search for Amazons into their adventurers' contracts" (Batya Weinbaum, *Islands of Women and Amazons: Representations and Realities* [Austin: University of Texas Press, 1999], 121). While the construct of the Amazon can be easily traced to the European imagination, as a projected European fantasy upon the Caribbean and the rest of the Americas, to what extent it also reflects Taino myths or Carib social arrangements where women lived separately from men and formed same-gender communities, remains unexplored. Women-only communities have continued to exist in Amerindian tales, the significance of which are extremely difficult to judge given the temporal and cultural distances, as well as masculine, patriarchal myopias that infuse historiography.
102. Recorded first by Columbus's doctor, Diego Alvarez Chanca, in his 1495 notes. See also Trexler, *Sex and Conquest*, 63.
103. Ibid.
104. Herskovits and Herskovits, *Trinidad Village*, 128.
105. Dann, *The Barbadian Male*, 60–63.
106. Chevannes, "Sexual Behavior of Jamaicans," 30.
107. Ibid.
108. The late 1970s also witnessed the emergence of the Gay Freedom Movement in Jamaica, the history of which is recaptured in the 2003 documentary film *Song of Freedom* produced and directed by Phillip Pike, Canada. The film definitively casts gay and lesbian relations in Jamaica in the 1980s as multiclass and not exclusive to the elite.
109. See Antonio E. de Moya and Rafael Garcia, "AIDS and the Enigma of Bisexuality in the Dominican Republic," in *Bisexuality and AIDS in International Perspective*, ed. Peter Aggleton (London: Taylor & Francis, 1996), 21–35; Leiner, *Sexual Politics in Cuba*; Lumsden, *Machos,*

Maricones, and Gays; David A. B. Murray, "Between a Rock and a Hard Place: The Power and Powerlessness of Transnational Narratives among Gay Martinican Men," *American Anthropologist* 102, no. 2 (2000), 261–270; Murray, *Opacity*.

110.   Tara L. Atluri, "When the Closet Is a Region: Homophobia, Heterosexism and Nationalism in the Commonwealth Caribbean" (Cave Hill, Barbados: Center for Gender and Development Studies, 2001).
111.   Annie Paul, "The Chi Chi Man Syndrome," *Sunday Herald*, 8–14 July 2001; Atluri, "When the Closet Is a Region"; Alexander, "Erotic Autonomy as a Politics of Decolonization"; Murray, *Opacity*.
112.   Donna Hope, "Of 'Chi-Chi' Men: The Threat of Male Homosexuality to Afro-Jamaican Masculine Identity" (paper presented at the 20th Annual Caribbean Studies Association Conference, St. Maarten, 2001).
113.   Ibid., 5.
114.   Chevannes, *Learning to Be a Man*; Kempadoo, "Adolescent Sex."
115.   Rosamund Elwin, ed., *Tongues on Fire: Caribbean Lesbian Lives and Stories* (Toronto: Women's Press, 1997).
116.   See, for example, Gloria Wekker's doctoral study ("'I Am Gold Money'") of "mati-ism" in Suriname and Jocelin Clemencia's "Women Who Love Women in Curaçao: From Cachapera to open Throats—A commentary in collage." *Feminist Studies*, 22(1),(1996):81–88."
117.   Rosamund Elwin, "Introduction: Tongues on Fire: Speakin' Zami Desire," in Elwin, *Tongues on Fire*, 10.
118.   Ibid., 9.
119.   Ibid., 10.
120.   Renà Blackwood, "Invisible Women: Identity Formation in Lesbians: A Study of Women from the Jamaican Homosexual Community" (M.Sc. thesis, University of the West Indies, 2000), 39, 61.
121.   Kempadoo, "Adolescent Sex."
122.   Sean Lokaisingh-Meighoo, "*Jahaji Bhai*: Notes on the Masculine Subject and Homoerotic Subtext of Indo-Caribbean Identity," *Small Axe: Journal of Criticism* 7 (2000), 77–92.
123.   Elizabeth Eggleton, Jean Jackson, and Karen Hardee, "Sexual Attitudes and Behavior among Young Adolescents in Jamaica," *International Family Planning Perspectives* 25, no. 2 (1999), 78–84.
124.   Cynthia Waszak and Maxine Wedderburn, "Baseline Community Youth Survey. VIP/Youth Project" (Kingston: United Nations Family Planning Association, 2000).
125.   Jacqueline Martis, "Tourism and the Sex Trade in St. Maarten and Curaçao," in Kempadoo, *Sun, Sex, and Gold*, 208.
126.   Some beginning work on colonial state ideologies about same-gender male sexual relations under indentureship is being conducted by Anil Persaud. Anil Persaud, "Fertility, Unnatural Sex and Fetishism: Creating Value in the Emancipated British Sugar Colonies" (paper presented at the 2003 Conference on Feminist Economics, University of the West Indies, Cave Hill Campus, 2003).
127.   Hilary Beckles, *Centering Woman: Gender Discourses in Caribbean Slave Society* (Kingston: Ian Randle Publishers, 1999), 69.
128.   Ibid., 68.

129.   Ibid., 62.
130.   Catherine Hall, "Gender Politics and Imperial Politics: Rethinking the Histories of Empire," in Shepherd, Brereton, and Bailey, *Engendering History*; Beckles, *Centering Woman*.

Chapter 3: Sex, Work, Gifts, and Money: Prostitution and Other Sexual-Economic Transactions

1.   Beckles, *Natural Rebels*, 143.
2.   Reddock, *Women, Labor and Politics in Trinidad and Tobago*, 20.
3.   Beckles, *Centering Woman*, 168, 65.
4.   David P. Geggus, "Slave and Free Colored Women in Saint Domingue," in *More Than Chattel: Black Women and Slavery in the Americas*, ed. David Barry Gaspar and Darlene Clark Hine (Bloomington: Indiana University Press, 1996), 259–278.
5.   Paulette Kerr, "Victims or Strategists? Female Lodging-House Keepers in Jamaica," in Shepherd, Brereton, and Bailey, *Engendering History*, 210.
6.   Ibid.
7.   Mathurin Mair (1974), quoted in Mohammed, "'But Most of All Mi Love Mi Browning,'" 43.
8.   Morrissey, *Slave Women in the New World*, 146.
9.   Bush, *Slave Women in Caribbean Society*, 112.
10.   See, for example, Wim Hoogbergen and Marjo de Theye, "Surinaamse Vrouwen in de Slavernij," in *Vrouwen in de Nederlandse Kolonien: 7de Jaarboek Voor Vrouwengeschiedenis*, ed. Jeske Reijs et al. (Nijmegen: SUN, 1986), 126–157; and H. Hoetink, "Suriname and Curaçao," in *Neither Slave nor Free: The Freedman of African Descent in Slave Societies of the New World*, ed. D. W. Cohen and J. P. Greene (Baltimore: John Hopkins University Press, 1972).
11.   Eva Abraham-van der Mark, "Marriage and Concubinage among the Sephardic Merchant Elite of Curaçao," in *Women and Change in the Caribbean*, ed. Janet Momsen (London: James Currey; Kingston: Ian Randle; Bloomington: Indiana University Press, 1993), 38–50.
12.   See, for example, Bridget Brereton, "The Promise of Emancipation," in *The Colonial Caribbean in Transition: Essays on Postemancipation Social and Cultural History*, ed. Bridget Brereton and Kevin A. Yelvington (Kingston: University of the West Indies Press; Gainesville: University Press of Florida, 1999); Shepherd, "Gender, Migration and Settlement"; and Reddock, *Women, Labor and Politics in Trinidad and Tobago*.
13.   Fernando Henriques, *Prostitution in Europe and the Americas* (New York: Citadel Press, 1965), 203.
14.   Yamila Azize Vargas and Kamala Kempadoo, "Tráfico de Mujeres para Prostitución, Trabajo Doméstico y Matrimonio (Trafficking in Women for Prostitution, Domestic Work and Marriage)" (San Juan:

STV and GAATW, 1996). See also the final report of the Global
Research Project: Marjan Wijers and Lin Lap-Chew, "Trafficking
in Women, Forced Labor and Slavery-Like Practices in Marriage,
Domestic Labor and Prostitution" (Utrecht: STV, 1997).

15.   Kempadoo, "Exotic Colonies"; Amy Raquel Paul, "'It Isn't Love, It's
       Business': Prostitution as Entrepreneurship and the Implications for
       Barbados" (Ph.D. diss., University of California–Los Angeles,
       1997); Brennan, "Everything Is for Sale Here"; and Amalia Lucía
       Cabezas, "Pleasure and Its Pain: Sex Tourism in Sosúa, the Dominican
       Republic" (Ph.D. diss., University of California, Berkeley, 1998).

16.   See Centro de Orientación e Investigación Integral (COIN),
       *Juntarnos. Memorias Primer Congreso Dominicano de Trabajadoras
       Sexuales* (Santo Domingo: COIN, 1996); Dusilley Cannings et al.,
       "It's Good to Know: The Maxi Linder Association in Suriname," in
       Kempadoo and Doezema, *Global Sex Workers*, 215–225; Christel C. F.
       Antonius-Smits et al., "Gold and Commercial Sex: Exploring the
       Link between Small-Scale Gold Mining and Commercial Sex in the
       Rainforest of Suriname," in Kempadoo, *Sun, Sex, and Gold*, 237–259.

17.   See, for example, George K. Danns, "Child Prostitution and Child
       Sexual Exploitation in Guyana: A Study of Children in Especially
       Difficult Circumstances" (Georgetown: UNICEF, 1998); Isis
       Duarte, Carmen Julia Gómez , and Marina Ariza, "Profiles on Mi-
       nors in Especially Difficult Circumstances in the Dominican
       Republic" (Santo Domingo: Instituto de Estudios de Población y
       Desarrollo, 1994); Sian Williams, "Sexual Violence and Exploitation
       of Children in Latin America and the Caribbean: The Case of
       Jamaica" (Kingston: 1999); Dunn, "Jamaica: Situation of Children
       in Prostitution"; Aziza Ahmed, "Children and Transactional Sex in
       Jamaica: Addressing Increased Vulnerability to HIV/AIDS"
       (M.Sc. thesis, Harvard School of Public Health, 2003).

18.   See, for example, Tony Hall's play *Jean and Dinah* based on the
       popular calypso from the 1950s by the Mighty Sparrow.

19.   Militarized prostitution in Belize is discussed in Cynthia Enloe,
       *Bananas, Beaches and Bases: Making Feminist Sense of International
       Politics* (Berkeley: University of California Press, 1989); and Stephanie
       C. Kane, "Prostitution and the Military: Planning AIDS Intervention
       in Belize," *Social Science and Medicine*, no. 36 (1993), 965–979.

20.   Fernando Henriques, *Stews and Strumpets: A Survey of Prostitution*
       (London: MacGibbon and Kee, 1961), 17.

21.   Kane, "Prostitution and the Military," 972.

22.   Penelope Campbell and Ann Marie E. Campbell, "HIV/AIDS
       Prevention and Education for Commercial Sex Workers in Jamaica:
       An Exploratory Study and Needs Assessment" (Kingston: National
       HIV/STI Prevention and Control Programme, Ministry of Health,
       Jamaica, 2001), 29.

23.   Laura Mayorga and Pilar Velasqez, "Bleak Pasts, Bleak Futures: Life
       Paths of Thirteen Young Prostitutes in Cartagena, Colombia," in
       Kempadoo, *Sun, Sex, and Gold*, 172.

24. Campbell and Campbell, "HIV/AIDS Prevention and Education for Commercial Sex Workers in Jamaica," 31.

25. Red Thread Women's Development Programme, "'Givin' Lil Bit Fuh Lil Bit': Women and Sex Work in Guyana," in Kempadoo, *Sun, Sex, and Gold*, 277. It should be noted, however, that particularly among those who work with tourists, a relationship that starts off as a brief materially driven encounter may grow into a long-term relationship or marriage, thus shifting from work to an intimate relationship.

26. This practice is not without its problems to a sex worker's health, as has been pointed out elsewhere—see Cannings et al., "It's Good to Know"; and Red Thread Women's Development Programme, "'Givin' Lil Bit Fuh Lil Bit'"—but nevertheless appears to be common throughout the region. See also Ives Marie Chanel and Cathy Shepherd (trans.), "Haitian and Dominican Women in the Sex Trade," *CAFRA News*, June 1994.

27. Red Thread Women's Development Programme, "'Givin' Lil Bit Fuh Lil Bit,'" 277.

28. Wendy Chapkis, *Live Sex Acts: Women Performing Erotic Labor* (New York: Routledge, 1997).

29. See, for example, Thanh Dam Truong, *Sex, Money and Morality: The Political Economy of Prostitution and Tourism in South East Asia* (London: Zed Books, 1990); Luise White, *The Comforts of Home: Prostitution in Colonial Nairobi* (Chicago: University of Chicago Press, 1990); and Lin Leam Lim, ed., *The Sex Sector: The Economic and Social Bases of Prostitution in Southeast Asia* (Geneva: International Labor Office, 1998).

30. While self-employment in parts of the developed world is often taken as a marker of empowerment, independence, and middle or upper class status (and in prostitution discussions is usually attached to the image of the "Happy Hooker"), in the Caribbean it is what many women and men do out of sheer necessity to keep their head above water, where even full-time employment is for many barely sufficient to cover basic needs.

31. Marjolein van de Veen, "Rethinking Commodification and Prostitution: An Effort at Peacemaking in the Battles over Prostitution," *Rethinking Marxism* 13, no. 2 (2001): 33–35.

32. According to van de Veen, Marx argued that the commodification of the laboring body under capitalist economic relations resulted in the worker's estrangement and alienation.

33. van de Veen, "Rethinking Commodification and Prostitution," 43; emphasis hers.

34. Senior, *Working Miracles*, 115.

35. Ibid., 104.

36. Wekker, "I am Gold Money," 186.

37. Ibid., 223. Vice versa, women are aware that even in cases where they are no longer emotionally involved with the fathers of the children, sexuality is the basis upon which child support can be accessed (Senior, *Working Miracles*, 137).

38. See Kempadoo and Doezema, *Global Sex Workers*.

39. Interview by author with the police officer who issued the work permits in 1993.

40. See Kempadoo, *Sun, Sex, and Gold*.

41. See Amalia Lucía Cabezas, "Women's Work Is Never Done: Sex Tourism in Sosúa, the Dominican Republic," in Kempadoo, *Sun, Sex, and Gold*, 93–124; and A. Kathleen Ragsdale and Jessica Tomiko Anders, "The Muchachas of Orange Walk Town, Belize," in Kempadoo, *Sun, Sex, and Gold*, 217–236.

42. Joan L. Phillips, "Tourism-Oriented Prostitution in Barbados: The Case of the Beach Boy and the White Female Tourist," in Kempadoo, *Sun, Sex, and Gold*, 183–200; Mayorga and Velasqez, "Bleak Pasts, Bleak Futures."

43. Red Thread Women's Development Programme, "'Givin' Lil Bit Fuh Lil Bit.'"

44. *Trinidad Guardian*, 2 August 1998.

45. Red Thread Women's Development Programme, "Report of a Study on Female Commercial Sex Workers in Guyana, and Project Proposal Arising from the Study" (Georgetown: Red Thread Women's Development Programme, 2002).

46. Antonius-Smits et al., "Gold and Commercial Sex."

47. See also studies by Cabezas, Brennan, and Paul on the Dominican Republic and Barbados.

48. See, for example, White, *The Comforts of Home*; John K. Anarfi, "Ghanaian Women and Prostitution in Cote D'ivoire," in Kempadoo and Doezema, *Global Sex Workers*, 104–113; Catherine Coquery-Widrovitch, "Prostitution: From 'Free' Women to Women with AIDS," in *African Women: A Modern History*, edited by Catherine Coquery–Widvovitch, translated by Beth Gillian Raps (Boulder: Westview Press, 1997), 117–128.

49. See Cabezas, "Women's Work Is Never Done" on the Dominican Republic, and Ragsdale and Anders, "The Muchachas of Orange Walk Town, Belize" on Belize.

50. Shirley Campbell, Althea Perkins, and Patricia Mohammed, "'Come to Jamaica and Feel All Right': Tourism and the Sex Trade," in Kempadoo, *Sun, Sex, and Gold*.

51. Martis, "Tourism and the Sex Trade in St. Maarten and Curaçao."

52. Antonius-Smits et al., "Gold and Commercial Sex."

53. See Red Thread Women's Development Programme, "Report of a Study on Female Commercial Sex Workers in Guyana."

54. Also noted in Marcus Colchester, *Guyana Fragile Frontier: Loggers, Miners and Forest Peoples* (London: Latin America Bureau; Kingston: Ian Randle Publishers, 1997).

55. Campbell, Perkins, and Mohammed, "'Come to Jamaica and Feel All Right.'"

56. Red Thread Women's Development Programme, "'Givin' Lil Bit Fuh Lil Bit.'"

57. Campbell, Perkins, and Mohammed, "'Come to Jamaica and Feel All Right.'"

58. Mayorga and Velasqez, "Bleak Pasts, Bleak Futures."
59. Red Thread Women's Development Programme, "Report of a Study on Female Commercial Sex Workers in Guyana."
60. This term has also been introduced in the context of sexual relations in South Africa. Hunter defines this as "a central factor driving multiple partnered sexual relationships" and as both similar and different from prostitution: "in both cases, non-marital sexual relationships, often with multiple partners, are underscored by the giving of gifts or cash. Transactional sex, however, differs in important ways: participants are constructed as 'girlfriends' and 'boyfriends' and are not 'prostitutes' or 'clients,' and the exchange of gifts for sex is part of a broader set of obligations that might not involve a pre-determined payment." Mark Hunter, "The Materiality of Everyday Sex: Thinking Beyond 'Prostitution,'" *African Studies* 61, no. 1 (2002): 100.
61. Kempadoo, "Adolescent Sex," 9.
62. See Dunn, "Jamaica: Situation of Children in Prostitution"; and Kempadoo, "Adolescent Sex."
63. Kempadoo, "Adolescent Sex," 30.
64. Ibid., 27.
65. Dunn, "Jamaica: Situation of Children in Prostitution," 51.
66. Ibid.
67. Kempadoo, "Adolescent Sex," 19.
68. Interview by author, 20 July 2001.
69. Interview by author with manager of the brothel.
70. Base, a cocaine derivative, is the most commonly used hard drug today in Curaçao, being cheaper and more accessible than cocaine. It is a by-product of cocaine that is cooked and purified, forming a white powder that is smoked and sold on the streets in small packets of five guilders. A former user described it as "the Caribbean heroine," being just as addictive and destructive to the body as the other substance. A base user on the island is known as a choller, and the place where the users smoke, hang out, and sometimes live is known as a cholhuis (choller-house/chol-house).
71. Information provided by a female drug user/sex worker in Otrabanda.
72. Interview by author with an Antillian man.
73. Campbell and Campbell, "HIV/AIDS Prevention and Education for Commercial Sex Workers in Jamaica," 25.
74. The medical exams for this group of men began with the police raid at a house party in Santa Maria. Neighbors had complained of the noise one weekend, and the police made a raid. Under questioning about their activities, the spokesman for the group declared that they were selling sex and agreed to register as prostitutes with the police, as well as to undergo regular medical examinations.
75. *Vito*, 5 April 1969 (written in Papiementu, translated by Jacqueline Martis into English).
76. See, for example, Deborah Pruitt and Suzanne LaFont, "For Love and Money: Romance Tourism in Jamaica," *Annals of Tourism Research* 22, no. 2 (1995), 422–440.

77. On beachboys in Barbados, see Phillips, "Tourism-Oriented Prostitution in Barbados." Also see Howard, *Coloring the Nation.*
78. See, for example, bell hooks, "Dreaming Ourselves Dark and Deep: Black Beauty," in *Sisters of the Yam: Black Women and Self-Recovery* (Boston: South End Press, 1993), 79–98; Cornel West, "Black Sexuality: The Taboo Subject," in *Race Matters* (Boston: Beacon Press, 1993), 81–92; and Linden Lewis, "Constructing the Masculine in the Context of the Caribbean" (Merida: Mexico, 19th Annual Caribbean Studies Conference, 1994).
79. Rosalie Schwartz, *Pleasure Island: Tourism and Temptation in Cuba* (Lincoln: University of Nebraska Press, 1997), 86. See also Kutzinski, *Sugar's Secrets.*
80. Red Thread Women's Development Programme, "Report of a Study on Female Commercial Sex Workers in Guyana."
81. Chanel and Shepherd, "Haitian and Dominican Women in the Sex Trade," 14.
82. Henriques, *Children of Caliban*, 113.
83. *Vito*, 23 November 1979.
84. Natasha Barnes, "Face of the Nation: Race, Nationalisms, and Identities in Jamaican Beauty Pageants," in *Daughters of Caliban: Caribbean Women in the Twentieth Century*, ed. Consuelo Lopez Springfield (Bloomington: Indiana University Press, 1997), 285–306.
85. Williams, *Stains on My Name, War in My Veins*, 171, 73.
86. Williams, *Charcoal and Cinnamon*, 17, 1.
87. Ibid., 2.
88. Howard, *Coloring the Nation*, 89.
89. In the chapter on sex tourism we return to this theme, for as we shall see, there is some complexity in the tourism sector around the appreciation of blackness, where very dark men and women are sometimes privileged over the "brown" women and men.
90. Mayorga and Velasqez, "Bleak Pasts, Bleak Futures"; Cabezas, "Pleasure and Its Pain."
91. Chevannes, *Learning to Be a Man*, 195.

Chapter 4: The Happy Camp in Curaçao: Legal Sex Work and the Making of the "SanDom"

1. In 1993, the owner of Campo Alegre, Gilberto Bakhuis, secured a new bar and gambling license for the premises. The complex was rechristened Mirage, although is still popularly known by its former name.
2. When first opened, the brothel was not walled but rather was surrounded by wire mesh. A Christmas postcard dating to 1955 shows the open character.
3. See Kempadoo, "Prostitution and Sex Work Studies" in the *Blackwell Companion to Gender Studies*, edited by Philomena Essed, Audrey Kobayashi, and David Theo Goldberg. (London: Blackwell, 2004), 255–265.

4. Liesbeth Hesselink, "Prostitution: A Necessary Evil, Particularly in the Colonies. Views on Prostitution in the Netherlands Indies," in *Indonesian Women in Focus*, ed. Elsbeth Locher-Scholten and Anke Niehof (Dordrecht/Providence: Floris Publications, 1987), 206.

5. Sietske Altink, Martine Groen, and Ine Vanwesenbeeck, *Sekswerk: Ervaringen Van Vrouwen in de Prostitutie* (Amsterdam: SUA, 1991); Hesselink, "Prostitution: A Necessary Evil."

6. See also Jan Visser, "Decriminalizing Prostitution: Dutch Preparations for a New Way of Regulating Commercial Sex" (paper presented at Sex Matters: The Xth World Congress of Sexology, Amsterdam, 1992).

7. Sietske Altink, *Stolen Lives: Trading Women into Sex and Slavery* (London: Scarlet Press, 1995); Heleen Buijs, "Dutch Prostitution Policy and Human Rights" (Strasbourg: European Committee for Equality between Women and Men, Council of Europe, 1991); Nelleke van der Vleuten, "Survey on 'Traffick in Women': Policies and Policy Research in an International Context," in *VENA Working Paper*, Research and Documentation Centre, Women and Autonomy, Leiden University (Leiden: VENA, 1991).

8. Licia Brussa, "Survey on Prostitution, Migration and Traffick in Women: History and Current Situation" (Strasbourg: European Committee for Equality between Women and Men. Council of Europe, 1991); Buijs, "Dutch Prostitution Policy and Human Rights."

9. Johan Hartog, *Curaçao* (Aruba: De Wit, 1968).

10. Tjeerd de Reus, *Geslachtsziekten Op Curaçao* (Assen: Van Gorcum, 1970); U. C. H. Martins, "Hoe Campo Alegre Ontstond," in *Koperen Polyfonie* (Yearbook, Universiteit van de Nederlandse Antillen, Curaçao 1984), 30–42.

11. Letters from the Ministry of Foreign Affairs, The Hague, Afdeling Volkenbondzaken no. 23230 and 33166 to the Governor of Curaçao, 11 August 1928, 6 November 1929.

12. Telegram from the Governor of Curaçao to the Minister of the Colonies in The Hague, 30 January 1930.

13. Report from the Attorney General to the Governor of Curaçao, 31 July 1935.

14. Letter to the Governor of Curaçao, 23 January 1930.

15. This refers to League of Nations Circular, 25 June 1936, C.L.116.1936.IV, and the correspondence connected to it, including Letters from the Minister of the Colonies to the Governor of Curaçao, 9 July 1936 (no. 23/409) and 23 July 1936 (no. 24/442); Report made by the Attorney General to the Governor of Curaçao, 12 August 1936 (no. 1400); Letter from the Governor of Curaçao to the Minister of the Colonies in The Hague, 13 August 1936 (no. 5726); Report from the Attorney General to the Governor, 31 October 1936 (no. 1517); and Letter from the Governor of Curaçao to the Minister of the Colonies in The Hague, 3 November 1936 (no. 5726b/331).

16. Politie Blad 1921, No. 66.

17. The committee members were Father H. A. B. Hulsman, the lawyer L. Ch. Kwartsz, Dr. P. H. Maal, Father J. B. van der Meer, and

Ds. J. Mietes. The deliberations of the commission were supported
by the director of the Public Health Department, Dr. W. M. Bonne,
and the chief police inspector, W. J. van der Kroeff. See Staten van
Curaçao, *Aanbeiding: Ontwerp-Landsverordening Tot Wijziging En
Aanvulling Van De Verordening Van Den 9den Juni 1921*, Zittingsjaar
1942–1943. Commissie ter Bestrijding van Prostitutie en Geslachts-
ziekten, "Rapport Aan Zijne Excellentie Den Gouverneur Van
Curaçao" (Willemstad: Commissie ter Bestrijding van Prostitutie
en Geslachts-ziekten, 1942).

18.   The chairman and secretary of the commission who presented the
report were Father Hulsman and E. A. J. Ellis, respectively.

19.   Staten van Curaçao, *Ontwerp: Landsverordening Tot Wijziging En
Aanvulling Van De Verordening Van Den 9den Juni 1921*, Zittingsjaar
1943–1944, 12. Translation mine. This included a broadening of
article 34 and changes to articles 43, 45, 48, 50, and 51.

20.   Ibid.; Staten van Curaçao, *Memorie Van Toelichting*, Zittingsjaar
1943–1944, 3.

21.   Staten van Curaçao, *Ontwerp-Landsverordening Tot Wijziging En
Aanvulling Van De Verordening Van Den 9den Juni 1921*.

22.   de Reus, *Geslachtsziekten Op Curaçao*, 76; Martins, "Hoe Campo
Alegre Ontstond."

23.   Staten van Curaçao, *Landsverordening Van Den 23sten September
1944 Tot Wijziging an Aanvullingvan De Verordening Van Den 9den
Juni 1921*, 31 October 1944.

24.   de Reus, *Geslachtsziekten Op Curaçao*, 78; Martins, "Hoe Campo
Alegre Ontstond," 38.

25.   In an exchange of letters between concerned members of the government and the governor, the participation of the bank and the in-
vestment by the Dutch state in the brothel are clearly detailed.
Letter to the Governor, 14 October 1949 (no. 131), and Reply from
the Governor, 23 December 1949 (no. 8618).

26.   Staten van Curaçao, *Nota Naar Aanleiding Van Het Eindverslag*,
Begrotingsjaar 1953.

27.   Reported in *Amigoe di Curaçao*, 24 November 1955.

28.   Ibid.

29.   Ibid.

30.   "Oordeel van Zijne Hoogw. Excellentie Mgr. A.v.d Veen Zeppenfeldt en de Zeev Eerw. Pater M. Hulsman" in *Curaçao*, citing
Zeppenfeldt's statement in 1945. Date unknown.

31.   Ibid., in reference to a report from the Government Committee of
Inquiry into the problem of public prostitution, Aruba, 6 November 1951.

32.   Interview by author with the deputy chief of police, 1993.

33.   Interview by author with a former sex worker in Suriname, 1995.
See also Cannings et al., "It's Good to Know."

34.   Martis, "Tourism and the Sex Trade in St. Maarten and Curaçao."

35.   John Lindsay-Poland, "U.S. Military Bases in Latin America
and the Caribbean," *Foreign Policy in Focus*, October 2001,
http://www.americaspolicy.org/briefs/2001/body_v6n35milbase.html.

"The USSOUTHCOM AOR includes the land mass of Latin
America south of Mexico; the waters adjacent to Central and South
America; the Caribbean Sea, its 12 island nations and European territories; the Gulf of Mexico; and a portion of the Atlantic Ocean. It encompasses 32 countries (19 in Central and South America and 13 in
the Caribbean) and covers about 15.6 million square miles. The region represents about one-sixth of the landmass of the world assigned
to regional unified commands"
(http://www.southcom.mil/pa/Facts/Profile.htm).
In the late 1990s, with the closing of the Panama base, the headquar-
ters of SouthCom were moved to Miami and its main bases in the
region were relocated to Puerto Rico. Curaçao was originally defined
as a FOL (forward operating location) where "U.S. Air Force, Army,
Navy, Coast Guard and Customs surveillance and tracking aircraft
will operate from the locations to monitor drug traffic from the An-
dean region through the Caribbean to the United States"
(http://www.mapinc.org/drugnews/v99.n496.a03.html). By 2003,
however, the SouthCom mission was less about drug trafficking and
was recast as "military operations and security cooperation activities
in support of the War on Terrorism"
(http://www.southcom.mil/pa/Facts/Facts.htm).
As part of the U.S. pullout from Panama, "six C-130 and four F-16
aircraft and about 170 airmen assigned to the 24th Wing, and representing two Air Force flying missions, moved 01 May 1999, respectively to airfields in San Juan, Puerto Rico, and Curaçao's
international airport" (http://www.globalsecurity.org).

36. *Beurs-en Nieuwsberichten*, 24 May 1995.
37. Martis, "Tourism and the Sex Trade in St. Maarten and Curaçao."
38. In February 1990, the Antillian journalist Joel Labadie published a
series of five critical articles in the local newspaper, *Amigoe*: "De
Vrouwen van *Campo Alegre*"; "Publieke Vrouwen in en buiten
Campo Alegre"; "Ethiek tegenover nut van bordeel: het dilemma van
Dr. MacKibbelaar van de GGD"; "Gilberto Bakhuis, Directeur
Campo Alegre: Het is geen bordeel en ook geen taboe"; and "Poli-
tiechef Ursula over 'Eeuwige Zonde.'" This quote prefaces part five.
39. The various reasons were expressed by respondents from the Haitian and Venezuelan consulates in Curaçao and, in regard to
Haitians, are reflected in the research on suitcase traders; see
Monique Lagro and Donna Plotkin, "The Suitcase Traders in the
Free Zone of Curaçao," (Port of Spain: Caribbean Development
and Co-operation Committee, Economic Commission for Latin
America and the Caribbean, 1990).
40. It should be noted here that in the 1990s, most of the male clients
in Curaçao were Dutch Antillian men.
41. Even in the brothel, Campo/Mirage, the only woman I interviewed
who described physical violence by clients as a serious problem was
dark-skinned. Racialized gendered violence within the sex trade on
the island, however, requires far more research.

42. Florence Kalm, "The Two 'Faces' of Antillean Prostitution" (paper presented at the American Anthropological Association Meeting, 1975, place/location of unknown).

43. "Prostitutie Op Aruba" (paper presented at the Caribbean Conference on Prostitution, Bonaire, 1978), Author unknown.

44. Staten van de Nederlandse Antillen *Notulen*, 1 June, 1951.

45. Letters (14 April and 6 and 23 June 1951) and petitions (16 and 30 May 1951) that were sent to the governor are held in an archive in Curaçao. The documents and the opposition voiced in them were recorded by the local newspaper, *Amigoe*, at the time.

46. "Prostitutie Op Aruba."

47. Kalm, "The Two 'Faces' of Antillean Prostitution," 5.

48. Ibid., 8.

49. See ibid.; "Prostitutie Op Aruba."

50. Steering Committee, "Prostitution in St. Maarten" (paper presented at the Caribbean Conference on Prostitution, Bonaire, 1978). See also Martis, "Tourism and the Sex Trade in St. Maarten and Curaçao."

51. Steering Committee, "Prostitution in St. Maarten."

52. During my fieldwork in 1993, several respondents working with the police force as well as the narcotics bureau described this pattern. See also Martis, "Tourism and the Sex Trade in St. Maarten and Curaçao."

53. This information was kindly provided to me by Michele Russel-Capriles, at the time a member of the Parliament of the Netherlands Antilles, in personal correspondence, 4 December 1995.

54. Martis, "Tourism and the Sex Trade in St. Maarten and Curaçao," 209.

55. Ibid., 211.

56. Martis notes that similar sentiments were expressed by the St. Maarten Women's Steering Committee at a 1996 conference on prostitution; see ibid., 209.

57. Report from Suriname, (paper presented at the Caribbean Conference on Prostitution, Bonaire, 1978.) Author Unknown. 1978, and Antonius-Smits et al., "Gold and Commercial Sex," 239.

58. Letter from the Antillian Government Council to the Governor, 14 October 1949 (no. 131).

59. Letter to the Government Council, Willemstad, 12 October 1951.

60. Staten van de Nederlandse Antillen, *Notulen* 1 June 1951.

61. The debate between the chairman and deputy prime minister was published in detail in Dutch daily newspapers (*Amigoe*, 28 August and 24 November 1955).

62. Draft petition, 30 August 1955.

63. *Beurs-en Nieuwsberichten*, 11 November 1954; *Amigoe di Curaçao*, "Onze maatschappelijke Kwaal No. 1" (date unknown); Minutes from the meeting of the Government Commission, 18 July 1955; *Amigoe*, 3, 8 and 22 September 1956; *Beurs-en Nieuwsberichten*, 6, 11, and 12 September 1956.

64. Circular from Father Brenneker. The date of the circular is unknown, but from the reference to the large number of Venezuelan prostitutes in Campo, one can presume that it was written during

the 1950s, given that since the early 1960s very few women from Venezuela were found among the registered Campo sex worker population. A letter written by the president of the Roman Catholic Women's League in Aruba also states that her interview with Father Hulsman, who chaired the 1942 Prostitution Commission, revealed that although Father Brenneker originally was "skeptical" about Campo, in 1951 he was definitely against the brothel (letter dated 14 April 1951).

65. From the resolution of the conference.
66. Ibid.
67. Letter to the Lieutenant Governor, 21 November 1991 (no. 91/168).
68. The UMLA (Union Mujeres Latinos Americanos) prides itself as an organization of professional Latin American women in Curaçao that holds public events to celebrate their specific positions and achievements. See media coverage in *Amigoe*, 8 March 1993.

Chapter 5: For Love or Money? Fantasies and Realities in Sex Tourism

1. 11 February 1996, http://www.paranoia.com/faq/prostitution/Boca-Chica.txt.html.
2. Polly Pattullo, *Last Resorts: The Cost of Tourism in the Caribbean* (Kingston: Ian Randle, 1996).
3. *Travel Industry World Yearbook*, (Spencertown, NY: Travel Industry Publishing Company, 1996); Pattullo, *Last Resorts*; Paul F. Wilkinson, *Tourism Policy and Planning: Case Studies from the Commonwealth Caribbean* (New York: Cognizant Communication Corporation, 1997).
4. S. Mather and G. Todd, *Tourism in the Caribbean*, Special Report No. 455 (London: Economist Intelligence Unit, 1993), 9, quoted in Wilkinson, *Tourism Policy and Planning*, 3.
5. Pattullo notes that in particular U.S. interests and capital dominate the Caribbean tourism industry. In the early 1990s, for example, foreign airlines controlled almost three-quarters of the seats to the region; North American and European tour operators dominated the bookings for the larger hotels, and 63 percent of hotel rooms in the region were foreign owned. Some changes in this control and ownership have occurred, however, with the rise of locally owned "SuperClubs" and all-inclusives such as Sandals, and joint ventures in Cuba between the government and foreign businesses.
6. Pattullo, *Last Resorts*, 38.
7. Frantz Fanon, *The Wretched of the Earth* (New York: Grove Press, 1963), 154.
8. See, for example, Hilbourne A. Watson, "Global Neoliberalism: The Third Technological Revolution and Global 2000: A Perspective on Issues Affecting the Caribbean on the Eve of the 21st Century," in

Contending with Destiny: The Caribbean in the 21st Century, ed. Kenneth Hall and Denis Benn (Kingston: Ian Randle, 2000), 382–446; Denis Benn and Kenneth Hall, eds., *Globalisation: A Calculus of Inequality* (Kingston: Ian Randle, 2000); Thomas Klak, ed., *Globalization and Neoliberalism: The Caribbean Context* (Boulder: Rowman and Littlefield, 1998).

9.   See Anthony P. Maingot, "The Offshore Caribbean," in *Modern Caribbean Politics*, ed. Anthony Payne and Paul Sutton (Kingston: Ian Randle, 1993), 259–276.

10.   Norman Girvan, "Globalisation and Counter Globalisation: The Caribbean in the Context of the South," in *Globalisation: A Calculus of Inequality*, ed. Denis Benn and Kenneth Hall (Kingston: Ian Randle, 2000).

11.   See, for example, Dean MacCannell, *The Tourist: A New Theory of the Leisure Class* (New York: Shocken Books, 1989); Malcolm Crick, "Representations of International Tourism in the Social Sciences: Sun, Sex, Sights, Savings, and Servility," *Annual Review of Anthropology* 18 (1989), 307–344; Mimi Sheller, *Consuming the Caribbean* (London and New York: Routledge, 2003).

12.   Beverley Mullings, "Globalization, Tourism, and the International Sex Trade," in Kempadoo, *Sun, Sex, and Gold*, 55–80.

13.   Clayton M. Press Jr., "Reputation and Respectability Reconsidered: Hustling in a Tourist Setting," *Caribbean Issues* 4 (1978): 115.

14.   Cecilia A. Karch and G. H. S. Dann, "Close Encounters of the Third Kind," *Human Relations* 34 (1981).

15.   Joan L. Phillips, "The Beach Boys of Barbados: Post-Colonial Entrepreneurs," in *Transnational Prostitution: Changing Global Patterns*, ed. Susanne Thorbek and Bandana Pattanaik (London: Zed Books, 2002), 42–55.

16.   For example, Pruitt and LaFont, "For Love and Money"; Jan Strout, "Women, the Politics of Sexuality and Cuba's Economic Crisis," *Socialist Review* 25, no. 1 (1995), 5–15; Julia O'Connell Davidson, "Sex Tourism in Cuba," *Race and Class* 38 (1996), 39–48; Coco Fusco, "Hustling for Dollars," *Ms. Magazine*, September/October 1996, 62–70; Elena Díaz, Esperanza Fernández, and Tania Caram, "Turismo y Prostitución en Cuba" (Havana: Facultad Latinoamericana de Ciencias Sociales, Universidad de Havana, 1996); Brennan, "Everything Is for Sale Here"; Cabezas, "Pleasure and Its Pain"; Julia O'Connell Davidson and Jacqueline Sanchez Taylor, "Fantasy Islands: Exploring the Demand for Sex Tourism," in Kempadoo, *Sun, Sex, and Gold*, 37–54; Campbell, Perkins, and Mohammed, "'Come to Jamaica and Feel All Right'"; Jacqueline Sanchez Taylor, "Dollars Are a Girl's Best Friend? Female Tourists' Sexual Behavior in the Caribbean," *Sociology* 35, no. 1 (2001), 749–764; Edward Herold, Rafael Garcia, and Antonio E. de Moya, "Female Tourists and Beach Boys: Romance and Sex Tourism," *Annals of Tourism Research* 28, no. 4 (2001), 978–997.

17.   See, for example, Kempadoo, "Exotic Colonies"; de Moya and Garcia, "Three Decades of Male Sex Work in Santo Domingo"; Martis,

"Tourism and the Sex Trade in St. Maarten and Curaçao."
Although some of this work is still to be published, papers by Denys
Figuero and Gisele Fosada on male sex work in Cuba were pre-
sented at a conference session at the Annual Meeting of the Society
for the Study of Social Problems (SSSP), August 2001. See also
Mark Padilla, Looking for Life: Male Sex Work, HIV/AIDS
and the Political Economy of Gay Sex Tourism in the Dominican
Republic (Ph.D. diss., Emory University, Atlanta, 2003).

18.   Chris Ryan and Michael C. Hall, *Sex Tourism: Marginal People and Liminalities* (London: Routledge, 2001), 4.
19.   Ibid., 6.
20.   See, for example, Martin Oppermann, ed., *Sex Tourism and Prostitution: Aspects of Leisure, Recreation and Work* (New York: Cognizant Communication, 1998).
21.   Jamaica Kincaid, *A Small Place* (New York: Penguin, 1988), 18–19.
22.   "World Sex Guide," 20 June 1995, http://www.paranoia.com/faq/prostitution/cuba_bits.txt.html.
23.   O'Connell Davidson and Sanchez Taylor, "Fantasy Islands," 43.
24.   Cabezas, "Women's Work Is Never Done."
25.   These letters described tourist experiences in the Caribbean countries of Aruba, Cuba, Curaçao, the Dominican Republic, Jamaica,
Puerto Rico, and Suriname. In most cases the authors did not identify
their home countries, but some authors did indicate that they lived
in Chicago, Los Angeles, Miami, New York, Nevada, Texas, Canada,
Germany, England, the Netherlands, or simply the United States.
26.   28 March 1997, http://www.paranoia.com/faq/prostitution/ Ha-
vana.txt.html.
27.   5 September 1996, http://www.paranoia.com/faq/prostitution/dr_travel2.txt.html.
28.   6 May 1997, http://www.paranoia.com/faq/prostitution/ Negril.txt.html.
29.   27 June 1995, http://www.paranoia.com/faq/prostitution/dr_travel.txt.html.
30.   O'Connell Davidson and Sanchez Taylor, "Fantasy Islands," 47.
31.   2 July 1995, http://www.paranoia.com/faq/prostitution/cuba_faq.txt.html.
32.   27 June 1995, http://www.paranoia.com/faq/prostitution/dr_travel.txt.html.
33.   July 26, 1998 http://www.worldsexguide.com/world/cuba/index.htm Letter 75, Cuba.
34.   16 April 1996, http://www.paranoia.com/faq/prostitution/Cienfue-gos.txt.html.
35.   Martin Oppermann, "Introduction," in Oppermann, *Sex Tourism and Prostitution*, 157.
36.   Herold, Garcia, and de Moya, "Female Tourists and Beach Boys."
37.   It should be kept in mind that these images combine with actual
prostitution activities in which the women's sexual labor is criminalized and their lives subject to intense harassment by police and government authorities, coercion and force by men seeking to make a

monetary profit from their exoticized bodies, and exploitation for the satisfaction of tourist's desires.

38.   20 October 1997, http://www.paranoia.com/faq/prostitution/dr_expert.txt.html.
39.   11 June 1997, http://www.paranoia.com/faq/prostitution/Havana.txt.html.
40.   October 1996, http://www.paranoia.com/faq/prostitution/aruba_general.txt.html.
41.   20 January 1997, http://www.paranoia.com/faq/prostitution/dr_travel.txt.html.
42.   6 May 1997, http://www.paranoia.com/faq/prostitution/Negril.txt.html.
43.   5 September 1996, http://www.paranoia.com/faq/prostitution/dr_travel2.txt.html.
44.   11 February 1996, http://www.paranoia.com/faq/prostitution/Boca-Chica.txt.html.
45.   7 March 1997, http://www.paranoia.com/faq/prostitution/Puerto-Rico.txt.html.
46.   No date, http://www.paranoia.com/faq/prostitution/Guanabo.txt.html.
47.   October 1996, http://www.paranoia.com/faq/prostitution/aruba_general.txt.html.
48.   Cabezas, "Women's Work Is Never Done," 111.
49.   http://www.jamaicatravel.com/cgi-bin/mboard/jamaica/thread.cgi?361,0, posted 22 December 1999.
50.   A. Kathleen Ragsdale and Jessica Tomiko Anders, "Sex and Romance Tourism in Belize: A Site Comparison Study" Preliminary Report to the Steering Committee of the Sex Trade in the Caribbean project (1998).
51.   Sanchez Taylor, "Dollars Are a Girl's Best Friend?"
52.   Phillips, "Tourism-Oriented Prostitution in Barbados," 188.
53.   Sanchez Taylor, "Dollars Are a Girl's Best Friend?" 752.
54.   Phillips, "Tourism-Oriented Prostitution in Barbados," 88.
55.   Giovanna Gray Torchio, "Beyond Appearances and Perspectives: A New Look at Female Sex Tourism in Jamaica" (Bachelor of Arts, Connecticut College, New London 2002).
56.   Pruitt and LaFont, "For Love and Money," 436–38.
57.   The "ruud bwai," according to Scott, is the "young, urban, black and angry" element of Jamaican culture, signifying "not merely a lack of the esteemed rationality and preferred values of respectable society, but a positive contempt for, and refusal of them," seen to menace and threaten the normal body politic. David Scott, *Refashioning Futures: Criticism after Postcoloniality* (Princeton: Princeton University Press, 1999), 210.
58.   "Rasta Love," *Outlook*, 22 October 2000, 14.
59.   The local reference to young, predominantly white undergraduate students who descend in large groups on Jamaican tourist resorts during their spring semester mid-term break. In Jamaica, "spring break"—from February to early May—is an important focus for the

tourist industry, and events that cater to this particular crowd are widely promoted. The local daily papers also regularly carry news about Spring Break during this period of the year. For example, *The Jamaica Observer* issued a special "Tourist Times" section in 2001, with the front-page headline "Spring Breakers Arrive" and a photograph of the Jamaican Tourist Board general manager offering "a warm handshake and a word of 'Welcome to Jamaica' to a group of young Americans (15–24 March 2001). Other headlines read "Spring Breakers Shun 'Boring' Montego Bay," *The Gleaner*, 17 May 2001, and "Spring Breakers Warned: 'Tone Down Lewd and Obscene Behavior,'" front page of the *Sunday Gleaner*, 25 February 2001.

60. Claims from the Dominican Republic about this issue are somewhat contradictory. According to Mark Padilla's doctoral research, female sex tourists do not pay as much as male sex tourists; hence, the Sankies turn to men. Others claim that the beachboys "received less money from male tourists than from female tourists," that "among the beach boys who are mainly concerned with making money, their main targets are women who are either older (past the age of forty) or younger women who are overweight." Herold, Garcia, and de Moya, "Female Tourists and Beach Boys."

61. "The Will of Jah," *Outlook*, 22 October 2000, 16.

62. Torchio, "Beyond Appearances and Perspectives."

63. In Jamaica during Spring Break, every year hundreds of police are explicitly recruited from around the island and stationed in Negril, many in plain clothes, with the mandate to patrol the beaches and town to ensure tourists are not robbed, sold drugs, or taken advantage of while drunk. In an interview with two policemen in Negril, they described a large part of their job as having to look out for dealers of ganga and cocaine. They claimed they could identify many of the offenders and would arrest them even in cases where a tourist woman may defend the man by claiming he is her boyfriend. They would not arrest spring breakers, but stated they were there to ensure that the young people did not get excessive with smoking or drinking or cause accidents to themselves or others by driving motorscooters while drunk.

Chapter 6: Trading Sex across Borders: Interregional and International Migration

1. Elizabeth Thomas-Hope, "Skilled Labor Migration from Developing Countries: Study on the Caribbean Region" (Geneva: International Migration Programme, International Labor Office, 2002); Norman Girvan, "Globalisation and Counter-Globalisation."

2. See, for example, Jessica Byron, "Migration, Nationalism, and Regionalism in the Caribbean," in Hall and Benn, *Contending with Destiny*, 80–90.

3.   Jorge Duany, "Beyond the Safety Valve: Recent Trends in Caribbean Migration," in *Caribbean Sociology: Introductory Readings*, ed. Christine Barrow and Rhoda Reddock (Kingston: Ian Randle, 2001), 861–876.

4.   See Azize Vargas and Kempadoo, "Tráfico de Mujeres para Prostitución."

5.   IOM Migration Information Programme, "Trafficking in Women from the Dominican Republic for Sexual Exploitation" (Geneva: International Organization on Migration, 1996). This figure is at best a guesstimate that by most researchers in the field is considered to be conservative.

6.   See, for example, Azize Vargas and Kempadoo, "Tráfico de Mujeres para Prostitución"; Antonius-Smits et al., "Gold and Commercial Sex"; Kane, "Prostitution and the Military."

7.   Informal reports to the author.

8.   Brennan, "Everything Is for Sale Here," 292.

9.   Ibid., 295–96.

10. Ibid., 293.

11. See Lagro and Plotkin, *The Suitcase Traders in the Free Zone of Curaçao*, 1, who estimated that the number who traveled the region on an inter-island scale during the late 1980s was between five thousand and six thousand.

12. Campbell, Perkins, and Mohammed. "Come to Jamaica and Feel Alright," 1999, 150.

13. Lagro and Plotkin, *The Suitcase Traders in the Free Zone of Curaçao*.

14. Interviews by author with police in Curaçao, 1993. See also ibid.

15. Lagro and Plotkin, *See Above*.

16. As, for example, was the case with "Nikki," a Guyanese woman who bought goods in other islands and sold them in Barbados, but who turned exclusively to sex work in Barbados, after her male trading partner disappeared with the profits. See Paul, "It Isn't Love, It's Business," 134.

17. Interview by author with the Haitian consul in Curaçao, 1993.

18. Paul, It isn't Love, It's Business, 121.

19. See Gail Pheterson, *The Prostitution Prism* (Amsterdam: Amsterdam University Press, 1996).

20. Interview by author with Lisa, 1993.

21. Interview by author with the escort agency owner, Curaçao, 1993.

22. Interviews by author with nurses who worked at Campo, 1993.

23. See, for example, Judith R. Walkowitz, *Prostitution and Victorian Society: Women, Class and the State* (Cambridge: Cambridge University Press, 1980); Philippa Levine, "Venereal Disease, Prostitution, and the Politics of Empire: The Case of British India," *Journal of the History of Sexuality* 4 (1994): 579–602; Eileen Scully, "Pre-Cold War Traffic in Sexual Labor and Its Foes: Some Contemporary Lessons," in *Global Human Smuggling: Comparative Perspectives*, ed. D. Kyle and R. Koslowski (Baltimore: Johns Hopkins University Press, 2001), 74–106.

24. Scully, "Pre-Cold War Traffic in Sexual Labor and Its Foes."

25. See ISIS-wicce, "Asian Campaigns," *Women's World* (1990/91a): 9–11.

26. Kathleen Barry, *Female Sexual Slavery* (New York: New York University Press, 1984), 40.

27. ISIS-wicce, "World-Wide Solidarity," *Women's World* (1990/91b), 8–9.

28. The commissioned report was published in Marjan Wijers and Lin Lap-Chew, *Trafficking in Women, Forced Labor and Slavery-Like Practices in Marriage, Domestic Labor and Prostitution* (Utrecht: STV, 1997).

29. Kamala Kempadoo, "Women of Color and the Global Sex Trade: Transnational Feminist Perspectives," *Meridians* 1, no. 3 (2001), 28–51.

30. Interview by author with a sex worker at Campo, 1993.

31. *El Nacional*, 20 April 1985; *Outwrite*, September 1985; *Express*, 21 May 1985; *Quehaceras*, June 1985.

32. See Antonius-Smits et al., "Gold and Commercial Sex."

33. This was the topic of the collection of writings in Kempadoo and Doezema, *Global Sex Workers*; the subject of research by the Dutch Foundation Against Trafficking (STV) and Women and the Global Alliance Against Trafficking in Women (GAATW)—see Wijers and Lap-Chew, *Trafficking in Women, Forced Labor and Slavery-Like Practices in Marriage, Domestic Labor and Prostitution*—and the topic of many recent debates taking place in feminist circles about the global sex trade. It is also the focus of discussions, workshops, and a three-year-long feminist participatory action research project by the GAATW on trafficking, as well as a forthcoming collection of analyses and research reports edited by this author, entitled "Trafficking and Prostitution Revisited."

34. Most studies mentioned in the foregoing that have tracked the regional migratory flows and movements of sex workers also discuss international paths.

35. See Patricia Robin Klausner, "The Politics of Massage Parlour Prostitution: The International Traffick in Women for Prostitution in New York City, 1970–Present" (Ph.D. diss., University of Delaware, 1987), especially chap. IV, on the organized movement of women from Argentina, through Puerto Rico, to New York, under operation "Broadsword."

36. See Chris de Stoop, *Ze Zijn Zo Lief, Meneer: Over De Vrouwenhandelaars, Meisjesbaletten En De Bende Van De Miljardair* (Leuven: Kritak, 1992); *Inside Story: The Women Trade*, BBC, 16 September 1992.

37. de Stoop, Ze Zijn, Zo Lief, Meneer.

38. Altink, Groen, and Vanwesenbeeck, *Sekswerk: Ervaringen van Vrouwen in de Prostitutie*, in particular, and *Keerzijde*, the newsletter publication of the STV (Foundation Against the Trafficking in Women), which documents current issues and situations as reported primarily in the Dutch media.

39. IOM Migration Information Programme, "Trafficking in Women from the Dominican Republic for Sexual Exploitation," 4.

40. See Licia Brussa, "Gezondheid in de Raamprostitutie: Evaluatie van het Medisch Spreekuur op de Achterdam in Alkmaar"

(Amsterdam: Mr. A. de Graaf Stichting, 1992); also see the annual
reports of Humanitas (*Jaarverslag 1991* [Rotterdam: Humanitas,
1992]) and the Stichting Prostitutie Projekten Den Haag (*Jaarver-slag 1990 en 1991* [The Hague: Stichting Prostitutie Projekten Den
Haag, 1993]). Interviews in 1993 by the author with social workers
attached to prostitution organizations in Amsterdam and The
Hague indicated the same trends.

41.   IOM Migration Information Programme, "Trafficking in Women
from the Dominican Republic for Sexual Exploitation," 6.

42.   COIN, *Juntarnos*.

43.   See also Gina Gallardo Rivas, "Buscando la Vida: Dominicanas en
el Servicio Doméstico en Madrid" (Santo Domingo: CIPAF, 1995).

44.   See *Le Monde Diplomatique*, December 2001.

45.   "Trafficking in Human Beings: Implications for the OSCE,"
ODIHR Background Paper, 9–10 September 1999,
www.osce.org/odhir/documents/background/trafficking.

46.   *Stop Traffic Digest* 1, no. 467, 28 November 2001.

47.   Trafficking into the United States for the sex industry was only
taken up in the late 1990s by the U.S. government, whereas in
Western Europe it has been the subject for interrogation by the
state and civil organizations since the mid-1980s.

48.   See Anneke van Ammelrooy, *Vrouwenhandel: De Internationale
Seksslavinnenmarkt* (The Hague: BZZToH, 1989); Agnes Delvaux,
"Achter de Sluier van het Schijnhuwelijk: Het Schijnhuwelijk in
Relatie tot Vrouwenhandel in Nederland en het Caraibische
Gebeid" (M.A. thesis, University of Leiden, 1990); and the follow-ing newspaper articles: Bert Bommels and Paul Grijpma, "Schijn-huwelijken: Grenzeloos problem voor politie en justitie," *Elsevier*, 2
March 1985, 16–23; "Schijn Bedreigt: Fictieve huwelijken,
vrouwenhandel en het Nederlanderschap," *Elsevier*, 6 June 1989.

49.   IOM Migration Information Programme, "Trafficking in Women
from the Dominican Republic for Sexual Exploitation."

50.   Referred to by the owner of Campo, nurses who worked at Campo,
and a doctor during interviews, 1993.

51.   Brennan, "Everything Is for Sale Here," 131.

52.   Lusette Fairbarn, "Muhe di Bida" in *Mundo Yama Sinta Mira:
Womanhood in Curaçao*, edited by Richenel Asano, Joceline
Clemencia, Jeanette Coch, and Eithel Martis (Curaçao: Fundashon
Publikashon, 1992.), 143–150. Summary in English on pg. 150.

53.   Brennan, "Everything Is for Sale Here," 131.

54.   See, for example, Phillips, "Tourism-oriented Prostitution in Barbados,"
Pruitt and Lafont, "For Love and Money."

55.   de Moya and Garcia, "Three Decades of Male Sex Work in Santo
Domingo," 134–35.

56.   Ibid., 135.

57.   Peter Stalker, *Workers without Frontiers: The Impact of Globalization
on International Migration* (Boulder, CO: Lynne Rienner, 2000).

58.   Thomas-Hope, "Skilled Labor Migration from Developing Coun-tries"; Duany, "Beyond the Safety Valve."

59. Duany, "Beyond the Safety Valve," 869.
60. See Carla Freeman, "Reinventing Higglering across Transnational Zones: Barbadian Women Juggle the Triple Shift," in *Daughters of Caliban: Caribbean Women in the Twentieth Century*, ed. Consuelo Lopez Springfield (Bloomington: Indiana University Press, 1997).
61. Ibid., 71.

Chapter 7: Dying for Sex: HIV/AIDS and Other Dangers

1. Alexander Irwin, Joyce Millen, and Dorothy Fallows, *Global AIDS: Myths and Facts* (Cambridge, MA: South End Press, 2003).
2. AIDS Epidemic Update, December 2001, http://www.unaids.org/epidemic.update/report-dec01/index.html. UNAIDS Fact Sheet 2002: Latin America and the Caribbean Joint United Nations Programme on HIV/AID (UNAIDS)
3. Bilali Camara, "20 Years of the HIV/AIDS Epidemic in the Caribbean: A Summary" (Port-of-Spain: CAREC/PAHO/WHO, 2001); J. Figueroa, "Breaking the Silence: AIDS—2000," *West Indian Medical Journal* 49, no. 3 (2000), 185–186.
4. Bilali Camara, "An Overview of the AIDS/HIV/STD Situation in the Caribbean," in *The Caribbean AIDS Epidemic*, ed. Glenford Howe and Alan Cobley (Kingston: University of the West Indies Press, 2000), 1–21.
5. CARICOM, "The Caribbean Regional Strategic Plan for HIV/AIDS: 1999–2004" (CARICOM, Secretariat, Guyana. 1999), 1.
6. *AIDS Window*, no. 1, 2000, 28.
7. Irwin, Millen, and Fallows, *Global AIDS*, 138.
8. See, for example, Keith Carter, "Female Sex Workers' Seroprevalence Survey, Georgetown, Guyana" (Georgetown: Unknown, 1993); E. Santo Rosario et al., "La Industria del Sexo por Dentro" (Santo Domingo: COIN, 1994); Julia Terborg, "AIDS en Prostitutie, Deelonderzoek I: Geregistreerde Prostituees" (Paramaribo: National AIDS Programma, Ministerie van Volsgezondheid, 1990); Julia Terborg, "AIDS en Prostitutie, Deelonderzoek II: Onderzoek Onder Mannelijke Klanten van de Dermatologische Dienst" (Paramaribo: National AIDS Programma, Ministerie Van Volsgezondheid, 1990); Claris O'Carroll-Barahona et al., "Needs Assessment Study among Street Based Female Commercial Sex Workers in Paramaribo, Suriname" (Paramaribo: National AIDS Programma, Ministerie van Volksgezondheid, 1994); Margarita Alegria et al., "HIV Infection, Risk Behaviors and Depressive Symptoms among Puerto Rican Sex Workers," *American Journal of Public Health* 84, no. 12 (1994), 2000–2002; Brader Braithwaite, "Gay Research Initiative on AIDS Prevention in the Caribbean" (Port of Spain: CAREC, 1996); Dusilley

Cannings and Jennifer Rosenweig, "Female Commercial Sex Worker's Project: Final Report" (Georgetown: National AIDS Programme Secretariat, Guyana, 1997); Toye H. Brewer et al., "Migration, Ethnicity and Environment: HIV Risk Factors for Women on the Sugar Cane Plantations of the Dominican Republic," *AIDS* 12, no. 14 (1998), 1879–1887; Campbell and Campbell, "HIV/AIDS Prevention and Education for Commercial Sex Workers in Jamaica"; Shiela Samiel, "Commercial Sex Work: Barbados" (Trinidad: Barbados National AIDS Commission and the Special Programme on Sexually Transmitted Infections [SPSTI, CAREC/GTZ], 2001); Alex P. Vega, Caroline Allen, and Geoffrey Stanford, "A Sexual Health Promotion Intervention and Caribbean Men Who Have Sex with Men" (Port of Spain: CAREC, 2001); Marjan de Bruin, "Teenagers at Risk: High-Risk Behavior of Adolescents in the Context of Reproductive Health" (Kingston: CARIMAC, University of the West Indies, 2001); Abraham Joshua Ken Bremnor, "Lifestyle Practices and HIV/AIDS in Trinidad and Tobago" (Port of Spain: Caribbean Union College, 2003); Sandra D. Reid, "Drug Use, Sexual Behavior and HIV Risk of the Homeless in Port-of-Spain, Trinidad," *West Indian Medical Journal* 48, no. 2 (1999), 57–60; Navindra E. Persaud et al., "Drug Use and Syphilis: Co-Factors for HIV Transmission among Commercial Sex Workers in Guyana," *West Indian Medical Journal* 48, no. 2 (1999), 52–56; Earl and Phillips Consulting Group, "Sexual Practice and Condom Use Study: The Eastern Caribbean" (Barbados: Population Services International, 2002).

9.   See Eileen J. Suarez Findlay, *Imposing Decency: The Politics of Sexuality in Puerto Rico, 1870–1920* (Durham: Duke University Press, 1999); Laura Briggs, *Reproducing Empire: Race, Sex, Science and U.S. Imperialism in Puerto Rico* (Berkeley and Los Angeles: University of California Press, 2002).

10. Navindra E. Persaud, "HIV Infection, Drug Use and HIV Risk Practices among Street-Based and Brothel-Based Female Commercial Sex Workers in Guyana" (unpublished report. Georgetown, Guyana, 1998), 8.

11. See, for example, Samiel, "Commercial Sex Work"; Bremnor, "Lifestyle Practices and HIV/AIDS in Trinidad and Tobago."

12. Camara, "20 Years of the HIV/AIDS Epidemic in the Caribbean."

13. A number of studies and reports on MSM have been produced, among them Braithwaite, "Gay Research Initiative on AIDS Prevention in the Caribbean"; Vega, Allen, and Stanford, "A Sexual Health Promotion Intervention and Caribbean Men Who Have Sex with Men"; Carlos F. Caceres, "HIV among Gay and Other Men Who Have Sex with Men in Latin America and the Caribbean: A Hidden Epidemic?" *AIDS* 16, Suppl. 3 (2002), 282–283.

14. In the Netherlands Antilles, the concept of "sexual networking" was developed as early as 1992. See Tineke Alberts, "Je Lust En Je Leven: Een Inventariserend Onderzoek Naar Relatievorming, Sexueel Gedrag en de Preventie van AIDS op Curaçao" (Willemstad: Nationale

AIDS commissie van de Nederlandse Antillen en de Geneeskundige-en Gezondheidsdienst van het Eilandgebied Curaçao, 1992). In the English-speaking Caribbean this concept found its way into the medical discourse in 2002. Personal communication with a researcher of the U.S. National Institute of Drug Abuse (NIDA) and the National Institutes of Health (NIH), March 2003. In April 2003, the NIH/NIDA held a symposium in which networking was a central concept.

15. Peter Figueroa, "Myths, Beliefs, Taboos: Current Attitudes Towards HIV/AIDS," *Cajanus* 29, no. 2 (1996), 53–61.
16. Kempadoo, "Adolescent Sex," 63.
17. D. T. Simeon et al., "Experiences and Socialization of Jamaican Men with Multiple Sex Partners," *West Indian Medical Journal* 48, no. 4 (1999): 212.
18. CAREC, "Guidelines for Upgrading of HIV/AIDS/STI Surveil-lance in the Caribbean" (Port of Spain: Caribbean Epidemiological Centre [CAREC], 2002), 74.
19. Irwin, Millen, and Fallows, *Global AIDS*.
20. Caroline Allen, "Social Science Approaches to Sexually Transmitted Diseases in the Caribbean," in *AIDS in the Caribbean*, ed. Glenford Howe and Alan Cobley (Kingston: University of the West Indies Press, 2000), 22–41.
21. See, for example, UNIFEM, "UNFPA Caribbean Youth Summit 1998: Adolescent Sexual and Reproductive Health and Rights" (UNIFEM Caribbean Office, Kingston, 1999).
22. Irwin, Millen, and Fallows, *Global AIDS*, 19.
23. de Zalduondo and Bernard, "Meanings and Consequences of Sexual-Economic Exchange."
24. Cindy Patton, *Globalizing AIDS* (Minneapolis: University of Minnesota Press, 2002), 40.
25. Ibid., 42.
26. Irwin, Millen, and Fallows, *Global AIDS*. A similar problem has been identified in late-nineteenth-century Puerto Rico, where the "tropical medical gaze" is seen to have been crucial in the produc-tion of racial difference between colonizer and colonized. See Briggs, *Reproducing Empire*.
27. Irwin, Millen, and Fallows, *Global AIDS*, 21.
28. CAREC, "Guidelines for Upgrading of HIV/AIDS/STI Surveil-lance in the Caribbean," 1.
29. Ibid., 7.
30. See also Paul Farmer, "Introduction," in Irwin, Millen, and Fallows, *Global AIDS*; Allen, "Social Science Approaches to Sexually Trans-mitted Diseases in the Caribbean"; Partners in Health, "2002 An-nual Report" (Boston: Partners in Health, 2003).
31. Alison Murray and Tess Robinson, "Minding Your Peers and Queers: Female Sex Workers in the AIDS Discourse in Australia and Southeast Asia," *Gender, Place and Culture* 3, no. 1 (1996): 45.
32. Ibid., 38.

33.   Annette Dula, "IWA Conference Paper" (Boulder: IWA, University of Colorado, 2000), 6.
34.   In Kenya, for example, hundreds of women were deliberately left to be exposed to HIV infection in order that scientific knowledge could be gathered about possible genetic immunity or a natural defense against HIV. The findings, that around 5 percent of the tested sex workers did not become HIV+ after years of exposure to the virus, have been hailed as a significant breakthrough in the medical world.
35.   Such as in a recent research project in Guyana.
36.   "HIV, AIDS and Other Sexually Transmitted Infections," in *Health in the Americas* (2002): 264.
37.   J. D. Stewart, "Is Medical Research Taking Us Where We Cannot Afford to Go?" *West Indian Medical Journal* 50, Suppl. 6 (2001), 14.
38.   http://www.actupny.org/reports/durban-access.html.
39.   *Guardian Weekly*, 11–17 July 2002.
40.   *BBC World News*, 3 July 2003.
41.   Claudette R. Francis, "The Psychosocial Dynamics of the AIDS Epidemic in the Caribbean," in Howe and Cobley, *The Caribbean AIDS Epidemic*, 192.
42.   Ahmed, "Children and Transactional Sex in Jamaica."
43.   Peter Figueroa, chief medical officer with the Jamaican Ministry of Health, is one of the proponents in the region who has openly and publicly called for the decriminalization of homosexuality and a review of laws governing prostitution with regards to HIV/AIDS prevention. As reported from a presentation he made during the 46th Annual Meeting of the Caribbean Health Research Council in 2001, "he urged policy makers to decriminalize and regulate 'sex work'" and "was advocating changes which rendered illegal the sexual relations between consenting adults in private because that situation was 'one of things which helps to drive the epidemic underground'" ("Figueroa Calls for Review of Sex Laws," *Daily Gleaner*, 27 April 2001, A2). See also Omar Francis, "The Legal and Ethical Issues Related to the Control of HIV," *West Indian Medical Journal* 50, no. 3 (2001), 183–185 who states that "restrictive laws force prostitutes underground and therefore undermine the educational programmes." Similar views were expressed to me by CAREC senior researcher Sheila Samiel during an informal interview in 2003.
44.   Kempadoo and Doezema, *Global Sex Workers*.
45.   Antonius-Smits, "Gold and Commercial Sex." See also Cannings et al., "It's Good to Know."
46.   Red Thread Women's Development Programme, "'Givin' Lil Bit Fuh Lil Bit'"; Cannings and Rosenweig, "Female Commercial Sex Worker's Project."
47.   CAREC/GTZ, "Research Protocol: HIV Infection and HIV Risk Practices among Female Sex Workers in Georgetown, Guyana" (Port of Spain: CAREC/GTZ, 2000), 1. See also Persaud, "HIV Infection, Drug Use and HIV Risk Practices."

48.   Andaiye, "The Red Thread Story," in *Spitting in the Wind: Lessons in Empowerment from the Caribbean*, ed. Suzanne Francis Brown (Kingston: Ian Randle, 2000), 51–98.

49.   See Red Thread Women's Development Programme, "'Givin' Lil Bit Fuh Lil Bit.'"

50.   CAREC/GTZ, "Research Protocol," 2.

51.   See Red Thread Women's Development Programme, "'Givin' Lil Bit Fuh Lil Bit'"; Red Thread Women's Development Programme, "Report of a Study on Female Commercial Sex Workers in Guyana."

52.   Red Thread Women's Development Programme, "Report of a Study on Female Commercial Sex Workers in Guyana," 14.

53.   Ibid.

54.   Cannings et al., "It's Good to Know."

55.   See, for example, the *CAREC Surveillance Report*, which provides statistics and details on communicable diseases in the CAREC member countries.

Chapter 8: Resistance, Rebellion, and Futures

1.   Nancy C. M. Hartsock, *The Feminist Standpoint Revisited and Other Essays* (Boulder: Westview Press, 1998), 221.

2.   Mohanty, "Cartographies of Struggle," 38.

3.   Lizabeth Paravisini-Gebert and Ivette Romero-Cesareo, eds., *Women at Sea: Travel Writing and the Margins of Caribbean Discourse* (New York: Palgrave, 2001).

4.   Carolyn Cooper, "Slackness Hiding from Culture: Erotic Play in the Dancehall," *Jamaica Journal* 22, no. 4 (1989/90), 12–20; Carolyn Cooper, *Noises in the Blood: Orality, Gender and the 'Vulgar' Body of Jamaican Popular Culture* (Durham: Duke University Press, 1995).

5.   Cooper, *Noises in the Blood*, 157.

6.   Ibid., 141, 11.

7.   Cooper, "Slackness Hiding from Culture," 19.

8.   Natasha Barnes, "Body Talk: Notes on Women and Spectacle in Contemporary Trinidad Carnival," *Small Axe: Journal of Criticism* 7 (2000): 95, 97.

9.   Tejaswini Niranjana, "'Left to the Imagination': Indian Nationalisms and Female Sexuality in Trinidad," *Small Axe: Journal of Criticism* 2 (1997): 18.

10.   Rawwida Baksh-Soodeen, "Power, Gender and Chutney," in *Matikor: The Politics of Identity for Indo-Caribbean Women*, ed. Rosanne Kanhai (St. Augustine: University of the West Indies School of Continuing Studies, 1999), 195.

11.   Ibid., 197.

12.   Ibid., 198.

13.   For example, the *Pisenlit* and Stickfighter characters in the Trinidad carnival, the *jamet/jammette* women (the name for Afro-Trinidadian women of the urban underclass that came to be a synonym for *prostitute* during the early twentieth century), the prostitute, the dance hall queen, the chutney-soca performer, and the working-class teenage girl.

14.   Pamela Franco, "The 'Unruly Woman' in Nineteenth-Century Trinidad Carnival," *Small Axe: Journal of Criticism* 7 (2000): 60.

15.   Ibid., 66, 70.

16.   Ibid., 76.

17.   Hartsock, *The Feminist Standpoint Revisited and Other Essays*, 240.

18.   Ibid., 244.

19.   This can be complemented by politics of gay and lesbian movements, such as J-FLAG in Jamaica and BGLAD in Barbados. A 2003 doctoral study by Jeanne Christensen that discusses Rastafari feminism also clearly points to another arena where a politics of sexual liberation among Caribbean women is articulated.

20.   COIN, *Juntarnos.*

21.   Laura Murray, "Global Sex Workers Act Locally," *Alliance News*, July/December 2001, 33.

22.   Ibid., 34.

23.   Antonius-Smits, "Gold and Commercial Sex," 241.

24.   Ibid.

25.   See Azize Vargas and Kempadoo, "Tráfico de Mujeres para Prostitución," and an unpublished report compiled by Azize Vargas on the GAATW/STV Latin American and Caribbean workshop on women's human rights in the context of trafficking and migration, held in the Dominican Republic, 12–16 June 1998.

26.   See Antonius-Smits, "Gold and Commercial Sex."

27.   See writings and publications about the sex workers' organizations MODEMU and the Maxi Linder Association in Kempadoo and Doezema, *Global Sex Workers*; Kempadoo, *Sun, Sex, and Gold.*

28.   Watson, "Global Neoliberalism."

Bibliography

Abraham-van der Mark, Eva. "Marriage and Concubinage among the Sephardic Merchant Elite of Curaçao." In *Women and Change in the Caribbean*, edited by Janet Momsen, 38–50. London: James Currey; Kingston: Ian Randle; Bloomington: Indiana University Press, 1993.

Ahmed, Aziza. "Children and Transactional Sex in Jamaica: Addressing Increased Vulnerability to HIV/AIDS." M.Sc. thesis, Harvard School of Public Health, 2003.

Alberts, Tineke. "Je Lust En Je Leven: Een Inventariserend Onderzoek Naar Relatievorming, Sexueel Gedrag en de Preventie van AIDS op Curaçao." Willemstad: Nationale AIDS commissie van de Nederlandse Antillen en de Geneeskundige-en Gezondheidsdienst van het Eilandgebied Curaçao, 1992.

Alegria, Margarita, Mildred Vera, Daniel H. Freeman, Rafael Robles, Maria del C. Santos, and Carmen L. Rivera. "HIV Infection, Risk Behaviors and Depressive Symptoms among Puerto Rican Sex Workers." *American Journal of Public Health* 84, no. 12 (1994): 2000–2.

Alegria, Ricardo. "The Study of Aboriginal Peoples: Multiple Ways of Knowing." In *The Indigenous People of the Caribbean*, edited by Samuel M. Wilson, 9–19. Gainesville: University Press of Florida, 1997.

Alexander, M. Jacqui. "Erotic Autonomy as a Politics of Decolonization: An Anatomy of Feminist and State Practice in the Bahamas Tourist Economy." In *Feminist Genealogies, Colonial Legacies, Democratic Futures*, edited by M. Jacqui Alexander and Chandra Talpade Mohanty, 63–100. New York: Routledge, 1997.

———. "Redrafting Morality: The Postcolonial State and the Sexual Offences Bill of Trinidad and Tobago." In *Third World Women and the Politics of Feminism*, edited by Chandra Talpade Mohanty, Ann Russo, and

Lourdes Torres, 133–52. Bloomington and Indianapolis: Indiana University Press, 1991.

Allaire, Louis. "Visions of Cannibals: Distant Islands and Distance Lands in Taino World Image." In *The Lesser Antilles in the Age of European Expansion*, edited by Robert L. Paquette and Stanley L. Engerman, 33–49. Gainesville: University Press of Florida, 1996.

Allen, Caroline. "Social Science Approaches to Sexually Transmitted Diseases in the Caribbean." In *AIDS in the Caribbean*, edited by Glenford Howe and Alan Cobley, 22–41. Kingston: University of the West Indies Press, 2000.

Alloula, Malek. *The Colonial Harem*. Minneapolis: University of Minnesota Press, 1986.

Altink, Sietske. *Stolen Lives: Trading Women into Sex and Slavery*. London: Scarlet Press, 1995.

Altink, Sietske, Martine Groen, and Ine Vanwesenbeeck. *Sekswerk: Ervaringen van Vrouwen in de Prostitutie*. Amsterdam: SUA, 1991.

Anarfi, John K. "Ghanaian Women and Prostitution in Cote D'ivoire." In *Global Sex Workers: Rights, Resistance, and Redefinition*, edited by Kamala Kempadoo, 104–13. New York: Routledge, 1998.

Andaiye . "The Red Thread Story." In *Spitting in the Wind: Lessons in Empowerment from the Caribbean*, edited by Suzanne Francis Brown, 51–98. Kingston: Ian Randle Publishers, 2000.

Antonius-Smits, Christel C. F. et al. "Gold and Commercial Sex: Exploring the Link between Small-Scale Gold Mining and Commercial Sex in the Rainforest of Suriname." In *Sun, Sex, and Gold: Tourism and Sex Work in the Caribbean*, edited by Kamala Kempadoo, 237–59. Lanham: Rowman and Littlefield, 1999.

Atluri, Tara L. "When the Closet Is a Region: Homophobia, Heterosexism and Nationalism in the Commonwealth Caribbean." Cave Hill, Barbados: Center for Gender and Development Studies, 2001.

Augier, F. R., and Shirley C. Gordon. *Sources of West Indian History*. London: Longman Caribbean, 1960.

Azize Vargas, Yamila, and Kamala Kempadoo. "Tráfico de Mujeres para Prostitución, Trabajo Doméstico y Matrimonio (Trafficking in Women for Prostitution, Domestic Work and Marriage)." San Juan: STV and GAATW, 1996.

Baksh-Soodeen, Rawwida. "Power, Gender and Chutney." In *Matikor: The Politics of Identity for Indo-Caribbean Women*, edited by Rosanne Kanhai, 194–98. St. Augustine: University of the West Indies School of Continuing Studies, 1999.

Bannerji, Himani. "But Who Speaks for Us? Experience and Agency in Conventional Feminist Paradigms." In *Unsettling Relations: The University as a Site of Feminist Struggles*, edited by Himani Bannerji, Linda Carty, Kari Delhi, Susan Heald, and Kate McKenna. Boston: South End Press, 1992.

Barnes, Natasha. "Body Talk: Notes on Women and Spectacle in Contemporary Trinidad Carnival." *Small Axe: Journal of Criticism* 7 (2000): 93–107.

———. "Face of the Nation: Race, Nationalisms, and Identities in Jamaican Beauty Pageants." In *Daughters of Caliban: Caribbean Women in the*

Twentieth Century, edited by Consuelo Lopez Springfield, 285–306. Bloomington: Indiana University Press, 1997.

Barriteau, Eudine. *The Political Economy of Gender in the Twentieth Century Caribbean.* New York: Palgrave, 2001.

Barrow, Christine. *Family in the Caribbean: Themes and Perspectives.* Kingston: Ian Randle; Oxford: James Currey, 1996.

Barry, Kathleen. *Female Sexual Slavery.* New York: New York University Press, 1984.

Beckles, Hilary. *Centering Woman: Gender Discourses in Caribbean Slave Society.* Kingston: Ian Randle Publishers, 1999.

———. *Natural Rebels: A Social History of Enslaved Black Women in Barbados.* London: Zed Books, 1989.

Benn, Denis, and Kenneth Hall, eds. *Globalisation: A Calculus of Inequality.* Kingston: Ian Randle, 2000.

Bisnauth, Dale. *The Settlement of Indians in Guyana 1890–1930.* London: Peepal Tree Press, 2000.

Blackwood, Renà. "Invisible Women: Identity Formation in Lesbians: A Study of Women from the Jamaican Homosexual Community." M.Sc. thesis, University of the West Indies, 2000.

Boucher, Philip P. *Cannibal Encounters: Europeans and Island Caribs, 1492–1763.* Baltimore: The Johns Hopkins University Press, 1992.

Bourdieu, Pierre. "First Lecture. Social Space and Symbolic Space: Introduction to Japanese Reading of Distinction." *Poetics Today*, no. 14 (1991): 628.

———. *Outline of a Theory of Practice.* Cambridge: Cambridge University Press, 1977.

Braithwaite, Brader. "Gay Research Initiative on AIDS Prevention in the Caribbean," 54. Port of Spain: CAREC, 1996.

Braithwaite, Edward K. *The Development of Creole Society in Jamaica, 1770–1820.* Oxford: Clarendon Press, 1971.

Bremnor, Abraham Joshua Ken. "Lifestyle Practices and HIV/AIDS in Trinidad and Tobago," 16. Port of Spain: Caribbean Union College, 2003.

Brennan, Denise E. "Everything Is for Sale Here: Sex Tourism in Sosúa, the Dominican Republic." Ph.D. diss., Yale University, 1998.

Brereton, Bridget. "The Promise of Emancipation." In *The Colonial Caribbean in Transition: Essays on Postemancipation Social and Cultural History*, edited by Bridget Brereton and Kevin A. Yelvington, 1–25. Kingston: University of the West Indies Press; Gainesville: University Press of Florida, 1999.

Brewer, Toye H., Hasburn Julia, Caroline A. Ryan, Stephen E. Hawes, Samuel Martinez, Jorge Sanchez, Martha Bulter de Lister, Jose Constanzo, Jose Lopez, and King K. Holmes. "Migration, Ethnicity and Environment: HIV Risk Factors for Women on the Sugar Cane Plantations of the Dominican Republic." *AIDS* 12, no. 14 (1998): 1879–87.

Briggs, Laura. *Reproducing Empire: Race, Sex, Science and U.S. Imperialism in Puerto Rico.* Berkeley and Los Angeles: University of California Press, 2002.

Brown, Janet, and Barry Chevannes. "'Why Man Stay So': Tie the Heifer, Loose the Bull. An Examination of Gender Socialization in the Caribbean." Kingston: University of the West Indies, 1998.

Brussa, Licia. "Gezondheid in de Raamprostitutie: Evaluatie van het Medisch Spreekuur op de Achterdam in Alkmaar." Amsterdam: Mr. A. de Graaf Stichting, 1992.

———. "Survey on Prostitution, Migration and Traffick in Women: History and Current Situation." Strasbourg: European Committee for Equality between Women and Men, Council of Europe, 1991.

Buijs, Heleen. "Dutch Prostitution Policy and Human Rights." Strasbourg: European Committee for Equality between Women and Men, Council of Europe, 1991.

Bush, Barbara. *Slave Women in Caribbean Society: 1650–1838*. Bloomington: Indiana University Press, 1990.

Butler, Judith. *Bodies that Matter: On the Discursive Limits of "Sex"*, New York: Routledge, 1993.

Byron, Jessica. "Migration, Nationalism, and Regionalism in the Caribbean." In *Contending with Destiny: The Caribbean in the 21st Century*, edited by Kenneth Hall and Denis Benn, 80–90. Kingston: Ian Randle, 2000.

Cabezas, Amalia Lucía. "Pleasure and Its Pain: Sex Tourism in Sosúa, the Dominican Republic." Ph.D. diss., University of California, Berkeley, 1998.

———. "Women's Work Is Never Done: Sex Tourism in Sosúa, the Dominican Republic." In *Sun, Sex, and Gold: Tourism and Sex Work in the Caribbean*, edited by Kamala Kempadoo, 93–124. Lanham: Rowman and Littlefield, 1999.

Caceres, Carlos F. "HIV among Gay and Other Men Who Have Sex with Men in Latin America and the Caribbean: A Hidden Epidemic?" *AIDS* 16, no. Suppl. 3 (2002): 23–33.

Camara, Bilali. "20 Years of the HIV/AIDS Epidemic in the Caribbean: A Summary." Port-of-Spain: CAREC/PAHO/WHO, 2001.

———. "An Overview of the AIDS/HIV/STD Situation in the Caribbean." In *The Caribbean AIDS Epidemic*, edited by Glenford Howe and Alan Cobley, 1–21. Kingston: University of the West Indies Press, 2000.

Campbell, Penelope, and Ann Marie E. Campbell. "HIV/AIDS Prevention and Education for Commercial Sex Workers in Jamaica: An Exploratory Study and Needs Assessment." Kingston: National HIV/STI Prevention and Control Programme, Ministry of Health, Jamaica, 2001.

Campbell, Shirley, Althea Perkins, and Patricia Mohammed. "'Come to Jamaica and Feel All Right': Tourism and the Sex Trade." In *Sun, Sex, and Gold: Tourism and Sex Work in the Caribbean*, edited by Kamala Kempadoo, 125–56. Lanham: Rowman and Littlefield, 1999.

Cannings, Dusilley, Juanita Altenberg, Judi Reichart, and Kamala Kempadoo. "It's Good to Know: The Maxi Linder Association in Suriname." In *Global Sex Workers: Rights, Resistance, and Redefinition*, edited by Kamala Kempadoo and Jo Doezema, 215–25. New York: Routledge, 1998.

Cannings, Dusilley, and Jennifer Rosenweig. "Female Commercial Sex Worker's Project: Final Report." Georgetown: National AIDS Programme Secretariat, Guyana, 1997.

CAREC. "Guidelines for Upgrading of HIV/AIDS/STI Surveillance in the Caribbean." Port of Spain: Caribbean Epidemiological Centre (CAREC), 2002.

CAREC/GTZ. "Research Protocol: HIV Infection and HIV Risk Practices among Female Sex Workers in Georgetown, Guyana." Port of Spain: CAREC/GTZ, 2000.

CARICOM. "The Caribbean Regional Strategic Plan for HIV/AIDS: 1999–2004." CARICOM Secretariat, Guyana, 1999.

Carter, Keith. 1993. "Female Sex Workers' Seroprevalence Survey, Georgetown, Guyana." Georgetown: Unknown, 1993.

Centro de Orientación e Investigación Integra (COIN). *Juntarnos. Memorias Primer Congreso Dominicano de Trabajadoras Sexuales*. Santo Domingo: COIN, 1996.

Chambers, Claudia, and Barry Chevannes. "Report on Six Focus Group Discussions: Sexual Decision-Making Project." Kingston: ISER-UCLA, University of the West Indies, 1994.

Chanel, Ives Marie, and Cathy Shepherd (trans.). "Haitian and Dominican Women in the Sex Trade." *CAFRA News*, June 1994, 13–14.

Chapkis, Wendy. *Live Sex Acts: Women Performing Erotic Labor*. New York: Routledge, 1997.

Chevannes, Barry. *Learning to Be a Man: Culture, Socialization and Gender Identity in Five Caribbean Communities*. Kingston: The University of the West Indies Press, 2001.

———. "Sexual Attitudes and Behavior of Jamaican Men." Kingston: Jamaican Family Planning Association, 1986.

———. "Sexual Behavior of Jamaicans: A Literature Review." *Social and Economic Studies* 42, no. 1 (1993): 1–45.

Chevannes, Barry, and Herbert Gayle. "Adolescent and Young Male Sexual and Reproductive Health Study, Jamaica: Report to the Pan American Health Organization." Kingston: University of the West Indies, 2000.

Clarke, Edith. *My Mother Who Fathered Me: A Study of the Families in Three Selected Communities of Jamaica*. Kingston: The University Press of the West Indies, 1999 (ca. 1957).

Clemencia, Joceline, "Women Who Love Women in Curaçao: From Cachapera to Open Throats–A Commentary in Collage." *Feminist Studies*, 22(1) (1996): 81–88.

Colchester, Marcus. *Guyana Fragile Frontier: Loggers, Miners and Forest Peoples*. London: Latin America Bureau; Kingston: Ian Randle Publishers, 1997.

Commissie ter Bestrijding van Prostitutie en Geslachts-ziekten. "Rapport Aan Zijne Excellentie Den Gouverneur Van Curaçao." Willemstad: Commissie ter Bestrijding van Prostitutie en Geslachts-ziekten, 1942.

Cooper, Carolyn. *Noises in the Blood: Orality, Gender and the 'Vulgar' Body of Jamaican Popular Culture*. Durham: Duke University Press, 1995.

———. "Slackness Hiding from Culture: Erotic Play in the Dancehall." *Jamaica Journal* 22, no. 4 (1989/90): 12–20.

Coquery-Widrovitch, Catherine. "Prostitution: From 'Free' Women to Women with AIDS." In *African Women: A Modern History*. edited by Catherine Coquery-Widrovitch, translated by Beth Gillian Raps. Boulder: Westview Press, 1997, 117–128.

Crick, Malcolm. "Representations of International Tourism in the Social Sciences: Sun, Sex, Sights, Savings, and Servility." *Annual Review of Anthropology* 18 (1989): 307–44.

Cumber Dance, Daryl. "Matriarchs, Doves and Nymphos: Prevalent Images of Black, Indian and White Women in Caribbean Literature." *Studies in Literary Imagination*, no. 26 (1993): 21.

Dann, Graham. *The Barbadian Male: Sexual Attitudes and Practice.* London: Macmillan Caribbean, 1987.

Danns, George K. "Child Prostitution and Child Sexual Exploitation in Guyana: A Study of Children in Especially Difficult Circumstances." Georgetown: UNICEF, 1998.

de Bruin, Marjan. "Teenagers at Risk: High-Risk Behavior of Adolescents in the Context of Reproductive Health," 40. Kingston: CARIMAC, University of the West Indies, 2001.

de Moya, Antonio E., and Rafael Garcia. "AIDS and the Enigma of Bisexuality in the Dominican Republic." In *Bisexuality and AIDS in International Perspective*, edited by Peter Aggleton, 21–35. London: Taylor & Francis, 1996.

————. "Three Decades of Male Sex Work in Santo Domingo." In *Men Who Sell Sex: International Perspectives on Male Prostitution and HIV/AIDS*, edited by Peter Aggleton, 127–40. Philadelphia: Temple University Press, 1999.

de Reus, Tjeerd. *Geslachtsziekten Op Curaçao.* Assen: Van Gorcum, 1970.

de Stoop, Chris. *Ze Zijn Zo Lief, Meneer: Over de Vrouwenhandelaars, Meisjesbaletten en de Bende van de Miljardair.* Leuven: Kritak, 1992.

de Zalduondo, Barbara O., and Jean Maxius Bernard. "Meanings and Consequences of Sexual-Economic Exchange: Gender, Poverty and Sexual Risk Behavior in Urban Haiti." In *Conceiving Sexuality: Approaches to Sex Research in a Postmodern World*, edited by Richard G. Parker and John H. Gagnon, 157–80. New York: Routledge, 1995.

Delvaux, Agnes. "Achter de Sluier van het Schijnhuwelijk: Het Schijnhuwelijk in Relatie tot Vrouwenhandel in Nederland en het Caraibische Gebeid." M.A. thesis, University of Leiden, 1990.

Díaz, Elena, Esperanza Fernández, and Tania Caram. "Turismo y Prostitución en Cuba." Havana: Facultad Latinoamericana de Ciencias Sociales, Universidad de Havana, 1996.

di Leonardo, Micaela. *Exotics at Home: Anthropology, Others, American Modernity.* Chicago: University of Chicago Press, 1998.

Duany, Jorge. "Beyond the Safety Valve: Recent Trends in Caribbean Migration." In *Caribbean Sociology: Introductory Readings*, edited by Christine Barrow and Rhoda Reddock, 861–76. Kingston: Ian Randle, 2001.

Duarte, Isis, Carmen Julia Gómez, and Marina Ariza. "Profiles on Minors in Especially Difficult Circumstances in the Dominican Republic." Santo Domingo: Instituto de Estudios de Población y Desarrollo, 1994.

Dula, Annette. "IWA Conference Paper." Boulder: IWA University of Colorado, 2000.

Dunn, Leith L. "Jamaica: Situation of Children in Prostitution: A Rapid Assessment," 89. Geneva: International Labor Organization/International Programme on the Elimination of Child Labor, 2001.

The Earl and Phillips Consulting Group. "Sexual Practice and Condom Use Study: The Eastern Caribbean," 43. Barbados: Population Services International, 2002.

Eggleton, Elizabeth, Jean Jackson, and Karen Hardee. "Sexual Attitudes and Behavior among Young Adolescents in Jamaica." *International Family Planning Perspectives* 25, no. 2 (1999): 78–84.

Elwin, Rosamund. "Introduction: Tongues on Fire: Speakin' Zami Desire." In *Tongues on Fire: Caribbean Lesbian Lives and Stories*, edited by Rosamund Elwin, 7–10. Toronto: Women's Press, 1997.

———, ed. *Tongues on Fire: Caribbean Lesbian Lives and Stories*. Toronto: Women's Press, 1997.

Engels, Frederick. *The Origin of the Family, Private Property, and the State*. Peking: Foreign Language Press, 1978 (ca. 1884).

Enloe, Cynthia. *Bananas, Beaches and Bases: Making Feminist Sense of International Politics*. Berkeley: University of California Press, 1989.

Espinet, Ramabai. "Representation and the Indo-Caribbean Woman in Trinidad and Tobago." In *Indo-Caribbean Resistance*, edited by Frank Birbalsingh, 42–61. Toronto: TSAR, 1993.

Fairbarn, Lusette, "Muhe Di Bada." In *Mundo Yama Sinta Mira*: Womanhood in Curaçao, edited by Richenel Asano, Joceline Clemencia, Jeanette Coch, and Eithel Marts, 143–50. Curaçao: Fundashon Publikashon, 1992.

Fanon, Frantz. *Black Skin, White Masks*, translated by Charles Lam Markmann. New York: Grove Press, 1967.

———. *The Wretched of the Earth*. New York: Grove Press, 1963.

Farmer, Paul. "Introduction." In *Global AIDS: Myths and Facts*, edited by Alexander Irwin, Errol Miller, and Dorothy Fallows, xvii–xxviii. Boston: South End Press, 2003.

Figueroa, J. "Breaking the Silence: AIDS—2000." *West Indian Medical Journal* 49, no. 3 (2000): 185–86.

Figueroa, Peter. "Myths, Beliefs, Taboos: Current Attitudes Towards HIV/AIDS." *Cajanus* 29, no. 2 (1996): 53–61.

Findlay, Eileen J. Suarez. *Imposing Decency: The Politics of Sexuality in Puerto Rico, 1870–1920*. Durham: Duke University Press, 1999.

Francis, Claudette R. "The Psychosocial Dynamics of the AIDS Epidemic in the Caribbean." In *The Caribbean AIDS Epidemic*, edited by Glenford Howe and Alan Cobley, 186–201. Kingston: University of the West Indies Press, 2000.

Francis, Omar. "The Legal and Ethical Issues Related to the Control of HIV." *West Indian Medical Journal* 50, no. 3 (2001): 183–85.

Franco, Pamela. "The 'Unruly Woman' in Nineteenth-Century Trinidad Carnival." *Small Axe: Journal of Criticism* 7 (2000): 60–76.

Frazier, E. Franklin, *The Negro Family in Chicago*. Chicago: University of Chicago Press, 1932, 32–33.

Freeman, Carla. "Reinventing Higglering across Transnational Zones: Barbadian Women Juggle the Triple Shift." In *Daughters of Caliban: Caribbean Women in the Twentieth Century*, edited by Consuelo Lopez Springfield, 243–51. Bloomington: Indiana University Press, 1997.

Fusco, Coco. "Hustling for Dollars." *Ms. Magazine*, September/October 1996, 62–70.

Gallardo Rivas, Gina. "Buscando la Vida: Dominicanas en el Servicio Doméstico en Madrid." Santo Domingo: CIPAF, 1995.

Geggus, David P. "Slave and Free Colored Women in Saint Domingue." In *More Than Chattel: Black Women and Slavery in the Americas*, edited by David Barry Gaspar and Darlene Clark Hine, 259–78. Bloomington: Indiana University Press, 1996.

Gilman, Sander L. "Black Bodies, White Bodies: Toward an Iconography of Female Sexuality in Late Nineteenth-Century Art, Medicine, and Literature." In *"Race," Writing, and Difference*, edited by Henry Louis Gates Jr., 223–61. Chicago: The University of Chicago Press, 1986.

Girvan, Norman. "Globalisation and Counter Globalisation: The Caribbean in the Context of the South." In *Globalisation: A Calculus of Inequality*, edited by Denis Benn and Kenneth Hall, 65–87. Kingston: Ian Randle Publishers, 2001.

———. "Reinterpreting the Caribbean." In *New Caribbean Thought*, edited by Brian Meeks and Folke Lindahl, 3–23. Kingston: The University of the West Indies Press, 2001.

Hall, Catherine. "Gender Politics and Imperial Politics: Rethinking the Histories of Empire." In *Engendering History: Caribbean Women in Historical Perspective*, edited by Verene A. Shepherd, Bridget Brereton, and Barbara Bailey, 48–59. New York: St. Martin's Press, 1995.

Hall, Stuart. "Negotiating Caribbean Identities." In *New Caribbean Thought*, edited by Brian Meeks and Folke Lindahl, 24–39. Kingston: University of the West Indies Press, 2001.

Hammonds, Evelyn M. "Toward a Genealogy of Black Female Sexuality: The Problematic of Silence." In *Feminist Genealogies, Colonial Legacies, Democratic Futures*, edited by M. Jacqui Alexander and Chandra Talpade Mohanty, 170–182. New York: Routledge, 1997.

Hartog, Johan. *Curaçao*. Aruba: De Wit, 1968.

Hartsock, Nancy C. M. *The Feminist Standpoint Revisited and Other Essays*. Boulder: Westview Press, 1998.

Henriques, Fernando. *Children of Caliban: Miscegenation*. London: Secker and Warburg, 1974.

———. *Family and Color in Jamaica*. London: Eyre and Spottiswoode, 1953.

———. *Prostitution and Society: Primitive, Classical and Oriental*. Vol. I. London: MacGibbon and Kee, 1962.

———. *Prostitution in Europe and the Americas*. New York: Citadel Press, 1965.

———. *Prostitution in Europe and the New World*. Vol. II. London: MacGibbon and Kee, 1963.

———. *Stews and Strumpets: A Survey of Prostitution*. London: MacGibbon and Kee, 1961.

Herold, Edward, Rafael Garcia, and Antonio E. de Moya. "Female Tourists and Beach Boys: Romance and Sex Tourism." *Annals of Tourism Research* 28, no. 4 (2001): 978–97.

Herskovits, Melville J. *Life in a Haitian Village*. New York: Octagon Books, 1964 (ca. 1937).

————. *The Myth of the Negro Past*. Boston: Beacon Press, 1958.

————. *Rebel Destiny: Among the Bush Negroes of Dutch Guiana*. New York: McGraw-Hill, 1934.

————. *Suriname Folk-Lore*. New York: Columbia University Press, 1936.

Herskovits, Melville J., and Frances S. Herskovits. *Trinidad Village*. New York: Alfred A. Knopf, 1947.

Hesselink, Liesbeth. "Prostitution: A Necessary Evil, Particularly in the Colonies. Views on Prostitution in the Netherlands Indies." In *Indonesian Women in Focus*, edited by Elsbeth Locher-Scholten and Anke Niehof, 205–24. Dordrecht/Providence: Floris Publications, 1987.

"HIV, AIDS and Other Sexually Transmitted Infections." In *Health in the Americas*, 262–66, 2002.

Hoetink, H. "Suriname and Curaçao." In *Neither Slave nor Free: The Freedman of African Descent in Slave Societies of the New World*, edited by D. W. Cohen and J. P. Greene. Baltimore/London: Johns Hopkins University Press, 1972.

Hoogbergen, Wim, and Marjo de Theye. "Surinaamse Vrouwen in De Slavernij." In *Vrouwen in de Nederlandse Kolonien: 7de Jaarboek Voor Vrouwengeschiedenis*, edited by Jeske Reijs, Els Kloek, Ulla Jansz, Annemaie de Wildt, Suzanne van Norden, and Mirjam de Baar, 126–51. Nijmegen: SUN, 1986.

hooks, bell. "Dreaming Ourselves Dark and Deep: Black Beauty." In *Sisters of the Yam: Black Women and Self-Recovery*. Boston: South End Press, 1993, 79–98.

Hope, Donna. "Of 'Chi-Chi' Men—the Threat of Male Homosexuality to Afro-Jamaican Masculine Identity." Paper presented at the 20th Annual Caribbean Studies Association Conference, St. Maarten, 2001.

Howard, David. *Coloring the Nation: Race and Ethnicity in the Dominican Republic*. Boulder: Lynne Rienner Publishers; Oxford: Signal Books, 2001.

Hulme, Peter. *Colonial Encounters: Europe and the Native Caribbean 1492–1797*. London: Routledge, 1992.

Hulme, Peter, and Neil L. Whitehead, eds. *Wild Majesty: Encounters with Caribs from Columbus to the Present Day*. Oxford: Clarendon Press, 1992.

Hunter, Mark. "The Materiality of Everyday Sex: Thinking Beyond 'Prostitution.'" *African Studies* 61, no. 1 (2002): 99–120.

Illouz, Eva. *Consuming the Romantic Utopia: Love and the Cultural Contradictions of Capitalism*. Berkeley: University of California Press, 1997.

IOM Migration Information Programme. "Trafficking in Women from the Dominican Republic for Sexual Exploitation." Geneva: International Organization on Migration, 1996.

Irwin, Alexander, Joyce Millen, and Dorothy Fallows. *Global AIDS: Myths and Facts*. Cambridge, MA: South End Press, 2003.

Jara, Rene, and Nicholas Spadaccini, eds. *Amerindian Images and the Legacy of Columbus*. Vol. 9, *Hispanic Issues*, edited by Nicholas Spadaccini. Minneapolis: University of Minnesota Press, 1992.

Jean, Jean-Pierre. "The 10th Department." *NACLA Report on the Americas*, January/February 1994, 41–45.

Kabbani, Rana. *Europe's Myths of Orient*. London: Pandora Press, 1986.

Kalm, Florence. "The Two 'Faces' of Antillean Prostitution." Paper presented at the American Anthropological Association meeting, 1975.

Kane, Stephanie C. "Prostitution and the Military: Planning AIDS Interven-
    tion in Belize." *Social Science and Medicine*, no. 36 (1993): 965–79.
Karch, Cecilia A., and G. H. S. Dann. "Close Encounters of the Third Kind."
    Human Relations 34 (1981): 249–68.
Keegan, William F. "Columbus Was a Cannibal: Myth and the First Encoun-
    ters." In *The Lesser Antilles in the Age of European Expansion*, 17–32.
    Gainesville: University Press of Florida, Boulder, 1996.
Kempadoo, Kamala. "Adolescent Sex: A Study in Three Communities in
    Jamaica." Kingston: UNICEF and UNFPA, Jamaica, 2001.
———. "Exotic Colonies: Caribbean Women in the Dutch Sex Trade."
    Ph.D. diss., University of Colorado, Boulder, 1994.
———. "Prostitution and Sex Work Studies" in the *Blackwell Companion to
    Gender Studies*, edited by Philomena Essed, Audrey Kobayashi, and
    David Theo Goldberg, London: Blackwell, 2004.
———. "'SanDom's' and Other Exotic Women: Prostitution and Race in the
    Caribbean." *Race and Reason: Journal of the Institute for African-American
    Studies, Columbia University* (1996): 48–54.
———. "Women of Color and the Global Sex Trade: Transnational Feminist
    Perspectives." *Meridians* 1, no. 3 (2001): 28–51.
———, ed. *Sun, Sex, and Gold: Tourism and Sex Work in the Caribbean*. Lanham:
    Rowman and Littlefield, 1999.
Kempadoo, Kamala, and Jo Doezema, eds. *Global Sex Workers: Rights, Resis-
    tance, and Redefinition*. New York: Routledge, 1998.
Kempadoo, Kamala, and Cynthia Mellon. "The Sex Trade in the Caribbean."
    Boulder: University of Colorado, CAFRA, and ILSA, 1998.
Kerr, Paulette. "Victims or Strategists? Female Lodging-House Keepers in
    Jamaica." In *Engendering History: Caribbean Women in Historical Perspec-
    tive*, edited by Verene A. Shepherd, Bridget Brereton, and Barbara Bai-
    ley, 197–212. New York: St. Martin's Press, 1995.
Khan, Aisha. "Journey to the Center of the Earth: The Caribbean as Master
    Symbol." *Cultural Anthropology* 16, no. 3 (2001): 271–302.
———. "What Is 'a Spanish'? Ambiguity and 'Mixed' Ethnicity in
    Trinidad." In *Trinidad Ethnicity*, edited by Kevin A. Yelvington.
    Knoxville: University of Tennesee Press, 1993. Reprinted in C. Barrow
    and R. Reddock. *Caribbean Sociology: Introductory Readings*. Kingston:
    Ian Randle, 2001, 287–304.
Kincaid, Jamaica. *A Small Place*. New York: Penguin, 1988.
Klak, Thomas, ed. *Globalization and Neoliberalism: The Caribbean Context*.
    Boulder: Rowman and Littlefield, 1998.
Klausner, Patricia Robin. "The Politics of Massage Parlour Prostitution: The
    International Traffick in Women for Prostitution in New York City,
    1970–Present." Ph.D. diss., University of Delaware , 1987.
Kutzinski, Vera M. *Sugar's Secrets: Race and the Erotics of Cuban Nationalism*.
    Charlottesville: University Press of Virginia, 1993.
Lagro, Monique, and Donna Plotkin. "The Suitcase Traders in the Free Zone
    of Curaçao." Port of Spain: Caribbean Development and Co-operation
    Committee, Economic Commission for Latin America and the
    Caribbean, 1990.

Leiner, Marvin. *Sexual Politics in Cuba: Machismo, Homosexuality, and AIDS*. Boulder: Westview Press, 1994.

Lewis, Linden. "Constructing the Masculine in the Context of the Caribbean." 19th Annual Caribbean Studies Association Conference, Merida Mexico: 1994.

———. "Nationalism and Caribbean Masculinity." In *Gender Ironies of Nationalism*, edited by Tamar Mayer, 261–81. New York: Routledge, 2000.

Lewis, Reina. *Gendering Orientalism: Race, Femininity and Representation*. London: Routledge, 1996.

Lim, Lin Leam, ed. *The Sex Sector: The Economic and Social Bases of Prostitution in Southeast Asia*. Geneva: International Labor Office, 1998.

Lindsay, Keisha. "Is the Caribbean Male an Endangered Species?" In *Gendered Realities: Essays in Caribbean Feminist Thought*, edited by Patricia Mohammed. Kingston: University of the West Indies Press, 2002, 56–82.

Lokaisingh-Meighoo, Sean. "*Jahaji Bhai*: Notes on the Masculine Subject and Homoerotic Subtext of Indo-Caribbean Identity." *Small Axe: Journal of Criticism* 7 (2000): 77–92.

Lumsden, Ian. *Machos, Maricones, and Gays: Cuba and Homosexuality*. Philadelphia: Temple University Press, 1996.

MacCannell, Dean. *The Tourist: A New Theory of the Leisure Class*. New York: Shocken Books, 1989.

Maingot, Anthony P. "The Offshore Caribbean." In *Modern Caribbean Politics*, edited by Anthony Payne and Paul Sutton, 259–76. Kingston: Ian Randle, 1993.

Mangru, Basdeo. "The Sex Ratio Disparity and Its Consequences under the Indenture in British Guiana." In *India in the Caribbean*, edited by David Dabydeen and Brinsley Samaroo, 211–30. London: Hansib/University of Warwick, 1987.

Martins, U. C. H. "Hoe Campo Alegre Ontstond." In *Koperen Polyfonie*, 30–42. Yearbook of Universiteit van Nederlandse Antilles, Curaçao, 1984.

Martis, Jacqueline. "Tourism and the Sex Trade in St. Maarten and Curaçao." In *Sun, Sex, and Gold: Tourism and Sex Work in the Caribbean*, edited by Kamala Kempadoo, 201–16. Lanham: Rowman and Littlefield, 1999.

Mayorga, Laura, and Pilar Velasqez. "Bleak Pasts, Bleak Futures: Life Paths of Thirteen Young Prostitutes in Cartagena, Colombia." In *Sun, Sex, and Gold: Tourism and Sex Work in the Caribbean*, edited by Kamala Kempadoo, 157–82. Lanham: Rowman and Littlefield, 1999.

McClintock, Anne. *Imperial Leather: Race, Gender and Sexuality in the Colonial Contest*. New York: Routledge, 1995.

Meunier, Jacques, and A. M. Savarin. *The Amazonian Chronicles*, translated by Carol Christensen. San Francisco: Mercury House, 1991.

Miller, Errol. *Men at Risk*. Kingston: Jamaica Publishing House, 1991.

Mohammed, Patricia. "'But Most of All Mi Love Mi Browning': The Emergence in Eighteenth and Nineteenth Century Jamaica of the Mulatto Woman as the Desired." *Feminist Review*, no. 65 (2000): 22–48.

———. "A Symbiotic Visiting Relationship: Caribbean Feminist Historiography and Caribbean Feminist Theory." In *Confronting Power, Theorizing*

Gender: Interdisciplinary Perspectives in the Caribbean, edited by Eudine Barriteau. Cave Hill: University of the West Indies Press, 2003, 101–125.

———. "Towards Indigenous Feminist Theorizing in the Caribbean." *Feminist Review* 59 (1998): 6–33.

———. "Writing Gender into History: The Negotiation of Gender Relations among Indian Men and Women in Post-Indenture Trinidad Society 1917–47." In *Engendering History: Caribbean Women in Historical Perspective*, edited by Verene A. Shepherd, Bridget Brereton, and Barbara Bailey, 20–47. New York: St. Martin's Press, 1995.

Mohammed, Patricia, and Althea Perkins. *Caribbean Women at the Crossroads: The Paradox of Motherhood among Women of Barbados, St. Lucia and Dominica*. Kingston: Canoe Press, University of the West Indies, 1999.

Mohanty, Chandra Talpade. "Cartographies of Struggle: Third World Women and the Politics of Feminism." In *Third World Women and the Politics of Feminism*, edited by Chandra Talpade Mohanty, Ann Russo, and Lourdes Torres, 1–47. Bloomington: Indiana University Press, 1991.

Morrissey, Marietta. *Slave Women in the New World: Gender Stratification in the Caribbean*. Lawrence: University Press of Kansas, 1989.

Mullings, Beverley. "Globalization, Tourism, and the International Sex Trade." In *Sun, Sex, and Gold: Tourism and Sex Work in the Caribbean*, edited by Kamala Kempadoo, 55–80. Lanham: Rowman and Littlefield, 1999.

Murray, Alison, and Tess Robinson. "Minding Your Peers and Queers: Female Sex Workers in the AIDS Discourse in Australia and Southeast Asia." *Gender, Place and Culture* 3, no. 1 (1996): 43–59.

Murray, David A. B. "Between a Rock and a Hard Place: The Power and Powerlessness of Transnational Narratives among Gay Martinican Men." *American Anthropologist* 102, no. 2 (2000): 261–70.

———. *Opacity: Gender, Sexuality, Race, and the 'Problem' of Identity in Martinique*. New York/Washington, D.C.: Peter Lang, 2002.

Murray, Laura. "Global Sex Workers Act Locally." *Alliance News*, July/December 2001, 32–38.

Niranjana, Tejaswini. "'Left to the Imagination': Indian Nationalisms and Female Sexuality in Trinidad." *Small Axe: Journal of Criticism* 2 (1997): 1–18.

O'Carroll-Barahona, Claris, Juanita Altenberg, Dusilley Cannings, Christel Antonius-Smits, and Ruben Del Prado. "Needs Assessment Study among Street Based Female Commercial Sex Workers in Paramaribo, Suriname." Paramaribo: National AIDS Programma, Ministerie can Volksgezondheid, 1994.

O'Connell Davidson, Julia, and Jacqueline Sanchez Taylor. "Fantasy Islands: Exploring the Demand for Sex Tourism." In *Sun, Sex, and Gold: Tourism and Sex Work in the Caribbean*, edited by Kamala Kempadoo, 37–54. Lanham: Rowman and Littlefield, 1999.

O'Connell Davidson, Julia. "Sex Tourism in Cuba." *Race and Class* 38 (1996): 39–48.

Oppermann, Martin. "Introduction." In *Sex Tourism and Prostitution: Aspects of Leisure, Recreation and Work*, edited by Martin Oppermann, 1–19. New York: Cognizant Communication Corporation, 1998.

————, ed. *Sex Tourism and Prostitution: Aspects of Leisure, Recreation and Work.* New York: Cognizant Communication Corporation, 1998.

Padilla, Mark. "Looking for Life: Male Sex Work, HIV/AIDS and the Political Economy of Gay Sex Tourism in the Dominican Republic." Ph.D. dissertation, Emory University, Atlanta, 2003.

Paquette, Robert L., and Stanley L. Engerman, eds. *The Lesser Antilles in the Age of European Expansion.* Gainseville: University Press of Florida, 1996.

Paravisini-Gebert, Lizabeth, and Ivette Romero-Cesareo, eds. *Women at Sea: Travel Writing and the Margins of Caribbean Discourse.* New York: Palgrave, 2001.

Parker, Andrew, Regina Maria Barbosa, and Peter Aggleton, eds. *Framing the Sexual Subject: The Politics of Gender, Sexuality, and Power.* Berkeley: University of California Press, 2000.

Partners in Health. "2002 Annual Report." Boston: Partners in Health, 2003.

Patton, Cindy. *Globalizing AIDS.* Minneapolis: University of Minnesota Press, 2002.

Pattullo, Polly. *Last Resorts: The Cost of Tourism in the Caribbean.* Kingston: Ian Randle, 1996.

Paul, Amy Raquel. "'It Isn't Love, It's Business': Prostitution as Entrepreneurship and the Implications for Barbados." Ph.D. diss., University of California–Los Angeles, 1997.

Paul, Annie. "The Chi Chi Man Syndrome." *Sunday Herald,* 8–14 July 2001.

Peake, Linda, and Alissa D. Trotz. *Gender, Ethnicity and Place: Women and Identities in Guyana, Routledge Studies in Development and Society.* New York: Routledge, 1999.

Persaud, Anil. "Fertility, Unnatural Sex and Fetishism: Creating Value in the Emancipated British Sugar Colonies." Paper presented at the 2003 Conference on Feminist Economics, University of the West Indies, Cave Hill Campus, 2003.

Persaud, Navindra E. "HIV Infection, Drug Use and HIV Risk Practices among Street-Based and Brothel-Based Female Commercial Sex Workers in Guyana." Unpublished report, Georgetown, Guyana, 1998.

Persaud, Navindra E., W. Klaskala, T. Tewari, J. Shultz, and M. Baum. "Drug Use and Syphilis: Co-Factors for HIV Transmission among Commercial Sex Workers in Guyana." *West Indian Medical Journal* 48, no. 2 (1999): 52–56.

Pheterson, Gail. *The Prostitution Prism.* Amsterdam: Amsterdam University Press, 1996.

Phillips, Joan L. "The Beach Boys of Barbados: Post-Colonial Entrepreneurs." In *Transnational Prostitution: Changing Global Patterns,* edited by Susanne Thorbek and Bandana Pattanaik, 42–55. London: Zed Books, 2002.

————. "Tourism-Oriented Prostitution in Barbados: The Case of the Beach Boy and the White Female Tourist." In *Sun, Sex, and Gold: Tourism and Sex Work in the Caribbean,* edited by Kamala Kempadoo, 183–200. Lanham: Rowman and Littlefield, 1999.

Piedra, Jose. "Loving Columbus." In *Amerindian Images and the Legacy of Columbus,* edited by Rene Jara and Nicholas Spadaccini, 230–65. Minneapolis: University of Minnesota Press, 1992.

Porter, Roy. "The Exotic as Erotic: Captain Cook in Tahiti." In *Exoticism in the Enlightenment*, edited by G. S. Rousseau and Roy Porter. Manchester: Manchester University Press, 1990.

Poynting, Jeremy. "East Indian Women in the Caribbean: Experience and Voice." In *India in the Caribbean*, edited by David Dabydeen and Brinsley Samaroo, 231–64. London: Hansib/University of Warwick, 1987.

Press, Clayton M., Jr. "Reputation and Respectability Reconsidered: Hustling in a Tourist Setting." *Caribbean Issues* 4 (1978): 109–19.

"Prostitutie Op Aruba." Paper presented at the Caribbean Conference on Prostitution, Bonaire, 1978.

Pruitt, Deborah, and Suzanne LaFont. "For Love and Money: Romance Tourism in Jamaica." *Annals of Tourism Research* 22, no. 2 (1995): 422–40.

Ragsdale, A. Kathleen, and Jessica Tomiko Anders. "The *Muchachas* of Orange Walk Town, Belize." In *Sun, Sex, and Gold: Tourism and Sex Work in the Caribbean*, edited by Kamala Kempadoo, 217–36. Lanham: Rowman and Littlefield, 1999.

———. "Sex and Romance Tourism in Belize: A Site Comparison Study Preliminary Report to the Steering Committee of the Sex Trade in the Caribbean Project," 1998.

Reddock, Rhoda. "Douglarization and the Politics of Gender in Trinidad and Tobago." In *Contemporary Issues in Social Science: A Caribbean Perspective*, edited by D. Deosaran, R. Reddock, and N. Mustapha. St. Augustine: University of the West Indies, Department of Sociology, 1994. Reprinted in C. Barrow and R. Reddock, *Caribbean Sociology: Introductory Readings*. Kingston: Ian Randle, 2001, 320–333.

———. "Freedom Denied: Indian Women and Indentureship in Trinidad and Tobago, 1845–1917." *Economic and Political Weekly*, no. 20 (1985): 79–67.

———. *Women, Labor and Politics in Trinidad and Tobago*. London: Zed Books, 1994.

Red Thread Women's Development Programme. "'Givin' Lil Bit Fuh Lil Bit': Women and Sex Work in Guyana." In *Sun, Sex, and Gold: Tourism and Sex Work in the Caribbean*, edited by Kamala Kempadoo, 263–90. Lanham: Rowman and Littlefield, 1999.

———. "Report of a Study on Female Commercial Sex Workers in Guyana, and Project Proposal Arising from the Study," 35. Georgetown: Red Thread Women's Development Programme, 2002.

Reid, Sandra D. "Drug Use, Sexual Behavior and HIV Risk of the Homeless in Port-of-Spain, Trinidad." *West Indian Medical Journal* 48, no. 2 (1999): 57–60.

Rogers, J. A. *Sex and Race: A History of White, Negro and Indian Miscegenation in the Two Americas: The New World*. 6th ed., Vol. III. New York: Helga M. Rogers, 1972.

Rosario, E. Santo, Antonio E. de Moya, Luis Moreno, Bayardo Gómez, Laurie Fox, Marcos Espinal, José Ducós, and Francisca Ferreira. "La Industria del Sexo por Dentro." Santo Domingo: COIN, 1994.

Rousseau, G. S., and Roy Porter, eds. *Exoticism in the Enlightenment*. Manchester: Manchester University Press, 1990.

Rubin, Gayle. "Thinking Sex: Notes for a Radical Theory of the Politics of Sexuality." In *Pleasure and Danger: Exploring Female Sexuality*, edited by Carol S. Vance, 267–319. London: Pandora Press, 1988.

Russell-Brown, Pauline, and Godfrey Sealy. "Gay Research Initiative on AIDS Prevention in the Caribbean: An Analysis of Discussions with Men Who Have Sex with Men." Port of Spain: CAREC, 1998/2000.

Ryan, Chris, and Michael C. Hall. *Sex Tourism: Marginal People and Liminalities*. London: Routledge, 2001.

Said, Edward. *Orientalism*. New York: Vintage Books, 1979.

Samiel, Shiela. "Commercial Sex Work: Barbados," 21. Trinidad: Barbados National AIDS Commission and the Special Programme on Sexually Transmitted Infections (SPSTI), CAREC/GTZ, 2001.

Sanchez Taylor, Jacqueline. "Dollars Are a Girl's Best Friend? Female Tourists' Sexual Behavior in the Caribbean." *Sociology* 35, no. 1 (2001): 749–64.

Sardar, Ziauddin, Ashis Nandy, and Merryl Wyn Davies. *Barbaric Others: A Manifesto on Western Racism*. London: Pluto Press, 1993.

Schwartz, Rosalie. *Pleasure Island: Tourism and Temptation in Cuba*. Lincoln: University of Nebraska Press, 1997.

Scott, David. *Refashioning Futures: Criticism after Postcoloniality*. Princeton: Princeton University Press, 1999.

Senior, Olive. *Working Miracles: Women's Lives in the English-Speaking Caribbean*. Cave Hill: ISER; London: James Currey; Bloomington: Indiana Press, 1991.

Sharpley-Whiting, T. Denean. *Black Venus: Sexualized Savages, Primal Fears, and Primitive Narratives in French*. Durham: Duke University Press, 1999.

Sheller, Mimi. *Consuming the Caribbean*. London and New York: Routledge, 2003.

Shepherd, Verene A. "Gender, Migration and Settlement: The Indentureship and Post-Indentureship Experiences of Indian Females in Jamaica, 1845–1943." In *Engendering History: Caribbean Women in Historical Perspective*, edited by Verene A. Shepherd, Bridget Brereton, and Barbara Bailey, 233–57. New York: St. Martin's Press, 1995.

———. *Women in Caribbean History: The British Colonised Territories*. Kingston: Ian Randle; Oxford: James Currey; Princeton: Markus Wiener, 1999.

Silvera, Makeda. "Man Royals and Sodomites: Some Thoughts on the Invisibility of Afro-Caribbean Lesbians" in *Tongues on Fire: Caribbean Lesbian Lives and Stories*, edited by Rosamund Elwin, Toronto: Women's Press, 1997, 41–48.

Simeon, D. T., E. LeFranc, B. Bain, and G. E. Wyatt. "Experiences and Socialization of Jamaican Men with Multiple Sex Partners." *West Indian Medical Journal* 48, no. 4 (1999): 212–15.

Smith, M. G. *West Indian Family Structure*. Seattle: University of Washington Press, 1962.

Smith, Raymond T. *The Matrifocal Family: Power, Pluralism and Politics*. New York: Routledge, 1996.

———. *The Negro Family in British Guiana: Family Structure and Social Status in the Villages*. London: Routledge and Kegan Paul, in association with the Institute of Social and Economic Research, University College of the West Indies, Jamaica, 1956.

Stalker, Peter. *Workers without Frontiers: The Impact of Globalization on International Migration.* Boulder, CO: Lynne Rienner, 2000.

———. *Landsverordening Van Den 23sten September 1944 Tot Wijziging an Aanvullingvan De Verordening Van Den 9den Juni 1921.* 31 October 1944.

———. *Memorie Van Toelichting.* Zittingsjaar 1943–1944, 3.

———. *Nota Naar Aanleiding Van Het Eindverslag.* Begrotingsjaar 1953.

———. *Ontwerp: Landsverordening Tot Wijziging En Aanvulling Van De Verordening Van Den 9den Juni 1921.* Zittingsjaar 1943–1944, 12.

Staten van de Nederlandse Antillen. *Notulen.* 1 June 1951.

The Steering Committee. "Prostitution in St. Maarten." Paper presented at the Caribbean Conference on Prostitution, Bonaire, 1978.

Stewart, J. D. "Is Medical Research Taking Us Where We Cannot Afford to Go?" *West Indian Medical Journal* 50, Suppl. 6 (2001): 14.

Strout, Jan. "Women, the Politics of Sexuality and Cuba's Economic Crisis." *Socialist Review* 25, no. 1 (1995): 5–15.

Terborg, Julia. "AIDS en Prostitutie, Deelonderzoek I: Geregistreerde Prostituees." Paramaribo: National AIDS Programma, Ministerie Van Volsgezondheid, 1990.

———. "AIDS en Prostitutie, Deelonderzoek II: Onderzoek Onder Mannelijke Klanten van de Dermatologische Dienst." Paramaribo: National AIDS Programma, Ministerie van Volsgezondheid, 1990.

Thomas-Hope, Elizabeth. "Skilled Labor Migration from Developing Countries: Study on the Caribbean Region," 31. Geneva: International Migration Programme, International Labor Office, 2002.

Torchio, Giovanna Gray. "Beyond Appearances and Perspectives: A New Look at Female Sex Tourism in Jamaica." Bachelor of Arts, Connecticut College, New London, 2002.

Trexler, Richard C. *Sex and Conquest: Gendered Violence, Political Order, and the European Conquest of the Americas.* Ithaca, N.Y.: Cornell University Press, 1993.

Truong, Thanh Dam. *Sex, Money and Morality: The Political Economy of Prostitution and Tourism in South East Asia.* London: Zed Books, 1990.

UNIFEM. "UNFPA Caribbean Youth Summit 1998: Adolescent Sexual and Reproductive Health and Rights." UNIFEM Caribbean Office, Kingston, 1999.

van Ammelrooy, Anneke. *Vrouwenhandel: De Internationale Seksslavinnenmarkt.* The Hague: BZZToH, 1989.

van de Veen, Marjolein. "Rethinking Commodification and Prostitution: An Effort at Peacemaking in the Battles over Prostitution." *Rethinking Marxism* 13, no. 2 (2001): 30–51.

van der Vleuten, Nelleke. "Survey on 'Traffick in Women': Policies and Policy Research in an International Context." In *VENA Working Paper, Research and Documentation Centre, Women and Autonomy, Leiden University.* Leiden, VENA, 1991.

Vance, Carole S. "Pleasure and Danger: Towards a Politics of Sexuality." In *Pleasure and Danger: Exploring Female Sexuality*, edited by Carole S. Vance, 1–27. London: Pandora Press, 1988.

Vega, Alex P., Caroline Allen, and Geoffrey Stanford. "A Sexual Health Pro-
motion Intervention and Caribbean Men Who Have Sex with Men,"
38. Port of Spain: CAREC, 2001.
Visser, Jan. "Decriminalizing Prostitution: Dutch Preparations for a New
Way of Regulating Commercial Sex." Paper presented at Sex Matters:
The Xth World Congress of Sexology, Amsterdam, 1992, 1–59.
Wacquant, Lois J. D. "Toward a Social Praxeology: The Structure and
Logic of Bourdieu's Sociology." In *An Invitation to Reflexive Sociology*,
edited by Lois J. D. Wacquant. Chicago: University of Chicago Press,
1992.
Waszak, Cynthia, and Maxine Wedderburn. "Baseline Community Youth
Survey. VIP/Youth Project." Kingston: United Nations Family Planning
Association, 2000.
Watson, Hilbourne A. "Global Neoliberalism: The Third Technological Rev-
olution and Global 2000: A Perspective on Issues Affecting the
Caribbean on the Eve of the 21st Century." In *Contending with Destiny:
The Caribbean in the 21st Century*, edited by Kenneth Hall and Denis
Benn, 382–446. Kingston: Ian Randle, 2000.
Weinbaum, Batya. *Islands of Women and Amazons: Representations and Realities.*
Austin: University of Texas Press, 1999.
Wekker, Gloria. "'I Am Gold Money' (I Pass through All Hands, but I Do
Not Lose My Value): The Construction of Selves, Gender and Sexuali-
ties in a Female, Working Class, Afro-Surinamese Setting." Ph.D. diss.,
University of California, Los Angeles, 1992.
———. "Of Mimic Men and Unruly Women: Exploring Sexuality and Gen-
der in Surinamese Family Systems." Paper presented at the Caribbean
Feminisms Conference, University of the West Indies, Cave Hill
Campus, 2002.
West, Cornel, ed., "Black Sexuality: The Taboo Subject." In *Race Matters* ,
81–92. Boston: Beacon Press, 1993.
White, Luise. *The Comforts of Home: Prostitution in Colonial Nairobi.* Chicago:
University of Chicago Press, 1990.
Whitten, Norman, and Rachel Corr. "Contesting the Images of Oppression:
Indigenous Views of Blackness in the Americas." *NACLA Report on the
Americas*, May/June 2001, 24–28.
Wijers, Marjan, and Lin Lap-Chew. *Trafficking in Women, Forced Labor and
Slavery-Like Practices in Marriage, Domestic Labor and Prostitution.*
Utrecht: STV, 1997.
Wilkinson, Paul F. *Tourism Policy and Planning: Case Studies from the
Commonwealth Caribbean.* New York: Cognizant Communication Cor-
poration, 1997.
Williams, Brackette. *Stains on My Name, War in My Veins: Guyana and the Pol-
itics of Cultural Struggle.* Durham: Duke University Press, 1991.
Williams, Claudette M. *Charcoal and Cinnamon: The Politics of Color in Spanish
Caribbean Literature.* Gainesville: University Press of Florida, 2001.
Williams, Sian. "Sexual Violence and Exploitation of Children in Latin
America and the Caribbean: The Case of Jamaica." Kingston:
1999.

Willis, Deborah, and Carla Williams. *The Black Female Body: A Photographic History*. Philadelphia: Temple University Press, 2002.

Wilson, Samuel M., ed. *The Indigenous People of the Caribbean*. Gainseville: University Press of Florida, 1997.

Yegenoglu, Meyda. *Colonial Fantasies: Towards a Feminist Reading of Orientalism*. Cambridge: Cambridge University Press, 1998.

Yelvington, Kevin A. *Producing Power: Ethnicity, Gender and Class in a Caribbean Workplace*. Philadelphia: Temple University Press, 1995.

Young, Robert J. C. *Colonial Desire: Hybridity in Theory, Culture and Race*. London: Routledge, 1995.

Index

Inter-racial sex, 32
Intimacy, 42, 61, 202, 203
IOM, *see* International Organization
    for Migration
Irregular conjugal relations, 15

J
Jewish men, concubinage and, 56

K
Kaimoo, 70
Kidnapping, 153

L
Labor
    child, 58
    demand for cheap
        sexualized, 156
    First World, 140
    forced, 39
    laws, 158
    male, recruitment of, 106
    migrant, gender-specific form
        of, 59
    migrations, 141
    power, 63
    relations, exploitative, 158
    waged, 56
La Gloria, 122
Lap dancing, 69
League of Nations, 91, 148
Legal taboos, 178
Lesbianism, uniqueness to
        Caribbean, 47
Lesbians, identity formation of, 48
Lodging-house proprietresses, 54
Loose sexuality, Africanness and, 17
Love, 42, 175
    marriages, 161
    romantic, 43
Lovemaking, vigorous style of, 133

M
Mail-order bride arrangements, 149
Male dominance, female
        assertiveness and, 21
Male hustling, 77, 130
Male labor, recruitment of, 106

Male-to-male sexual relationship, 46
Male sex tourists, difference between
    women tourists and, 128
Man royal, 48
Marginalization, 79
Marijuana, 75
Marriage(s)
    between Europeans and slaves, 55
    bogus, 159
    common-law, 19
    ideals about, 175
    love, 161
    migration and, 159
    models of, 204
    opportunities for sexual
        satisfaction outside, 18
    system(s)
        dual, 17
        European monogamous, 19
Masculinity
    colonial, 139
    Jamaican, 130
Mati work, 27, 84
Matrifocality, 18, 20
Mean's health conditions,
        monitoring of, 98
Medical violence, 180
Men
    bisexual, 174, 176
    discrimination toward, 170
    naturally promiscuous, 203
    need for sex by, 108
    self-identification, 191
    sexually deviant, 168
Messengers of health, 185
Mestizo, 32
Migrant labor, gender-specific form
    of, 59
Migration, interregional and
        international, 141–166
    economies of scale, 164–166
    factors facilitating international
        movement into sex trade,
        153–159
    marriage and migration, 159–163
    migrant work, 163–164
    migration versus trafficking,
        148–153

CPSIA information can be obtained
at www.ICGtesting.com
Printed in the USA
BVHW08s0156110818
524184BV00001B/37/P